Managing for Quality
in the Hospitality Industry

Managing for Quality in the Hospitality Industry

John H. King, Jr.

President and Chief Executive Officer
HDS Services

Ronald F. Cichy, Ph.D., NCE, CHA

Director and Professor
The School of Hospitality Business
Michigan State University

PEARSON
Prentice
Hall

Upper Saddle River, New Jersey 07458

Library of Congress Cataloging-in-Publication Data

King, John H.,
  Managing for quality in the hospitality industry / by John H. King, Jr. and Ronald F. Cichy.
    p. cm.
  ISBN 0-13-094589-7
  1.   Total quality management.   2.   Quality control.   3.   Hospitality industry—Management.   I. Cichy, Ronald F. II. Title.
HD62.15.K556 2005
647.94'068'4—dc22

                                                              2004020562

Executive Editor: Vernon R. Anthony
Associate Editor: Marion Gottlieb
Editorial Assistant: Beth Dyke
Senior Marketing Manager: Ryan DeGrote
Senior Marketing Coordinator: Elizabeth Farrell
Marketing Assistant: Les Roberts
Director of Manufacturing and Production: Bruce Johnson
Managing Editor: Mary Carnis
Production Liaison: Jane Bonnell
Production Editor: John Shannon, Pine Tree Composition, Inc.
Manufacturing Manager: Ilene Sanford
Manufacturing Buyer: Cathleen Petersen
Creative Director: Cheryl Asherman
Senior Design Coordinator: Miguel Ortiz
Cover Designer: Amy Rosen
Composition: Pine Tree Composition
Printer/Binder: Banta Harrisonburg
Cover Printer: Phoenix Color Corp.
Cover Photo: Courtesy of HDS Services. In a high performance hospitality service organization, the organization's internal customers are the most important in delivering exceptional experiences for external customers.

Pearson Prentice Hall™ is a trademark of Pearson Education, Inc.
Pearson® is a registered trademark of Pearson plc
Prentice Hall® is a registered trademark of Pearson Education, Inc.

Pearson Education LTD.   Pearson Education Canada, Ltd.
Pearson Education Australia PTY, Limited   Pearson Educación de Mexico, S.A. de C.V.
Pearson Education Singapore, Pte. Ltd.   Pearson Education—Japan
Pearson Education North Asia Ltd.   Pearson Education Malaysia, Pte. Ltd.

10   9   8   7   6   5   4   3   2   1

ISBN 0-13-094589-7

Contents

Chapter 9   Strategic Quality Plan   167

Chapter 10   Assessing Quality   191

Chapter 11   Implementing Quality   213

Chapter 12   Leading Quality   237

Chapter 13   Quality Life   253

Chapter 14   Final Thoughts   269

Glossary   279

Index   291

Your Tools of the Trade   299

Foreword

This text looks forward with a vision for quality. Carolyn Rigterink, Director of Management Development for HDS Services, read each page of this text. Afterwards, she wrote: "John King and Dr. Cichy have brought theory and practice together in this wonderful text. This book is a must read for all hospitality/service business managers and should be on every manager's desk, because it takes you to the heart of understanding what it means to manage quality and offers a practical approach to implementing the process. In my experience in training managers in the hospitality industry, I am frequently asked to explain how the process works, so they can better understand how to take it to their associates. We now have the practical guide."

Thomas C. Galyon, President and CEO of the Corpus Christi Convention & Visitors Bureau said, after reading the book: "Quality is the measurement by which all things are judged. This book explains it in understandable terms."

From an industry standpoint, I personally found the text to be well written (not overly technical) and directed for use by both students and company executives. It also plays well to the myriad of private club COOs/general managers and restaurateurs who are not a part of a chain, but are large enough to realize the importance of quality and are looking for a book that details the process. My fellow Wall of Fame member, Mike Getto, Director, Franchise Development for GuestHouse International, said he only wished that 48 years ago when he was a student he would have had the opportunity to use and learn from a text such as this.

Dan Mathews, Senior Vice President and Chief Operating Officer of the National Automatic Merchandising Association, wrote, "I have known John King and Ron Cichy personally for many years. I have followed their careers. They not only teach and write about quality and leadership superbly, they live it with superb results. Success does indeed breed success—read this book and breed your own success." I agree. As a consultant for many businesses, I have seen it take place.

Paul Fayad, President and Chief Executive Officer of HHA Services, after reading the book said, "Finally a 'How To' manual that aids new managers in understanding and implementing quality in the hospitality industry. John King and Dr. Cichy simplify the most important elements in managing quality in the hospitality industry. A must read manual for all students and new managers in the hospitality industry." John R. Zangas, then Associate Director of Sales for The Ritz-Carlton Dearborn, wrote, "The John King / Ron Cichy text offers a complete history and analysis of quality management and a roadmap for implementation in any organization." John Zangas is currently the Director of Hotel Sales—Detroit Marriott Troy.

John R. Weeman, Jr., President of Weeman Partners in Development, said, "This book offers a unique opportunity to make the management of quality in the hospitality industry 'alive' for students." Added Kevin Brown, Chief Executive Officer of Lettuce Entertain You Enterprises, Inc., "This is what students need to learn, study, and know." "Managing quality in the hospitality industry will provide the next generation of students a positive roadmap for the future," noted Jared Flayer, Regional Vice President of Operations for HDS Services. We are all students for quality.

Philip J. Hickey, Jr., Chairman and CEO of RARE Hospitality International, Inc., and J. G. Ted Gillary, CCM, Executive Manager of the Detroit Athletic Club, generously contributed materials to this book to complement the HDS Services materials. Maggie Bonner from the U.S. Air Force also added a number of very positive suggestions after she read the manuscript. All of these individuals helped prepare the very best book for you.

After he reviewed the work, while he was still Vice President, Quality, for The Ritz-Carlton Hotel Company, Patrick Mene wrote: "The hospitality industry should be grateful for your manuscript. Your logic, processes and tools go to the heart of managing for quality in the hospitality industry. Managing *for* Quality in the Hospitality Industry is a more appropriate title." The authors have Patrick Mene to thank for the title of the book you now hold.

And we have the authors to thank for the years of dedicated teaching and research into managing for quality that resulted in the labor of love that you now hold. I now invite you to join the rest of us on *your* journey for *your* total quality life and managing for quality. The result will be a continuous improvement of your life and the life of your organization.

Jerry A. McVety
President of McVety & Associates

Preface

We were urged to write this book by the students in our Total Quality Management in the Hospitality Industry class at Michigan State University, a course that we have team taught since 1994. In 2001, the title of the course was updated to Managing for Quality in the Hospitality Business—like the evolution of quality in an organization, the course is a journey. It is constantly evolving, and it is never presented exactly the same way twice.

We share an evolutionary and experiential teaching methodology with American philosopher and writer John Dewey. This pedagogy involves creating a hypothetical company dedicated to managing and continuously improving quality. Students then role play as owners of the company and as members of the company's Senior Quality Improvement Team (SQIT). The students understand how they contribute to the achievement of the hypothetical company's vision and come away with the knowledge that quality is not a "me" or "I" achievement, but a "we" achievement.

Our course contains an amazing set of interdisciplinary elements (i.e., strategic management, leadership, human resources, food and beverage services, athletic and recreation services, marketing, written and verbal communication, finance, and other metrics) which we consider necessary to the pedagogy. The basic atmosphere of the educational process in our course is freedom; the basic methodology is experimental. As a result we have observed countless instances where a new set of values emerges in the students. The use of HDS Services as an industry example offers a real life application that students can take as a benchmark, or at least a comparison, for use in later business situations.

In manufacturing it is easier to test the degree of quality through hard measurement. This text demonstrates how to take the same processes and apply them to service and hospitality businesses. The HDS journey with Managing for Quality is a real life example of successful application of the principles. This company is recognized by its clients, external customers, associates, and suppliers as achieving success with the quality effort. The result is a company managed by self-directed teams whose members have grown significantly in their skill set.

The professors are not simply the lecturing experts in our course. We prepare the environment, present the concepts and tools, point to the vision and goals, but the students teach themselves and each other through a process of discovery and reinforcement. The students hear the voices of quality and find their individual pathways to excellence.

Our course does not view students as an element in a series of overarching concerns. Rather, it sees students as an experimental touchstone of both educational methods and the human experience. We have learned as much from our students as they have told us they have learned from us. We genuinely believe that college students possess different and higher qualities than most attribute to them; we have seen evidence of this fact time and time again.

This book, which is used in our course, begins with an overview of managing for quality and presents this process within the three broad sets of expectations in any organization—the expectations of internal customers, external customers, and financial results. The data gathered during the course journey validates the end assessment that customers' expectations were met. Quality management often requires a paradigm shift in the ways one views the process of change and how to do things right. High performance service organizations put the customers first, beginning with internal customers and then focusing on external customers. The needs and expectations of these two groups are translated into expectations that govern the organization's culture.

We also view associates as an organization's hidden strengths. These internal customers are the primary focus because they create and deliver service for all other customers. The effectiveness of internal customers depends on synergy, empowerment, and teamwork. The development of associates' leadership skills allows them to make decisions that put action into the organization's vision, mission, and core values. Just like internal customers, external customers must be understood in terms of their needs, wants, and expectations. Furthermore, customer complaints can lead to the identification of quality improvement opportunities which will result in customer satisfaction.

The management and improvement of quality is a continuous journey. The process is a realistic but sobering realization that this is not a quick fix. Tools of the Trade help measure and monitor quality improvements. These are important because assessing quality is essential from both the internal and external customers' perspectives. Your Tools of the Trade appear as a tearout section at the end of this book. The assessment helps us determine what the customers want and to implement quality management processes.

The book also covers strategic quality planning. This planning begins with a personal vision and is transformed into a shared vision within the organization. The mission, core values, and vision of an organization are the drivers behind the strategic goals and critical processes. Together they define what we believe in and they help build commitment to the long term goal.

Finally, we discuss leadership. Leadership is intimately related to managing and improving quality. Understanding one's personal leadership qualities, keys, and secrets helps drive the process of continuous improvement. The principles of managing for quality also apply to one's personal life. By implementing these principles in one's personal life, the quality will be improved. These principles then can be extended to the work place.

Acknowledgments

We would like to acknowledge the contributions of the many individuals and organizations that helped us prepare this book. Students in our improving quality course over the past years have strongly urged us to write a book that could help them better understand the differences between organizations that have quality as their voices and those that only pay quality lip service. The leaders at all levels at HDS Services contributed to the book through their examples, attitudes, and professional approach to business. They epitomize a team approach to decision making and provide a high degree of excellence to both internal and external customers. They have served as caring mentors for our students, helping us to provide the very best learning experience firmly grounded in the reality of the hospitality business. They also have shared their expertise as visiting professors in the classroom.

We thank the other visiting industry speakers from The Ritz-Carlton Hotel Company, Port Huron Hospital, and Ford Motor Company who have helped us prepare the future leaders of the hospitality industry by graciously sharing their wisdom and experiences. We also thank the industry leaders who willingly contributed their wisdom and organizations' materials for inclusion in this book. These leaders include those mentioned in the list of reviewers, as well as throughout the book.

We also owe a debt of gratitude to Jae-Min Cha and John Windom, who reviewed and provided input for this book, as well as contributed to the learning experiences of the students in a positive and professional way. We also thank Eileen Dobrotka from HDS Services for her expertise and kind assistance in the formatting of this book.

Lastly, we would like to dedicate *Managing for Quality in the Hospitality Industry* to our families, who have helped us better understand quality and have encouraged us to progress in our journey of continuous improvement and significance. They have taught us that there is more to life than success. The fundamental reason for living is to be significant, and our families have encouraged each of us to focus on significance rather than success. We acknowledge the supreme importance of our families and express our sincere gratitude to them.

John H. King, Jr.
Northville, Michigan

Ronald F. Cichy, Ph.D.
Okemos, Michigan

Reviewers

Anthony Agbeh
Program Coordinator/Professor
Ferris State University
Big Rapids, MI

Nora Berkey-Campell
Northern Virginia CC
Annandale, VA

Margaret E. Bonner
HQ Air Force Services Agency
Clubs Division
Washington, DC

Kevin Brown
Chief Executive Officer
Lettuce Entertain You Enterprises, Inc.
Chicago, IL

Jae-Min Cha
Graduate Student
The School of Hospitality Business
Michigan State University
East Lansing, MI

Dan W. Darrow
President
Palm Hospitality Company, a subsidiary
 of The Walt Disney Company
Orlando, FL

Richard D. Farrar
Vice President, Owner & Franchise
 Services
Marriott International, Inc.
Washington, DC

Paul Fayad
President and Chief Executive Officer
HHA Services
St. Clair Shores, MI

Jared Flayer
Regional Vice President of Operations
HDS Services
Farmington Hills, MI

Don Fletcher
President and Chief Executive Officer
Port Huron Hospital
Port Huron, MI

Jerry Fournier
Executive Vice President
HDS Services
Farmington Hills, MI

Thomas C. Galyon
President and CEO
Corpus Christi Convention and Visitors
 Bureau
Corpus Christi, TX

Michael Hutson Getto
Director of Franchise Development
GuestHouse International
Santa Barbara, CA

J. G. Ted Gillary, CCM
Executive Manager
Detroit Athletic Club
Detroit, MI

Philip J. Hickey, Jr.
Chairman and CEO
RARE Hospitality International, Inc.
Atlanta, GA

Allegra Johnson, CCM
Club Manager
Dunwoody Country Club
Dunwoody, GA

Sue Lantzsch
Regional Vice President of Operations
HDS Services
Farmington Hills, MI

Dan H. Mathews, Jr.
Senior Vice President and Chief Operating Officer
National Automatic Merchandising Association
Chicago, IL

Jerry A. McVety
President
McVety & Associates
Farmington Hills, MI

Patrick Mene
Vice President, Quality
The Ritz-Carlton Hotel Company
Atlanta, GA

Linda Rhodes-Pauly, MS, RD
Vice President Business Development
HDS Services
Farmington Hills, MI

Carolyn Rigterink
Director of Management Development
HDS Services
Farmington Hills, MI

Paul A. Smith
Owner
Hitching Post Inn Resort & Conference Center
Cheyenne, WI

Susan K. Smith
President
Food Concepts, Inc.
Denver, CO

Daniel L. Ward, CTA
International Business College
Fort Wayne, IN

John R. Weeman, Jr.
President
Weeman Partners in Development
Irving, TX

Clifford Wener
Associate Professor/Coordinator
Business Management and Food Service Management
College of Lake County
Grayslake, IL

Mary Westcott
Vice President Operations
HDS Services
Farmington Hills, MI

Bob Wills
Executive Vice President Operations
HDS Services
Farmington Hills, MI

John Windom
Graduate Student
The School of Hospitality Business
Michigan State University
East Lansing, MI

John R. Zangas
Director of Hotel Sales
Detroit Marriott—Troy
Troy, MI

About the Authors

John H. King, Jr. and his team embarked on their quality journey in 1991. He is the president and chief executive officer of HDS Services, a national management and consulting services company. He has been with the company for almost four decades, holding various positions including food services manager, director of operations, vice president, executive vice president, and president since 1975. He earned a BS degree in pre-med from Washington and Jefferson College and attended Michigan State University for one year to obtain a business degree.

Since 1994, Mr. King has been a visiting professor for senior-level and graduate students in *The* School of Hospitality Business, an industry-specific School within The Eli Broad College of Business and The Eli Broad Graduate School of Management at Michigan State University. In May 1995, he was honored with the Richard J. Lewis Quality of Excellence Award from The Eli Broad College of Business at Michigan State University for his team-taught innovative course in Total Quality Management.

Mr. King is a member of the Board of Directors of HDS Services. He also chairs the company's Operating Committee, which drives most of the company's activity. Mr. King chairs the Senior Quality Improvement Team as well, and he serves on the Executive Committee of the corporate alliance between HDS Services and HHA Services, a plant operations/environmental services organization specializing in health care. Mr. King has been a speaker on the topic of managing and improving quality for executives of several organizations, including HHA Services and the Michigan Association of Homes and Services for the Aging (MAHSA).

Ronald F. Cichy, Ph.D. is the director and a professor in *The* School of Hospitality Business. Previously, he was the director of educational services for the Educational Institute of the American Hotel & Motel Association. Dr. Cichy has also served on the faculties of the University of Denver and Lansing Community College. He earned a Ph.D. from Michigan State University (MSU) in food science and human nutrition and an MBA and BA from the University's School of Hotel, Restaurant and Institutional Management.

Dr. Cichy earned the designations of Certified Hotel Administrator (CHA) and Certified Food and Beverage Executive (CFBE) from the Educational Institute in 1983, and the designation of Certified Hospitality Educator (CHE) in 1992. In 1996, he was named an Outstanding Alumnus by MSU's College of Human Ecology. In 1999, he received the prestigious Lamp of Knowledge for outstanding hospitality educator by the Educational Institute. In 2003, Dr. Cichy was named a Distinguished Alumnus by the Broad College of Business at MSU. He also earned the National Automatic Merchandising Association's Certified Executive (NCE) in 2003.

Dr. Cichy's industry experience includes positions in lodging and foodservice operations as a hotel manager, food and beverage manager, banquet chef, and sales representative. He has written more than 125 articles for foodservice and lodging audiences. In addition to co-authoring *Managing for Quality in the Hospitality Industry*, he is a co-author of three other books: *Managing Beverage Service, Managing Service in Food and*

Beverage Operations–Third Edition, and *Foodservice Systems Management.* He also has authored *Food Safety: Managing the HACCP Process, Quality Sanitation Management, Sanitation Management: Strategies for Success,* and *The Spirit of Hospitality.*

Dr. Cichy is active professionally as a member of the Board of Trustees of the Educational Foundation of the American Hotel & Lodging Association and as a member of the AH&LA's Presidents Academy Board of Regents. He is a member of the Board of Directors of the Michigan Hotel, Motel and Resort Association, and he is on the Board of Directors for the National Automatic Merchandising Association's Foundation. He has served as a consultant for national and international lodging and foodservice organizations, for Fortune 500 companies including MASCO and General Motors, and for other organizations including the City of Detroit, Accident Fund of America, Toyota, Isuzu, Eagle Ottawa, and the U.S. Air Force. He has traveled extensively throughout the United States, Australia, Canada, Europe, Japan, and Mexico to design and conduct executive education programs.

Managing for Quality in the Hospitality Industry

Chapter 1

An Overview of Managing for Quality

Quality is the standard of measurement. It is the measurement of excellence. Quality is clean, fresh, and well appointed. Managing for quality looks at issues of safety and presentation from the perspectives of the customers.

Susan K. Smith
President
Food Concepts, Inc.
Denver, CO

Learning Objectives

1. Develop a personal definition of quality.
2. Understand the two categories of customers in an organization.
3. Discuss the three criteria for "doing things right."
4. Describe the process of benchmarking and its advantages.
5. Define a learning organization.
6. Understand five positive results from the process of managing for quality.

Introduction

Managing for quality means meeting the customer's expectations in the product or service being purchased. It also means reducing hassles, defects, deficiencies, barriers, obstacles, or problems perceived by the customer in the product or service. Examples of such problems are mistakes, delays, or delivering less than what was expected. When the customer's requirements are met and deficiencies are reduced, quite simply, quality has been managed.

The concept of management of quality is an outgrowth of the **Total Quality Management (TQM)** philosophy of management.

This philosophy states that bottom line performance will take care of itself in an organization that is committed to, and practices, quality effort. While some believe that TQM is out of fashion and others think that it was a failure, the truth is that organizations that practice identifying customer requirements and minimize or eliminate deficiencies perceived by customers survive in the short run and thrive in the long run. When this fundamental quality concept becomes a part of the organization's very fabric and way of doing business, the customer and the organization both win.

There are many examples of managing for quality in today's businesses. One is the unquestioning way sales associates at Nordstrom's accept returned merchandise that does not meet customer expectations. Hospitality examples include the presentation of the main course by an executive chef to dear friends celebrating a special occasion in a restaurant (Exhibit 1.1), the timely check-in at a hotel, recognition of a club member by name in a private club dining room, and the welcoming greeting by a long-time server offered to a returning family at a summer resort.

Exhibit 1.1   The presentation of the main course by the executive chef to dear friends celebrating a special occasion in a restaurant is an example of managing for quality. *(Source: HDS Services. Used with permission.)*

Organizations are systems or a series of interrelated critical processes that work in concert to manage and improve quality. Managing for quality does not simply happen; the organizational culture of a company makes it happen. When quality is considered in every process, management is able to completely redirect its focus away from the bottom line because quality products and services sold in the proper markets automatically increase the organization's financial performance. Quality is not solely based on appearance and financial success.

The System for Managing and Improving Quality

According to TQM theory, to begin managing and improving quality you must first know your customers and understand how the requirements of customers drive the efforts of an organization. All of the critical processes established and monitored in an organization and all of the changes made to improve quality are done to serve the customers better. The process of managing and improving quality takes place within three broad sets of expectations in any organization: **internal customers' expectations, external customers' expectations,** and **financial expectations.** The ongoing identification of these expectations, regularly monitoring how well the organization delivers on the expectations, and balancing the three expectations become central to the mission of the organization.

High-performance service organizations embrace a **paradigm** that places the customers first, beginning with internal customers and then shifting to external customers. The needs and expectations of these two groups are translated into processes and systems that govern the organization's culture and are considered in the development of the organization's vision, mission, and values. *Internal customers must be advocates for external customers if the organization is to manage for quality.* The driver (i.e., values, vision, and mission) in a hotel organization for the teams of internal customers must be the quality requirements of the organization's external customers (Exhibit 1.2).

Exhibit 1.2   A hotel organization's values, vision, and mission, as driven by the teams of internal customers, must be the quality requirements of the organization's external customers. *(Source: HDS Services. Used with permission.)*

Just like internal customers, external customers must be understood in terms of their requirements. The quality perceived by external customers determines the level of improvements needed, so it is essential to monitor and evaluate the quality delivered to external customers. Generally, if asked in a sincere and genuine way, external customers will give honest feedback to a representative of the organization. This feedback can be used in conjunction with customer complaints and can lead to the identification of quality improvement opportunities.

Continuous quality improvement is the key to managing and improving quality for both internal and external customers. The CQI journey never ends; the objective is to deliver results that are better today compared to those of yesterday. This concept utilizes cross-functional (i.e., across departments) teams of associates and managers to constantly innovate and improve quality as perceived by customers. Management's role in the CQI journey is to facilitate the progress of the internal customers, giving them the necessary resources to deliver the required improvements. Here are some of the resources used to achieve quality management that will be discussed in later chapters at greater length:

- **Tools of the trade.** These help measure and monitor quality improvements. They are simply ways to track how we are doing. (See Chapter 8.)
- **Strategic quality planning.** This begins with a personal vision, which transforms into a shared vision within the organization. Both personal and shared visions answer the question "What do I want to create?" Along with the mission and core values of the organization, this vision is the driver behind strategic goals and critical processes. (See Chapter 9.)
- **Assessing quality.** This is essential from both the internal and external customers' perspectives. External customers can be assessed using the tools of the trade. Management usually accomplishes assessing internal customers in a similar way. This assessment helps determine the requirements of the customers as well as how the organization is doing in the delivery of requirements at levels that meet or exceed the customers' expectations. Regular and ongoing assessments lead to improvements and call attention to precise steps in processes that need to be fixed. (See Chapter 10.)
- **Implementing quality.** The six steps of implementing quality include educating, assessing, addressing the burning issues, determining critical processes and how to measure progress, redesigning the process, and continuing improvement. Assessment is an ongoing part of the implementation of quality. (See Chapter 11.)
- **Leading quality.** This is the responsibility of everyone in the organization since leadership is intimately related to managing and improving quality. Understanding one's personal leadership qualities helps drive the process of continuous improvement, both in the individual and in the organization. Knowing these qualities can help identify strengths and improve weaknesses in the individual and organization. (See Chapter 12.)
- **Quality life.** This results from the effective application of principles to one's personal life. While at first glance this may not seem to be related directly to managing and improving quality in an organization, quality life principles have a direct impact on the individual who ultimately must make a contribution to the organization as a team member and internal customer of the organization. (See Chapter 13.)

It is a system that has evolved at HDS Services since 1991, and it has been applied in our senior-level class, Managing Quality in Hospitality Business, at Michigan State University since 1995. We have seen the results in the HDS Services system and have observed the outcomes in our course. If you have a vision for improving quality in your organization, our system can help you. If you are passionate about quality improvement from a personal standpoint, we will show you some tools and strategies that have worked for us.

First, however, we must begin with an overview of quality. The objective for the rest of this chapter is to give the reader a general idea of what quality is and how the process of managing for quality works. You also will learn about leaders' roles in bringing quality and the principles of managing for quality to every level of the organization.

Doing the Right Things

While some believe that **quality** is defined as "the best, the finest, the greatest, the most expensive, or most superior," others correctly define quality as "doing the right things right." In a service organization, doing the right thing simply means balancing the three sets of expectations in the organization: the expectations of **internal customers/associates** (staff members and managers), external customers (those who purchase the organization's products and services), and financial (owners and investors–public or private).

Internal customers are associates who are selected, oriented, and trained to create and deliver the products and services of the organization. **External customers** are the people that purchase an organization's products and services. When external customers select an organization to help meet their needs and exceed their expectations, they pay with their hard-earned money as well as with their irreplaceable time, and, therefore, they expect and deserve value. **Financial expectations** vary between organizations. Businesses expect to make a profit for the stakeholders, while non-profit organizations frequently expect to generate a surplus. This profit or surplus is used to build the organization by investing for future needs and in future growth.

Doing the right things in an organization can be illustrated by the model in Exhibit 1.3. The expectations are listed at the three converging points of the triangle. Each line is the same length, indicating equal importance of the three expectations.

Exhibit 1.3 A model for doing the right things. *(Source: Verne Harnish, Gazelles, Inc. Used with permission.)*

The other half of the definition of quality is "doing things right." Doing things right simply means meeting customer needs and expectations more rapidly and at a reduced cost.

At the Detroit Athletic Club, a 118-year-old private club in downtown Detroit, Michigan, the strategic planning process provides a unified vision throughout the organization. The leadership of the club learns about club member expectations through annual satisfaction surveys, 5-year comprehensive surveys (including satisfaction and importance measures as well as future vision), and annual "Town Hall" meetings between the volunteer board of directors, management, and the general membership.

Once expectations are clearly understood, the gap between what is expected and what is delivered can be analyzed and actions taken to close the gap. The expectations of internal customers are assessed through monthly PEP (performance excellence process) meetings to discuss performance, workplace issues, and the goals and objectives of the departments. In addition, each quarter an all-staff meeting is hosted by the executive manager to discuss priority concerns. Two additional ways to gather information from the internal customers are the annual staff member survey and the monthly Personal Progress Interviews conducted with key internal customers. Once again, the gaps between expectations and results are identified and interventions are implemented to reduce the differences. This takes time but it helps clearly visualize what are the right things to do.

Quality and Leadership

In today's society, we all have time pressures that seem to be forever increasing. We feel that we are all required to do more within shorter periods of time and with fewer resources. And while we still have the same number of hours in each day, we are expected to achieve more in that finite period of time. People need help from organizations to meet the obligations of these time pressures, and many businesses have developed to fulfill this need. We take our shirts to the laundry or dry cleaner; we wash our cars at automatic car washes; and we dine in restaurants or purchase prepared-foods-to-go from supermarkets or delicatessens on the way home from a busy day at work.

At the same time, our expectations have become more progressive and more sophisticated. Remember when you were a child and your mother was planning your birthday party? If you are old enough now, you may remember her purchasing all of the ingredients for your birthday cake—flour, eggs, sugar, vanilla, shortening, milk, cocoa. She would carefully mix the ingredients and bake, frost, and decorate your birthday cake. That was the expectation then. Expectations changed, however. After some time, your mother probably went to the store and bought a cake mix. She would simply add an egg, some oil, and liquid, and then bake it. She still frosted the cake and wrote your name on it along with a birthday greeting. After more time passed, your mother was more likely to phone the supermarket or bakery and order your cake. In all three of these situations, expectations concerning your mother's time changed and became progressively more demanding; the constant expectation, however, was that you, your family, and your friends would celebrate your birthday at home with a cake. Today, children expect their birthdays will be celebrated at a fun, child-oriented restaurant, with pizza, video games, and mechanical rides. Imagine the disappointed child guests who are invited to a birthday party in the home of one of their friends and "forced" to play Pin the Tail on the Donkey. Boring! Why? Because their expectations have become more sophisticated, based on what they have previously experienced.

This example shows that quality is dynamic rather than static. The definition of quality is fluid and evolutionary. Therefore, it is not possible to keep the level of quality of a product or service the same and expect to continue to please more demanding customers; managing for quality is ultimately related to **leadership.** Without leadership there is no quality and without quality there is no leadership.

Leadership involves the process of taking people somewhere with an idea, creating a compelling vision to help them see into the future, and then leading them to that future. An organization's vision must be based on the needs and expectations of its customers. It should be forward looking, outcome oriented, customer focused, realistic, and put into writing. High performance service organizations are **customer driven** and cannot define their visions until the customers are understood. A team of managers, associates, external customers, and owners/investors can be utilized effectively to define the customer-driven vision.

When members of the team are brought together to help define the vision and they understand how they contribute to the achievement of the vision, there will be a corresponding increase in personal commitment to make the vision a reality. This personal commitment will help associates convince others in the organization to internalize the vision and present it to customers. The overall result will be the creation of a customer service culture in the organization. For example, a member service culture in a private club dining room is one of the reasons that members are willing to pay an initiation fee and monthly dues (Exhibit 1.4).

The leader in a customer-driven service organization must possess a curious mind when it comes to quality and continuous improvement. A visionary leader is one who helps facilitate the ongoing search for better ways of doing things, specifically creating and delivering customer service that meets customer needs

Exhibit 1.4 A member service culture in a private club dining room. *(Source: HDS Services. Used with permission.)*

and exceeds customer expectations. Once leaders realize that they do not have all the answers concerning quality improvement, they will be more likely to accept the ideas for improvement from the people who are on the front line creating and delivering quality customer service. These improvements are guided by the vision and delivered by the associates.

It was rather recently that quality became a service issue. Assuming the same or similar product qualities across organizations (e.g., given the same supplier, the fresh whitefish sold by your restaurant is *not* substantially different from the fresh whitefish sold by the restaurant just down the road), the point of competitive advantage is the level of service quality delivered by each organization.

Service quality, then, becomes a critical strategy under the broad umbrella of managing quality. But how did the management of quality develop into such a strong force in excellent service organizations? Because the leaders of these organizations came to the realization that quality and customer loyalty are not based on the service provider's expectations and standards; they are based solely on the needs and expectations of the customers.

Customers

Quality-driven organizations are customer-driven organizations, but how can customers be the driving force behind everything an organization does? If we look at this in reverse and examine an organization whose policies, processes, and general way of doing business are based entirely on management's thinking, we will observe an organization that will alienate and lose its customers and eventually cease to exist.

Successful organizations listen to their customers, both internal and external, and involve their suppliers in some of the key decision-making processes in the organization. We refer to this as "listening to the voices of quality" or "the pathway to excellence." If everyone is involved in the process there will be more ideas from which to choose.

This, according to Dr. Edwards Deming, who is known as the father of quality, is one of the most important obligations of management. (See Chapter 2.) If a customer described a hassle he was experiencing to the senior management of an organization and they implemented a change to reduce or eliminate the hassle, the customer would be thankful for their action and proud that his complaint or suggestion created positive change for many of the organization's other external customers.

The above situation is an example of involving your customer in this process; they have the opportunity of **partnering** and creating opportunities for synergism and growth. Partnerships and alliances also provide a perfect environment for expanding the knowledge and understanding of managing for quality in the organization.

Benchmarking, or learning from other organizations to raise the quality levels of our own products and services, is related to partnering. Benchmarking helps an organization study a process at another organization and adapt, modify, and apply the process at their own organization. This learning opportunity demands time and commitment from key internal customers within the learning organization and the organization's culture and core values must include **thinking outside the box.**

All organizations and their associates must accept the fact that change is necessary and is a part of progress in today's world. Demands for change are both far-reaching and rapid. One way to realize rapid, dramatic change is through benchmarking. For example, the Detroit Athletic Club (DAC) benchmarks the best of other private clubs, as well as the best practices in the hotel and restaurant industry, to help establish the types of products and services that the club should be offering members. By benchmarking, the leadership of the club thinks "outside the box" (Exhibit 1.5). When this benchmark data is added to what members are saying they expect of the club, there is a clear path toward managing for quality. By setting goals that require the organization to leave its comfort zone and stretch toward the achievable, dramatic improvements often take place.

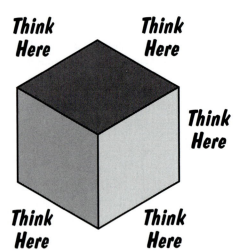

Exhibit 1.5 Think "outside the box" through benchmarking. *(Source: HDS Services. Used with permission.)*

So why do so many people resist change? First, they maintain their stability by hanging on to familiar and old ways of doing things. Also, when things change, we have to give up something in return; most people do not like to do this. Sometimes a change is implemented that makes one department more efficient, but it puts pressure on other departments because their people are required to make changes that are more time consuming. This points out the importance of getting everyone involved in the decision-making process.

Starting the Process of Managing and Improving Quality

When starting the process of managing and improving quality, remember that there is no right or wrong way to achieve quality. However, in all cases, three common threads can be identified in organizations that excel in managing and improving quality: 1) leadership by top management, 2) a view that quality is a long-term process, and 3) a passion for gathering and acting on feedback from customers.

An organization's top management sets the direction and pace. The process for managing and improving quality is more likely to succeed if there is a strong message that there is a **commitment** to make quality the core of the organization's culture.

Once an **assessment** of the organization's current level of quality takes place, the level of quality it hopes to achieve can be articulated and shared with those who can help make it happen. The organization's mission, vision statement, and core values should be reviewed during this assessment since these provide the context for evaluating current levels of quality. It is important that those in the organization understand where it is they want to go and how they are going to get there.

Many have suggested that an organization's **values** are the foundation for any progress since values describe how people in the organization intend to behave and act. The **mission** of the organization should present the following information in written form: who is in the organization, what the organization does, and who the customers (both internal and external) are. Once the mission is developed, a vision statement can be written to describe the organization's aspirations for the future. Everyone in the organization should have the opportunity to provide input on the development of the values, mission, and vision. Some organizations successfully combine their vision and mission into one statement. Once these are developed, the organization can start to assess the level of quality at present.

Cross-functional teams are the best resources for determining the present level of quality. These teams are developed from people in various functional departments (i.e., production, human resources, service, and technology). A good place to start the process of defining the current level of quality is to define a procedure for creating and submitting ideas to improve customer service and control costs and enhance profitability. In many cases cross-functional teams concentrate on finding an easy fix to get rapid, positive results. These positive results propel and encourage both individuals and teams to further explore ways to enhance customer service. This second step is repeated until overall improvement is achieved through the continuous identification of and elimination of root causes of service problems. This procedure is often called the **Deming Circle,** named after Dr. Deming, who first advocated its use.

Once teams are formed, they continue to need direction from leaders or from the team members themselves. (Self-directed teams are exclusively directed by team members; they do not rely on the organization's leaders for direction.) Team members must constantly remind themselves and others that all activities should be customer-driven and they help link the management of quality to the organization's strategy, mission, values, and vision. Unless the process of managing for quality is linked to strategic goals, quality efforts will not be realized. Clear goals also help make the team's start-up phase relatively brief so that results can be seen quickly. These early results help propel teams onward to tackle and overcome more difficult customer service challenges.

The process of managing for quality exists and flourishes within what has been characterized as a **"learning organization."** In his best seller, *The Fifth Discipline,* Peter M. Senge describes the concept of organizational learning as the way an organization recreates itself. People in learning organizations have shared knowledge, insights, and goals. Individual learning is important, but the sum of organizational learning is greater than its individual components.

These organizations also have an **organizational memory** for keeping these shared insights, knowledge, and goals. Associates in a learning organization commit to living the organizational culture. Organizational learning takes place at the individual, team, and organization levels. Learning organizations learn that if things go wrong, a hard look at the system is required; it is not a matter of who is responsible. Learning organizations look at the critical processes within the system to determine why the error occurred and implement ways to fix the process.

For managing and improving quality to be successful, it must be tailored to the unique needs, wants, and expectations of the service organization and the customers it serves. A commitment to managing and improving quality unique to the organization's culture and tied to the organization's history and vision for the future will add value to customer service. The uniqueness of the organization, its customers, and its associates, combined with a customized process for managing and improving quality, will encourage the creation and delivery of customer service that will help sustain a competitive advantage.

As Exhibit 1.6 shows, managing and improving quality results in a reduction in costs. This savings occurs because there are fewer mistakes, less rework, fewer delays, and a more efficient use of resources. Consequently, productivity improves because resources are used more efficiently and the organization's customer base increases because it is offered better quality at a lower price. The organization is able to stay competitive by concentrating on customers and their requirements rather than the bottom line. It builds its business through providing empowerment and satisfaction to internal customers. This boosts the retention of associates and improves products and services for external customers.

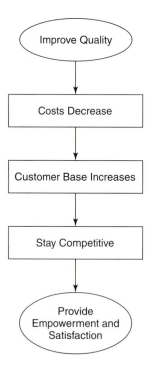

Exhibit 1.6 The results of improving quality. *(Source: Peter Capezio and Debra Morehouse.* Total Quality Management—The Road of Continuous Improvement. *Rockhurst College. Shawnee Mission, Kansas: National Press Publications. Used with permission.)*

The most important, and perhaps only, rule in service organizations is to take care of customer needs and expectations. Doing so results in delighted customers. Not doing so results in failure—for the organization and its internal customers. The process of managing for quality never ends. The process is not a destination but a journey of evolutionary improvement in a high performance service organization.

Summary

This chapter has given an insight into what quality is and how important it is to do things right, rather than using inspection to gain quality. Within the quality improvement system, the organization's leadership plays a critical role in improving quality and the leaders and associates must be committed totally to these principles. Recognizing who the customers are and what their role is in communicating expectations represent the key links in the process of managing and improving quality.

Key Terms

Assessing Quality—The requirements of the customers, as well as how the organization is doing in the delivery of requirements at levels that meet or exceed the customers' expectations.

Assessment—The organization's mission, vision statement, and core values should be reviewed during this assessment since these provide the context for evaluating current levels of quality.

Benchmarking—Benchmarking helps an organization study a process at another organization and adapt, modify, and apply the process at their own organization.

Commitment—The process for managing and improving quality is more likely to succeed if there is a strong message that there is a commitment to make quality the core of the organization's culture.

Continuous Quality Improvement (CQI)—Key to managing and improving quality for both internal and external customers; the objective is to deliver results that are better today compared to those of yesterday.

Cross-Functional Team—Composed of people in various functional departments to determine the present level of quality and work on improvements.

Customer Driven—High performance service organizations cannot define their visions until their customers are understood.

Deming Circle—Cross-functional teams encourage rapid results by having teams explore ways to enhance customer service. This is repeated until improvement is achieved through identification and elimination of problems.

External Customers—The people that purchase an organization's products and services.

Financial Expectations—These vary between organizations. Businesses expect to make a profit for the stakeholders, while non-profit organizations frequently expect to generate a surplus. This profit or surplus is used to build the organization by investing for future needs and in future growth.

Implementing Quality—Six steps include educating, assessing, addressing the burning issues, determining critical processes and how to measure progress, redesigning the process, and continuous improvement.

Internal Customers/Associates—Associates who are selected, oriented, and trained to create and deliver the products and services of the organization.

Leadership—The process of taking people somewhere with an idea, creating a compelling vision to help them see into the future, and then leading them to that future.

Leading Quality—Responsibility of everyone in the organization, since leadership is intimately related to managing and improving quality.

Learning Organization—Process of managing for quality exists and flourishes within the organization.

Mission—Defines the purpose of the organization and what the organization does.

Organizational Memory—The culture that takes place at the individual, team, and organization levels.

Paradigm—A way of seeing the world; places the customers first, beginning with internal customers and then shifting to external customers.

Partnering—Creates opportunities for synergism and growth; partnerships and alliances also provide a perfect environment for expanding the knowledge and understanding of managing for quality in the organization.

Quality—Doing the right things right.

Quality Life—Results from the effective application of quality principles to one's personal life; it also has a direct impact on the individual who ultimately must make a contribution to the organization as a team member and internal customer of the organization.

Strategic Quality Planning—Begins with a personal vision, which transforms into a shared vision within the organization. This vision is the driver behind strategic goals and critical processes.

Thinking Outside the Box—Demands time and commitment from key internal customers within the learning organization and the organization's culture and core values.

Tools of the Trade—Help measure and monitor quality improvements.

Total Quality Management (TQM)—Bottom line performance will take care of itself in an organization that is committed to and practices managing for quality.

Values—Describe how people in the organization tend to behave and act.

Review Questions

1. What is your personal definition of quality?
2. Who are the two most important customers in an organization and why?
3. What are the three criteria that form the basis of "doing things right"?
4. What is benchmarking?
5. What is Peter Senge's concept of the "learning organization"?
6. What are five positive results from managing the process to improve quality?

Activities in Your Organization

Listed below are some activities designed to reinforce the key chapter concepts in your organization. If you are a student and not currently working in the industry, interview an industry leader about one of these topics.

1. Your organization is a system with interrelated processes that directly affect the quality of the products and services created and delivered to your customers. Think about your organization and make some notes after you read each of the following questions:
   - Do you know your customers and understand the requirements of your customers?

- Do you understand the three broad sets of expectations in any organization—internal customers' expectations, external customers' expectations, and financial expectations? Briefly state what they are.
- What is your quality management paradigm?
- How do you view the organization's associates?
- How frequently are effective teams and their synergy used in your organization?
- How are external customers understood in terms of their requirements?
- Where is the organization on its CQI journey?
- Which tools of the trade help those in the organization measure and monitor quality improvements?
- How does strategic quality planning take place in your organization?
- What does your organization do to assess quality from both the internal and external customers' perspectives?
- Once the initial assessments are completed, how does your organization implement quality?
- Who in your organization is leading quality?

The answers to these questions give you insight into what your organization is currently doing to manage and improve quality. In many respects, the answers are the starting points for improvement.

2. Refer to Exhibit 1.3 and consider the three expectations in the model. How does your organization take into account the expectations of internal customers? What are these expectations? How does the organization discover and meet the expectations of external customers? How does the organization live up to the financial expectations? How are these expectations balanced in your organization?

3. Answer the following questions related to leadership and quality management:
   - As a leader who is personally committed to managing and improving quality in your organization, how will you articulate a compelling vision to help others see into the future and then lead them to that future?
   - What process will you use to define your organization's vision of quality and what it means to the organization's customers?
   - How will you become customer driven and understand your organization's customers? How will you determine customer expectations and customer requirements?
   - How will you select products and services that satisfy the needs and meet the expectations of the customers?
   - How will you involve members of the team to help define the vision and function in their roles as service creators and deliverers?
   - What will you do to create a customer service culture in the organization?
   - What will you do to solicit and accept the ideas for improvement from the people who are on the front line creating and delivering quality customer service?

Reference

Senge, Peter. *The Fifth Discipline: The Art and Practice of the Learning Organization.* New York: Doubleday/Currency, 1990.

Relevant Web Sites

There are many sites on the Web that relate to the topics presented in this chapter. Here are a few of our favorites:

Five Premises of TQM:
   http://www.rresults.com/tqm.html
Hotel Financial Performance Benchmarking:
   http://www.hotel-online.com/News/PR2003_2nd/May03_PKFBenchmarking.html
IQPIC—General Quality Web Site:
   http://www.iqpic.org
TQM Magazine:
   http://thesius.emeraldinsight.com/vl=12015191/cl=71/nw=1/rpsv/tqm.htm
What Is TQM?
   http://www.ed.gov/databases/ERIC_Digests/ed396759.html

Chapter

2

Champions of Quality

An organization's senior leaders should set directions and create customer focus, clear and visible values, and high expectations. The directions, values, and expectations should balance the needs of all your stakeholders. Leaders should ensure the creation of strategies, systems, and methods for achieving excellence, stimulating innovation, and building knowledge and capabilities.

Baldrige National Quality Program
Statement on Visionary Leadership

Learning Objectives

1. Understand Dr. W. Edwards Deming's Fourteen Obligations of Top Management, how executives use these obligations (cite examples from a previous work environment), and explain which of his obligations is used least often and/or questioned by executives of the modern era.

2. Explain the evolution of the Malcolm Baldrige National Quality Award and the basic criteria on which success is based. Also be able to name the company in the hospitality service industry that has won the award twice. Discuss Patrick Mene's VANO manager and the differences between a VANO manager and a manager with a Baldrige Award winning organization.

3. Speculate and describe how "Six Sigma" could be applied to the hospitality industry and how its success could be used as an effective marketing tool.

4. Describe the common themes among historic and modern-day quality gurus.

The twentieth century saw many quality-driven changes in corporate culture. Initial efforts involved a high degree of inspection, but they eventually evolved into the teachings of Dr. W. Edwards Deming (Exhibit 2.1) by mid-century and then into the work of modern gurus toward the end of the 1980s and 1990s. Knowing the origins and evolution of the principles of managing quality will give us a better understanding of the driving forces and their results. We are including the efforts and philosophies of the current leaders in the field because they offer a slightly different methodology and prioritization of internal customer focus.

Exhibit 2.1 Dr. W. Edwards Deming. *(Source: AP/Wide World Photos. Used with permission.)*

History of Managing for Quality

The management for quality has its origins in the pioneer work of several quality leaders, namely W. Edwards Deming, Joseph M. Juran, Armand Feigenbaum, Philip Crosby, Karou Ishikawa, and Genichi Taguchi. During the early decades of the twentieth century, the United States was completely transformed by the Industrial Revolution. The automobile companies, Ford Motor in particular, enjoyed tremendous success in developing the mass production process, a process based strictly on the interchangeability of labor and parts. Once there was duplication and strong marketing, however, the competitive advantage the United States had enjoyed for years changed. At that time, the mid-twentieth century, General Motors was able to continue to dominate the industrial world, however, by becoming product based, flexible, and geared for growth.

After World War II, two other changes occurred in the industrial sector: customers were suddenly looking for product differentiation and there was a drastic shortening of the product lifecycle. Most U.S. companies did not recognize this customer-based shift in expectations, but the Japanese were able to take advantage of this through incremental improvements.

The Quality Gurus

Deming

As American leadership turned deaf ears to customer's expectations, W. Edwards Deming went to Japan to help improve the quality of Japanese manufacturing, specifically automobiles. He helped post-World War II Japan rebuild its economy by introducing a philosophy and a statistical methodology to improve quality. The philosophy was based on continuous improvement; the methodology centered on statistics and probability, later known as statistical quality control, and was developed by Walter Shewhart and his associates at Bell Labs in the 1930s. Unlike the Japanese, it took decades for American businesses to recognize the Deming process for quality improvement.

In the early 1980s a TV documentary—*If Japan Can, Why Can't We?*—was shown on NBC. At this time, Ford Motor Company and other U.S. automakers were experiencing intensive competition from Japanese automakers. Ford Motor Company's CEO, Donald Petersen, invited Dr. Deming to Detroit to present his strategies for long-term process improvement in manufacturing. Deming told the automakers that 98 percent of the quality challenge was building the skills and knowledge of an organization's associates. To meet this challenge, Deming introduced the concepts of teamwork within departments, cross-functional (i.e., cross-departmental) teams, ongoing training, and strategic partnerships with goods and services vendors. At the heart of Deming's philosophy was the creation of a culture of quality within a company.

The foundations of Deming's challenge to improve quality were later used to develop other quality movements. For example, the Six Sigma process, a statistical measure that indicates 3.4 defects per million, or 99.9997 percent perfection, at Motorola and General Electric stemmed from Deming's earlier work.

Deming defined **Fourteen obligations of top management,** which are listed in Exhibit 2.2. These form the core of his quality system and define ways for an organization to transform itself into an organization focused on quality.

The Fourteen Obligations of Top Management

1. Create constancy of purpose for improvement of products and services.
2. Adopt the new philosophy .
3. Cease dependence on inspection to achieve quality.
4. End the practice of awarding business on the basis of price tag alone. Instead, minimize total cost by working with a single supplier.
5. Improve, constantly and forever, every process for planning, production, and service.
6. Institute training on the job.
7. Adopt and institute leadership.
8. Drive out fear.
9. Break down barriers between staff areas.
10. Eliminate slogans, exhortations, and targets for the work force.
11. Eliminate numerical quotas for the work force and numerical goals for management.
12. Remove barriers that rob people of pride of workmanship. Eliminate the annual rating or merit system.
13. Institute a vigorous program of education and self-improvement for everyone.
14. Put everybody in the company to work to accomplish the transformation.

Exhibit 2.2 Dr. Deming's Fourteen Obligations *(Source:* Out of Crisis *by W. Edwards Deming. Copyright © 1982, 1986 by W. Edwards Deming. Reprinted by permission of MIT Press.)*

According to Deming, top management must embody a constancy of purpose in the organization's vision and this vision must detail the commitment for constant improvement of products and services based on the needs and expectations of customers. Adopting this new philosophy involves focusing on the needs and expectations of the customers and realizing that these needs or expectations change over time. Ceasing dependence on inspections changes the reward system in the organization. Organizations focused on quality reward people for improving quality during the process, rather than solely relying on fixing quality problems once the process is completed. In other words, doing the job right the first time is preferred to the impossible task of inspecting quality in a product at the end of a process.

The goal of working with a single supplier is to develop a long-term, mutually beneficial alliance with a supplier that has adopted principles of quality management. This requires the creation of a partnership with a high level of trust. Constant improvement centers on an ongoing analysis of each process and continually rewarding creativity and commitment to the improvement of both product and service quality.

Deming's sixth obligation refers to training. Training should be ongoing and a responsibility of everyone in the organization rather than an add-on. It is the most important responsibility that managers and associates have in their role as mentors to others. Deming's seventh obligation, leadership, is tied to the idea of training. It includes creating an organizational culture in which associates are encouraged and developed by organizational leaders. Leaders should set an example, actively listen, and be empathetic. When fear is driven out of the organization, the culture becomes one in which associates can fail and learn and improve their quest for quality. This obligation is often one of the most difficult to accomplish; a leader must have a special set of talents in order to generate this level of trust.

Deming also says top management must break down barriers. Barriers are broken down when input from all team members (associates, suppliers, and managers) is utilized to create, evaluate, and improve products and services. Cross-functional teams help meet this obligation by incorporating ideas and views from many people from different areas of the organization.

Slogans, exhortations, and targets are often viewed by associates as the "program of the day, week, or month." These should be used to channel internal competition, that can create barriers to internal teamwork, into competition centered on external competitors. Furthermore, top management must place less emphasis on numerical quotas and goals, if they must exist, and more emphasis and effort on improving quality.

Another type of barrier management must break down are those barriers that rob people of pride of workmanship. These are counter to the ownership of quality. It is better to create an organizational culture where internal customers can make a positive difference, provide meaningful contributions, and continuously improve themselves and quality. Education and self-improvement provide continuous opportunities to improve. These opportunities must be available for all, according to Deming's philosophy. Including everybody in making the transformation to an organization that focuses on quality will ensure wide-reaching contributions that will create a plan of action based on the organization's vision and align and commit everyone toward the goal of continuously improving quality.

Juran

Dr. Joseph M. Juran's (Exhibit 2.3) contribution to the field of quality centers on his philosophy that quality requires commitment and action from top management, training in the management of quality, and quality improvements at a revolutionary rate. He suggested a way to organize an interconnected quality network to maximize an organization's delivery of quality products and services. Juran's *Quality Control Handbook,* first published in 1951, detailed this philosophy in his **Ten Steps to Quality Improvement** (Exhibit 2.4).

Another of Juran's unmatched contributions in the field of quality was his contribution to designing the **Malcolm Baldrige National Quality Award.** This

Exhibit 2.3   Dr. Joseph M. Juran.   *(Source: Juran Institute, Inc. Used with permission.)*

1. Create an awareness of and commitment to improve.
2. Establish goals for improvement, utilizing input from cross-functional sources.
3. Rally people in the organization around the common goal of improving quality.
4. Train associates by creating a learning organization focused on quality.
5. Continuously learn and improve as problems are solved and projects are completed.
6. Regularly communicate progress toward quality improvement goals.
7. Recognize those who contribute to improving quality.
8. Communicate results as the process of managing quality discovers information.
9. Measure progress toward the goals of improving quality.
10. Integrate improvement into the systems of the organization.

Exhibit 2.4   Dr. Juran's Ten Steps to Quality Improvement.   *(Source: "Ten Steps to Quality Improvement" from* Juran's Quality Control Handbook *by Joseph M. Juran. Used by permission of the McGraw-Hill Companies.)*

award, established by the U. S. Congress in 1987, was named after a former U.S. Secretary of Commerce and recognizes U.S. companies who have achieved excellence through implementation of quality-improvement programs. It was created to enhance the competitiveness of U.S. businesses by promoting quality through awareness and recognition of quality achievements of U.S. businesses. The Baldrige Award program is managed by the **National Institute of Standards and Technology,** an agency of the U.S. Department of Commerce's Technology Administration, in cooperation with private industry.

There were originally three categories of the award: manufacturing, service, and small business. In 1999, two new categories were added—education and health care. Each year, up to three awards may be presented in each of the categories.[1]

[1]For more information, please contact: Baldrige National Quality Program, National Institute of Standards and Technology, Administration Building, Room A600, 100 Bureau Drive, Stop 1020, Gaithersburg, MD 20899-1020.

The Baldrige Quality Award emphasizes the following core values and concepts:

- Visionary leadership
- Customer-driven excellence
- Organizational and personal learning
- Valuing internal customers and partners
- Agility
- Focus on the future
- Managing for innovation
- Management by fact
- Social responsibility
- Focus on results and creating value
- Systems perspective

The assessment tool used by the Baldrige National Quality Program, shown in Exhibit 2.5, can help an organization's leaders assess present performance and learn what can be improved.

ARE WE MAKING PROGRESS?

YOUR OPINION IS MOST IMPORTANT TO US. THERE ARE 40 STATEMENTS BELOW. FOR EACH STATEMENT, CHECK THE BOX THAT BEST MATCHES HOW YOU FEEL (STRONGLY DISAGREE, DISAGREE, NEITHER AGREE NOR DISAGREE, AGREE, STRONGLY AGREE). HOW YOU FEEL WILL HELP US DECIDE WHERE WE MOST NEED TO IMPROVE. WE WILL NOT BE LOOKING AT INDIVIDUAL RESPONSES BUT WILL USE THE INFORMATION FROM OUR WHOLE GROUP TO MAKE DECISIONS. IT SHOULD TAKE YOU ABOUT 10 TO 15 MINUTES TO COMPLETE THIS QUESTIONNAIRE.

Senior leaders, please fill in the following information:

_____

Name of organization or unit being discussed

CATEGORY 1: LEADERSHIP	Strongly Disagree	Disagree	Neither Agree nor Disagree	Agree	Strongly Agree
1a. I know my organization's mission (what it is trying to accomplish).	❑	❑	❑	❑	❑
1b. My senior (top) leaders use our organization's values to guide us.	❑	❑	❑	❑	❑
1c. My senior leaders create a work environment that helps me do my job.	❑	❑	❑	❑	❑
1d. My organization's leaders share information about the organization.	❑	❑	❑	❑	❑
1e. My senior leaders encourage learning that will help me advance in my career.	❑	❑	❑	❑	❑
1f. My organization lets me know what it thinks is most important.	❑	❑	❑	❑	❑
1g. My organization asks what I think.	❑	❑	❑	❑	❑

Exhibit 2.5   An Assessment Tool from the Baldrige National Quality Program.

CATEGORY 2: STRATEGIC PLANNING	Strongly Disagree	Disagree	Neither Agree nor Disagree	Agree	Strongly Agree
2a. As it plans for the future, my organization asks for my ideas.	❑	❑	❑	❑	❑
2b. I know the parts of my organization's plans that will affect me and my work.	❑	❑	❑	❑	❑
2c. I know how to tell if we are making progress on my work group's part of the plan.	❑	❑	❑	❑	❑

CATEGORY 3: CUSTOMER AND MARKET FOCUS	Strongly Disagree	Disagree	Neither Agree nor Disagree	Agree	Strongly Agree

(Note: Customer refers to the people who use the products of your work.)

	Strongly Disagree	Disagree	Neither Agree nor Disagree	Agree	Strongly Agree
3a. I know who my most important customers are.	❑	❑	❑	❑	❑
3b. I keep in touch with my customers.	❑	❑	❑	❑	❑
3c. My customers tell me what they need and want.	❑	❑	❑	❑	❑
3d. I ask if my customers are satisfied or dissatisfied with my work.	❑	❑	❑	❑	❑
3e. I am allowed to make decisions to solve problems for my customers.	❑	❑	❑	❑	❑

CATEGORY 4: MEASUREMENT, ANALYSIS, AND KNOWLEDGE MANAGEMENT	Strongly Disagree	Disagree	Neither Agree nor Disagree	Agree	Strongly Agree
4a. I know how to measure the quality of my work.	❑	❑	❑	❑	❑
4b. I know how to analyze (review) the quality of my work to see if changes are needed.	❑	❑	❑	❑	❑
4c. I use these analyses for making decisions about my work.	❑	❑	❑	❑	❑
4d. I know how the measures I use in my work fit into the organization's overall measures of improvement.	❑	❑	❑	❑	❑
4e. I get all the important information I need to do my work.	❑	❑	❑	❑	❑
4f. I get the information I need to know about how my organization is doing.	❑	❑	❑	❑	❑

Exhibit 2.5   continued

CATEGORY 5: HUMAN RESOURCE FOCUS	**Strongly Disagree**	**Disagree**	**Neither Agree nor Disagree**	**Agree**	**Strongly Agree**
5a. I can make changes that will improve my work.	❏	❏	❏	❏	❏
5b. The people I work with cooperate and work as a team.	❏	❏	❏	❏	❏
5c. My boss encourages me to develop my job skills so I can advance in my career.	❏	❏	❏	❏	❏
5d. I am recognized for my work.	❏	❏	❏	❏	❏
5e. I have a safe workplace.	❏	❏	❏	❏	❏
5f. My boss and my organization care about me.	❏	❏	❏	❏	❏

CATEGORY 6: PROCESS MANAGEMENT	**Strongly Disagree**	**Disagree**	**Neither Agree nor Disagree**	**Agree**	**Strongly Agree**
6a. I can get everything I need to do my job.	❏	❏	❏	❏	❏
6b. I collect information (data) about the quality of my work.	❏	❏	❏	❏	❏
6c. We have good processes for doing our work.	❏	❏	❏	❏	❏
6d. I have control over my work processes.	❏	❏	❏	❏	❏

CATEGORY 7: BUSINESS RESULTS	**Strongly Disagree**	**Disagree**	**Neither Agree nor Disagree**	**Agree**	**Strongly Agree**
7a. My customers are satisfied with my work.	❏	❏	❏	❏	❏
7b. My work products meet all requirements.	❏	❏	❏	❏	❏
7c. I know how well my organization is doing financially.	❏	❏	❏	❏	❏
7d. My organization uses my time and talents well.	❏	❏	❏	❏	❏
7e. My organization removes things that get in the way of progress.	❏	❏	❏	❏	❏
7f. My organization obeys laws and regulations.	❏	❏	❏	❏	❏
7g. My organization has high standards and ethics.	❏	❏	❏	❏	❏
7h. My organization helps me help my community.	❏	❏	❏	❏	❏
7i. I am satisfied with my job.	❏	❏	❏	❏	❏

Exhibit 2.5   continued

Would you like to give more information about any of your responses? Please include the number of the statement (i.e., 2a. or 7d.) you are discussing.

_____
_____
_____
_____
_____
_____
_____
_____
_____
_____
_____

Exhibit 2.5   continued

This assessment tool also may be downloaded at www.baldrige.nist.gov. Once the assessment is completed, the areas for improvement can be identified.

Baldrige Center of Performance Excellence

As mentioned earlier, organizations are systems and it is helpful to take a systems perspective in any organization, regardless of industry, or segment within a particular industry. A **systems perspective** includes the core values and concepts of the system. The Baldrige core values and concepts are embodied in seven categories shown in Exhibit 2.6:

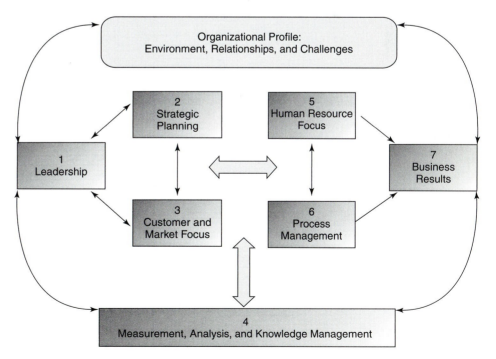

Exhibit 2.6   The Baldrige Criteria for Performance Excellence Framework. (*Source: www.baldrige.nist.gov.*)

1. Leadership
2. Strategic planning
3. Customer and market focus
4. Measurement, analysis, and knowledge management
5. Human resource focus
6. Process management
7. Business results
   - Customer-focused results
   - Product and service results
   - Financial and market results
   - Human resource results
   - Organizational effectiveness results
   - Governance and social responsibility results

According to the Baldrige criteria, leadership occurs when the senior executives of an organization help others understand customer requirements for quality products and services. At the historic Detroit Athletic Club discussed in Chapter 1, for example, the PEP (Performance Excellence Process) engages the entire club leadership and requires total commitment from the Board of Directors and the club's department heads. During the monthly PEP meetings, internal customers discuss goals, objectives, performance issues, and workplace issues. Leaders also must establish a definition of service quality that is easy to communicate and understand. They need to capture valuable data by gathering information and analyzing it to refine the definitions of what customers want and expect. Other data will measure how well the organization delivered on what was expected.

Short- and long-term strategic planning is optional when done by quality improvement teams, but when employed, strategic planning provides important information. At the Detroit Athletic Club, the strategic planning process provides a unified vision throughout the organization. It addresses questions such as:

- Why do we exist as an organization?
- Where are we going as an organization?
- What are the restraints (e.g., financial, governance process, committee structure, location, economic environment) that will temper our decisions?

The human resources piece of the framework shown in Exhibit 2.6 focuses on associate selection, orientation, training, validation of training by both internal and external customers, and coaching. Business results include measurement of what customers want and expect most: high-quality products, timely and reliable creation and delivery of services, friendly and efficient associates, and value for the money and time spent. Customer satisfaction must be measured regularly through focus groups, feedback from customer contact associates, surveys and comment cards, and direct observation. (Business results also cover financial and market, human resources, and company specific operating results.)

Baldrige Award Winners in the Food and Hospitality Industry

Once an application for the Baldrige Award is submitted and evaluated by a team of examiners from several industries, the organization is visited by a team that spends one week evaluating quality. As of 2003, only one hospitality company, the Ritz-Carlton Hotel Company of Atlanta, Georgia, has won the award in the service category. The Ritz-Carlton Hotel Company first won the Malcolm Baldrige National Quality Award in 1992 and then again in 1999.

From the greeting and service provided at the front door of the hotel (Exhibit 2.7) until you check-out and depart, the Ritz-Carlton Hotel Company prides itself on quality. They manage approximately 40 luxury hotels throughout the world

Exhibit 2.7 From the greeting and service provided at the front door of the hotel until you check-out and depart, the Ritz-Carlton hotel delivers quality. *(Source: Getty Images, Inc. Used with permission.)*

and they employ about 18,000 people. Patrick Mene, Vice President of Quality for Ritz-Carlton, is an avid proponent of the principles of quality improvement. Mr. Mene indicates there are two types of managers, the Ritz-Carlton manager and the **VANO (visual appearance/accounting numbers only) manager.**

The VANO manager believes:

1. A sales transaction is just a number.
2. The level of internal and external customer satisfaction does not impact profit.
3. Quality is solely the visual appearance of the facility.
4. Profit is the difference between sales and costs.
5. Today's profit is the primary objective, no matter what.

The Ritz-Carlton manager believes we need to produce a work environment that:

1. Helps people live better.
2. Treats people with dignity
3. Involves people in the planning of the work that affects them, to increase the pride and joy they derive from their work.

In other words, management's concentration on the internal customer will enable the associates at Ritz-Carlton to take care of the external customers by exceeding their expectations. This will happen if the internal customers are trained, given all the necessary information about the service and products, provided with the necessary tools and resources, involved in the planning process, share the vision of management, trust management, and are recognized for their efforts.

In 2002, HDS Services applied for the Michigan Quality Council's Leadership Award, which has adopted the Baldrige criteria. The council evaluated the application submission, a 50-page document, and determined that HDS did not qualify for the site evaluation. The company's Senior Quality Improvement Team (SQIT) was notified and was predictably disappointed at the outcome. However, when the evaluation documents were received and subsequently reviewed, it was very obvious that the report had tremendous value in terms of improving quality in the future. The SQIT unanimously approved a motion to continue the process of annual application to the council. HDS Services has since taken the position that they are applying to learn, and consequently improve each year, rather than win the award. If the company were to win, it would be perceived as a bonus.

Feigenbaum

Armand V. Feigenbaum introduced his **cost of nonconformance** philosophy and rationale regarding why an organization should commit to quality. Feigenbaum also refined the concept of **work process flow** and showed how improvement in one component of a process helps improve other areas of the organization. Feigenbaum's approach to quality is driven by those who purchase products and services. His philosophy of managing and improving quality, in the form of six key points, is shown in Exhibit 2.8.

1. **Total quality control (TQC)** is a system for integrating quality development, maintenance, and improvement into the groups of an organization. This integration enables marketing, engineering, production, and service to operate at the most economical levels to provide customer satisfaction.
2. Quality control (QC) represents a management tool that sets quality standards, evaluates performance against the established standards, acts when standards are not met, and makes plans to improve the standards.
3. Product quality is affected by both technological and human factors. The human factors are more important.
4. QC impacts all aspects of production from defining customers' needs to following up to ensure satisfaction.
5. The operating costs of quality can be categorized as prevention costs (planning and preventing nonconformance and defects), appraisal costs (evaluating quality based on standards), internal failure costs (costs such as spoilage that do not meet the specifications), and external failure costs (for example, loss of market share resulting when a defective product reaches the customer).
6. Quality is controlled in the process, not simply after production has been completed.

Exhibit 2.8 Armand V. Feigenbaum's Six Key Points. *(Source: Verne Harnish, Gazelles, Inc. Used with permission.)*

Crosby

In his role as ITT Corporation's first Vice President of Quality, Philip Crosby promoted the concept of zero defects to the company's executives as part of the **Crosby Complete Management System.** He believed that it is less expensive to "do things right the first time" and that the achievement of quality is relatively easy. His 14 steps to quality improvement are presented in Exhibit 2.9.

Ishikawa and Taguchi

As mentioned earlier, quality improvement processes originated after World War II as the Japanese manufacturing industries attempted to rebuild. The early focus was on process controls to identify defects at the source. Once this early inspection phase was largely completed, manufacturers moved into the second, or quality control phase.

1. Management must commit to centering its quality focus on the needs of its customers.
2. The quality improvement teams with representatives from each department oversee the continuous quality improvement process.
3. Measurement tools are utilized to establish baselines and where current and potential problems can be found.
4. Costs of quality are carefully defined and used as a management tool.
5. Quality awareness and personal concerns of all staff are heightened through training in quality improvement principles.
6. Once trained, corrective action is taken closest to the source of defects.
7. Zero defects planning analyzes the relevant activities using a committee.
8. Associates are educated by trained supervisors to know and practice their roles in the quality improvement process.
9. A zero defects day launches the quality improvement program company-wide and signals a change.
10. Individuals and groups establish their own quality improvement goals.
11. Associates inform management of the obstacles they face and the types of supportive work environments needed to deliver defined quality results.
12. All who participate are recognized for their commitment to quality improvement.
13. Quality councils are formed of groups of people who spotlight quality and share information about the process of continuous improvement.
14. The quality improvement process is continuous and never ends.

Exhibit 2.9 Philip Crosby's 14 Steps for Implementing Quality Improvements. (*Source:* Quality Is Free, *by Philip Crosby. Used by permission of The McGraw-Hill Companies.*)

Karou Ishikawa convinced senior members of Japanese management to follow the advice of quality circle members and grant them the necessary autonomy to survive and thrive. In quality circles, the responsibility for developing, implementing, and monitoring quality in an organization largely rests with members of these circles. Ishikawa also uniquely described the customer as both internal (within the organization) and external, and he promoted the necessity of a company-wide shared vision.

Genichi Taguchi developed a formula, incorporated into the **Taguchi Loss Function,** to calculate the costs associated with a lack of quality. According to Taguchi's theory, when a deviation from quality occurs, an economic loss follows in geometric proportion. The effect of the loss is cumulative and dramatic. Losses are reduced and eliminated through the use of cross-functional teams, focused communication, benchmarking, identification of alternative methods and plans, and the use of systems to monitor quality.

Quality control departments regularly monitored and reported product quality using statistical charts, such as cause-and-effect diagrams (these were developed by Ishikawa and show causes and outcomes of defects), control charts (show a process flow with upper and lower limits and when these limits are violated), flow charts (also known as process flow diagrams, depicting all of the steps in a process), histograms (used to measure the frequency of occurrence), Pareto charts (bar charts used to assign priorities), run (trend) charts (plot the results of a process over time), and scatter diagrams (show the relationship between two variables).

Modern-Day Quality Efforts—Gurus

The quality effort did not become a major topic in the United States until the 1970s and 1980s. During these decades the high-profile U.S. automobile industry lost a sizeable amount of its global market share, particularly at home, due to the products of the "Big Three" deteriorating in quality. At the same time, the Japanese automakers had gained significant ground because of drastic improvement in Japan's automotive quality since the late 1950s. Thus, there was a major shift in market share.

The sleeping giant finally woke up to the fact that managing the quality improvement process was the primary ingredient in the Japanese success, and Ford Motor was the first auto manufacturer to take action with its "Quality is Job One" initiative in the early 1980s. Many of Dr. Deming's management principles were adopted at Ford, and the company was successful in stopping its decline in market share. Not only did Ford improve quality in the components it manufactured, but quality compliance was enforced for its suppliers as well. Other manufacturers, however, failed to realize that managing for quality was a journey and expected immediate success.

Another factor in the shift in market share between U.S. and Japanese companies was Japan's culture, which is more compatible to managing for quality. They are more paternalistic. In contrast, our social system promoted independent thinking . In addition, American management was more results oriented in these earlier decades and Japanese management was more process oriented. In America, however, we have learned that the quality of the process leads to quality outcomes.

American industrial companies soon began implementing these quality principles as well as initiatives such as **Six Sigma.** Six Sigma, a concept derived from statistics, uses the Greek letter Sigma to measure how far from perfection a product deviates. Reaching Six Sigma indicates there are 3.4 errors per million opportunities. In other words, Six Sigma is 99.9997 percent (rather than 100 percent) perfect. Six Sigma indicates how well a process is performing, that is, producing its product or service.

The fundamental goal of Six Sigma is to improve the process through **DMAIC,** a process that Defines, Measures, Analyzes, Improves, and Controls existing processes, and **DMADV,** a process that Defines, Measures, Analyzes, Defines, and Verifies. DMAIC searches for incremental improvement in a process that falls below customer expectations, as reflected in the process specifications. DMADV is utilized if a current process needs more than simple incremental improvement or when developing a new process.

Motorola coined the term Six Sigma in 1986. (A Motorola team from Tianjin is pictured in Exhibit 2.10 celebrating its victory.) To indicate mastery of the Six Sigma process, Motorola also developed a belt ranking system similar to the rankings used in karate:

- Green Belts - Team leaders
- Black Belts - Technical leaders
- Master Black Belts - Technical leaders with theoretical mathematical understanding of the statistical methods (highest level of organizational and technical proficiency)

Motorola, General Electric, and other companies have used this initiative successfully for many years and continue to do so. These industry leaders are achieving unprecedented levels of quality improvements through cross-functional design and manufacturing teams, reduction in cycle time, statistical

Exhibit 2.10 A Motorola team from Tianjin celebrating its victory. *(Source: Motorola, Inc. Used with permission.)*

process applications, and Six Sigma quality to achieve total customer satisfaction. Six Sigma is a quality improvement pioneered by Motorola in the 1980s and refined by AlliedSignal and General Electric in the 1990s.

Starwood Hotels & Resorts Worldwide, Inc. was the first company in the hospitality industry to adopt Six Sigma in 2001. In statistics, the Greek letter sigma (σ) stands for standard deviation; that is, a statistical way to describe how much variation exists in a set of data, a group of items, or a process. If a hotel's room service delivers only about 68 percent of the meals on time, the process of delivery scores only a "2σ." There would have to be on-time service delivery 99.9997 percent of the time to meet Six Sigma standards.

Six Sigma helps establish a data-driven approach to continuously improving a process by reducing ineffective and inefficient process quality. It also helps raise productivity, which results in increased bottom line profitability. To improve the effectiveness of a process, managers can use the five steps listed in the DMAIC acronym: Define, Measure, Analyze, Improve, and Control.

The application of Six Sigma to the hotel and lodging industry also includes the following:

- **Voice of Customer (VOC)**
- **Critical to Quality (CTQ)**

Many hotel companies claim they are guest focused, yet they show little solid evidence to substantiate the claim. A hotel company that is truly committed to guest-focused operations has multiple guest feedback channels. The company also has a structured methodology for integrating the data into its product development and guest service delivery processes. VOC is the process of gathering, analyzing, and integrating guest input back into the organization's decision making. The way to capture the VOC extends from monitoring phone calls during reservations to guest surveys and guest focus groups. VOC includes the gathering of input from present guests' voices regarding products and services as well as the voices of potential guests, staff members (i.e., internal customers), and suppliers.

Critical to Quality (CTQ) is an integral part of confirming the guests' requirements. To define CTQ in Six Sigma terms, VOC data are collected and compared to the guests' CTQ requirements. Then, the gap between the requirements and the current quality level of the hotel organization's products and services is analyzed. Once the gap is identified and quantified, the Six Sigma internal customer team can begin to focus on measuring, analyzing, improving, and controlling this gap using the DMAIC process.

Six Sigma is not a new quality improvement technique, but its application is innovative in the hotel and lodging industry, and it is likely to change the face of the quality improvements of hospitality business products and services.

What economic affect does Six Sigma have on a company's bottom line? It depends on where they started. General Electric's CEO, Jack Welch, was involved in implementing Six Sigma in the mid 1990s, and in the company's annual report for 1999 he reported a multibillion dollar savings directly attributable to this effort. Other companies have been less successful financially, but other business dynamics can play a part in this as well. For example, if the quality effort is concentrated on a product that has little marketability.

Motorola also developed a program to make their systems more available to their customers. They call it the **5Nines Program** and it represents a commitment to total customer satisfaction. The 5Nines acronym refers to end-to-end availability 99.999% (5Nines) of the time or no more than five minutes of total downtime per year for customers. Motorola developed this program because the company was concerned about the availability of easy-to-use communication systems. Motorola realized that these communication systems were essential to the total satisfaction of its customers. Motorola is hopeful that 5Nines will result in a competitive advantage through the simplification of operations and world-class availability.

Common Themes of the Gurus

When reviewing the quality philosophies and messages from each of the historic quality gurus and modern-day users, several common themes emerge:

- People in organizations that regularly improve quality have a vision of a future that is better than the present.
- There is a shared commitment to the quality vision through a common goal of continuous improvement, which results in action by all to make the vision come to life and thrive.
- The organization is viewed as a system and progress toward improving quality is measured in a series of processes in the organization.
- The organization fundamentally exists to meet the needs/requirements of the customers, both internal (paid to create the products and services) customers and external (pay for the products and services) customers.
- Ongoing training of internal customers is essential, and it takes teamwork to create a network of this most important resource of the organization.
- People long for the ability to share in the plan and creation of the organization's vision, and they want to be recognized for their efforts in improving quality.

Even though the gurus are separated by decades of time, their consistent messages form the basis for any quality improvement program in an organization, regardless of industry segment or product or service created and sold.

Summary

In order to fully understand what needs to be done to manage and improve quality today, one must have a basic knowledge and appreciation of the history of quality. Today's quality management and improvement efforts are built on the foundation laid by the quality gurus in the twentieth century. Similarly, it is essential to understand today's companies that are taking quality to the next level by adding to the knowledge and skills in this area.

Key Terms

5Nines Program—5Nines represents a commitment to total customer satisfaction. The 5Nines acronym refers to end-to-end availability 99.999% (5Nines) of the time or no more than five minutes of total downtime per year for customers.

Cost of Nonconformance—Philosophy of Armand V. Feigenbaum and his rationale regarding an organization's commitment to quality.

Critical to Quality (CTQ)—CTQ is an integral part of confirming the guests' requirements. To define CTQ in Six Sigma terms, voice of the customer (VOC) data are collected and compared to the guests' CTQ requirements. Then, the gap between the requirements and the current quality level of the organization's products and services is analyzed. Once the gap is identified and quantified, the Six Sigma internal customer team can begin to focus on measuring, analyzing, improving, and controlling this gap using the define, measure, analyze, improve and control process.

Crosby Complete Management System—Crosby's 14 steps to implementing quality improvements in an organization.

Deming's Fourteen Obligations of Top Management—These form the core of Deming's quality system and define ways for an organization to transform itself into an organization focused on quality.

DMADV—A process that Defines, Measures, Analyzes, Defines, and Verifies.

DMAIC—A process that Defines, Measures, Analyzes, Improves, and Controls existing processes.

Juran's Ten Steps to Quality Improvement—A way to organize an interconnected quality network to maximize an organization's delivery of quality products and services.

Malcolm Baldrige National Quality Award—Established by the United States Congress in 1987, was named after a former U.S. Secretary of Commerce and recognizes U.S. companies who have achieved excellence through implementation of quality-improvement programs. It was created to enhance the competitiveness of U.S. businesses by promoting quality through awareness and recognition of quality achievements of U.S. businesses.

National Institute of Standards and Technology—An agency of the U.S. Department of Commerce's Technology Administration.

Six Sigma—A concept, derived from statistics, that uses the Greek letter Sigma to measure how far from perfection a product deviates.

Systems Perspective—Includes the core values and concepts of a system; leadership, strategic planning, customer and market focus measurement, analysis, and knowledge management, human resource focus, process management, and business results.

Taguchi Loss Function—Formula developed to calculate the costs associated with lack of quality.

Total Quality Control (TQC)—A system for integrating quality development, maintenance, and improvement into the groups of an organization.

VANO Manager—Visual, Appearance/Accounting, Numbers Only manager
Voice of Customer (VOC)—VOC is the process of gathering, analyzing, and integrating guest input back into the organization's decision making.
Work Process Flow—Feigenbaum's concept of how improvement in one component of a process helps improve other areas of the organization.

Review Questions

1. What are Dr. Deming's 14 obligations?
2. What is the difference between the company's vision and its mission?
3. What are the criteria for the Malcolm Baldrige's National Quality Award?
4. What is Six Sigma?
5. Why did Dr. Deming take his principles of management to Japan?
6. What is a VANO manager?
7. What are the common themes of the gurus of quality?

Activities in Your Organization

Listed below are some activities you can do in your organization. These are designed to reinforce the key chapter concepts. If you are a student and not currently working in the industry, interview an industry leader about one of these topics.

1. Use Dr. Deming's list of 14 Obligations to analyze your organization. Explain how these obligations are not currently being addressed/used in your organization. This analysis will pinpoint barriers to managing and improving quality. Explain how these obligations are being addressed/used in your organization. This analysis will identify strategies that need to be reinforced to manage and improve quality.
2. Review the 10 steps to quality improvement developed by Dr. Juran. Using these steps, honestly evaluate your organization's status relative to each one. Also ask a number of the organization's leaders to evaluate the organization's current status using the 10 steps. Then, using the Malcolm Baldrige National Quality Award criteria, develop an outline of action items for you and the other leaders to use in your organization to improve quality.
3. Analyze your management style using the VANO vs. the Ritz-Carlton management styles. Where are your strengths? Where are the areas that you could improve? Develop a plan to capitalize on your strengths and improve your weaknesses.

References

Ehrlich, B. H. *Transactional Six Sigma and Lean Servicing: Leveraging Manufacturing Concepts to Achieve World-Class Service.* Boca Raton, Florida: CRC Press LLC, 2002.

Senge, Peter. *The Fifth Discipline. The Art and Practice of the Learning Organization.* New York: Doubleday/Currency, 1990.

Verne Harnish, Gazelles, Inc.

Takenaka, Yuichiro, and Ronald Cichy, "Six Sigma Makes Sense." *Michigan Lodging.* September 2003. 13(9): 6.

Relevant Web Sites

Deming Electronic Network:
  http://deming.eng.clemson.edu/pub/den/deming_map.htm
Dr. Deming's Site for Total Quality Management:
  http://www.well.com/user/vamead/demingdist.html
Dr. Deming's Main Web Site:
  http://www.deming.org/
Juran and Deming Article (by Phil Landesberg):
  http://curiouscat.net/library/pdf/inthebeginning.pdf
Malcolm Baldrige Quality Award:
  http://www.emporia.edu/ibed/jour/jour14om/sarat.htm
Michigan Quality Award (Lighthouse):
  http://www.michiganquality.org/recog/Brochure/
More Malcolm Baldrige Quality Award:
  http://www.quality.nist.gov/
Ritz-Carlton Hotel Company:
  http://www.ritzcarlton.com/
Ritz-Carlton Hotel Company's Award Application Summary, 1999:
  http://www.quality.nist.gov/PDF_files/RCHC_Application_Summary.pdf
Six Sigma and Starwood Hotels and Resorts:
  http://www.starwood.com/development/fran_detail.html?category=OPSU&topNav=OS
Starwood Hotels and Resorts Worldwide, Inc. Web Site:
  http://www.starwood.com/
Who Is Dr. Edwards Deming?:
  http://www.lii.net/deming.html

Chapter

3

Quality Management

Implementation of the quality principles in your organization requires time; however, the end result will bring customer loyalty, satisfaction, increased market share, and financial contribution.

Sue Lantzsch
Regional Vice President Operations
HDS Services
Farmington Hills, MI

Quality is sustainable, tangible value and it's worth repeating over and over if you care enough.

Dan W. Darrow
President, Palm Hospitality Company
A subsidiary of the Walt Disney Company
Orlando, FL

Learning Objectives

1. Understand why and how shifts in paradigms occur and how to become a change maker.
2. Contrast a traditional organization with a high performance service organization.
3. Understand process thinking and continuous improvement.
4. Define the core principles of quality and how needs and expectations equal requirements.
5. Know the kinds of customers and the characteristics of each.

Shifting Paradigms

Imagine that you are the manager of an organization—a business, a volunteer group, or even a family. Your days are spent in your role as a law enforcement officer. Also imagine that when immediate problems must be solved, you are the troubleshooter or firefighter to put out the fire of the moment. You view associates as the "help," workers who are there to help you achieve your goals. You are reactive and feel minute-by-minute that the organization is running you. You become frustrated, stressed, and angry and you believe "if it ain't broke, don't fix it" because you are up to your neck in problems that already need fixing. One day, you say, "forget it," and quit.

Fortunately, there is a better way; rather than quitting, you could undergo a management strategy paradigm shift. A paradigm is an outstandingly clear or typical example—an archetype. It is an original model or pattern of which all things of the same type are representations. In other words, management paradigms are the eyeglasses through which managers view the world. The fictitious situation above illustrates a typical management paradigm. An alternative paradigm requires you to view management as innovation. In the alternative model, one we call **the better way,** a manager sees change happening and wants to help make it happen. At the very least, the manager accepts change early.

The HDS Example (1991): A Testimonial

In 1991, several senior operations executives came to the president of HDS Services and informed him that HDS was falling behind in the area of quality services and products. Corporate standards were excellent, but the systems, techniques, and processes required to achieve these standards were noticeably missing. The organization had been experiencing some difficulty competing in certain high profile retail markets, and the new managers on board did not possess the same standards of excellence that senior management had developed over the years.

This senior operations team convinced the president that there could be value in their attending a weeklong presentation on the principles of quality improvement in Chicago. They attended the conference, returned to the corporate office, and convinced the team that the organization should seriously consider adopting this quality effort. The Chicago experience was virtually responsible for a massive paradigm shift within HDS Services. A quality improvement presentation was made to the executives of HDS Services in October 1991, and the content of this presentation was well received by the team and made a lasting impression on everyone. Many quality-related management tools and principles had never been used at HDS Services; the basic principles of quality management had never been formally practiced and there wasn't a formal vision or company mission statement.

We decided to accept the challenge of transforming HDS into a quality improvement company and took a formal adoption recommendation to the executive staff committee, which at the time was a nine member committee responsible for developing corporate policy, long-range planning, and the annual strategic business plan. The next meeting was in November 1991, but because it was so late in the year and the 1992 business plan was already in development, we were concerned that the management of quality may get pushed back until mid-1992.

In two weeks our presentation was developed, and, with ample preliminary information distributed, we were able to conduct a full, in-depth discussion at the executive staff committee meeting regarding this paradigm shift. Could we adopt all of the new management principles and put them into action in a company with an enormous list of operational paradigms? Could senior management shift to a "bottom up" management style in their leadership throughout the organization?

As it turned out, they were more than ready for a change. In fact, the committee voted unanimously to adopt the proposed changes in management principles in their entirety. We devoted the entire day to full discussions of the changes and their application to HDS and the managed services industry. We discussed how the strategic management of quality works in general, how we would implement the principles throughout the HDS system nationwide, how our organizational structure would change, and we completed a detailed financial impact analysis. We incorporated it in our 1992 business plan and the financial plan as well. However, there were some questions we could not answer at the time, such as: Would there be any return on our investment in the latter part of 1992 if we were successful in implementing the quality improvement process early on in the year? Obviously, we took the conservative approach to budgetary allowances and elected to place all investment returns in future years. Returns would be generated in the form of associate productivity, increased sales, and general savings in overhead expense. We were reminded that the race for quality has no finish line.

Before the end of November 1991, the president took the HDS quality improvement presentation and the 1992 proposed business plan to the Executive Committee of the Board. This three-person committee was responsible for most major corporate policy decisions, and certainly all plans for major financial commitments. The entire plan was reviewed in total detail at this meeting, but the focus was on how the board would have to shift its management style paradigm, and how they would go about accomplishing this goal. The plan was approved; in fact, the entire business plan was approved in early December 1991, which was an acceleration from the normal time frame of events.

Change Fighters

When individuals are faced with the choice between changing their minds and proving there is no need to, almost everyone gets busy working on the proof. People fight change for many reasons, and this resistance is often the largest reason why change does not happen. Why do people resist change? One reason is fear. Aristotle said that "fear is pain arising from anticipation of evil." Fear can be overcome, however, if people are moved out of their comfort zone. Another reason people fight change is insecurity; when we shift paradigms, people get nervous.

It is tough to climb beyond what we know. A third reason people resist change is that change means extra work for the leader and members of the team. Finally, some people resist change simply because they like the old way. As Will Rogers wrote, however, "Even if you are on the right track, you'll get run over if you just sit there."

Change Makers

Because people can be so resistant to change, it is very important to pay attention to how change occurs. To overcome the resistance to change, you have to spell out expectations exactly. Explain the advantages of the proposed change to the resisters, *from the resisters' perspectives.* At the least, you will have communicated the message and given others a chance to ask questions after thinking about the proposed change. Usually, when people know where they are going and understand the goal and WIIFM (what's in it for me), they will buy into the change.

Most people worry about the effect the proposed change will have on them personally. The more quickly you explain the advantages (and disadvantages, if any) of the impending change, the more quickly people can embrace it. By involving people in the decisions about the changes that affect them, they learn about the challenges associated with the change. In other words, leaders must develop positive attitudes in their internal customers in order to reduce the level of resistance to change.

Understanding is a powerful tool in transforming change resisters into change makers. Communication cannot take place too soon or too often during the process. Listening to the concerns, frustrations, and ideas of those involved in the process of change helps all partake in the transition process. Everyone must take responsibility and be accountable for getting the job done if the better way is to work and work well.

Traditional Versus High Performance Organizations

Traditional organizations frequently embody the characteristics of Niccolo Machiavelli, a bureaucrat who lived in Florence, Italy, about 500 years ago during the Renaissance Period. It is rumored that those who managed traditional organizations were all trained in the Machiavelli School of Management and became **Machiavellian Managers.** The needs and expectations of their companies, and the managers, drove all actions. Such managers operated by impulse, which was often accompanied by anger and rage. These manipulators responded poorly to criticism by anyone. They were impatient and their expectations of others were unrealistically high. The organization operated within a culture of fear and hostility. Associates were afraid that when problems occurred they would be blamed, so they waited for precise directions from top management before acting.

By contrast, **high performance service organizations** view quality as a strategic objective that is part of the organization's overall strategic business plan. These organizations integrate quality into their cultures. It is the cornerstone of a system that monitors and continuously improves how those that come to the organization to purchase products and services have their needs met and expectations exceeded. These organizations define a vision for how satisfying customer needs and meeting or exceeding customer expectations will take place. This vision results in common goals that each person can understand and contribute to positively.

High performance service organizations utilize teamwork in the form of cross-functional teams working together to eliminate the hassles and continuously improve. The "how to's" of teamwork are communicated during training so that associates and managers learn how to function together as a team. High performance service organizations embrace **empowerment;** each person is given the responsibility for quality, not just simply informed of what is expected. Empowerment may be the most important guiding principle of high performance service companies. To be empowered is to be selected, enabled, involved, and committed. Selected associates are invited to join the organization based on their unique skills and talents and the needs of the organization. Enabled associates are trained and have had their training validated by other trained associates as well as the organization's customers. Involved associates are asked for their input and ideas regularly (Exhibit 3.1). Committed associates are invited and encouraged to develop.

The differences between a high performance service organization and a traditional company are dramatic. These differences are presented in Exhibit 3.2.

The indicators in Exhibit 3.2 clearly show why the high performance service organization is more successful. High performance service organizations separate themselves from the clutter of the competition by setting quality improvement as the number one goal. The quality of anything that the organization produces and delivers in the form of products and services can be improved. High performance service organizations also have a "bottom-up" management style: ideas percolate

Exhibit 3.1 Empowerment includes the solicitation of input and the asking for ideas. *(Source: HDS Services. Used with permission.)*

up through the organization, rather than being hammered down by top management. That fact alone results in a startling transformation. The organization becomes "ours" rather than "theirs." Of the two, the high performance service organization is customer focused, tries to prevent problems and hassles, has a goal of 100 percent customer satisfaction, views a commitment to quality as critical throughout each process, utilizes the synergy of teams, welcomes the participation by all with ideas for improvement, and promotes and celebrates empowerment.

Indicator	High Performance Service Organization	Traditional Company
Driving Force	Needs and expectations of customers	Needs and expectations of the company
Underlying Philosophy	Problems are prevented before they occur	Problems are detected after they occur
Guiding Principle	Nothing less than 100% satisfaction will do	Maximum acceptable levels of error and waste are defined
The Basis of Quality	A commitment to quality throughout the process	Inspection is the key to quality
Method of Operation	Cooperative, inter-departmental cross-functional teams	Autonomous, independent, competitive departments
Management—Associate Relationship	High associate participation, resulting in individuals and teams that are empowered	Associates are directed by management in a top-down fashion
Primary Goal	Long-term staying power	Short-term profit

Exhibit 3.2 The differences between a high performance service organization and a traditional company. *(Source: Capezio, Peter and Debra Morehouse.* Total Quality Management—The Road of Continuous Improvement, *Rockhurst College National Press Publications. Shawnee Mission, Kansas: Used with permission.)*

It is no surprise, then, that high performance service organizations transform themselves and last for generations. If one had to choose the type of organization in which to invest his or her career, the type of organization with which to do business, or the type of organization in which to invest as part of a personal retirement portfolio, the choice is, again, obvious.

How to Spot a High Performance Organization

High performance service organizations are known for their quality. That is, they do the right things the right way. High performance service organizations stand out because they practice continuous improvement of processes and systems. How do they know that they are improving? They measure results and compare what was achieved to what was planned. And then they figure out ways to close the gap, to narrow the spread between the actual and the desirable. High performance companies tap into the power of their external customer loyalty evidenced by the fact that when they leave, they have already planned to return and bring their friends.

These organizations use tools as objective measurements for the levels of product and service produced. These measurements establish baselines and track improvements. The tools are selected and utilized based upon two fundamental concepts: 1) process thinking (Exhibit 3.3) and 2) continuous improvement. Process thinking indicates a way of looking at *what* happens when a hassle occurs and crosses traditional functional areas in an organization.

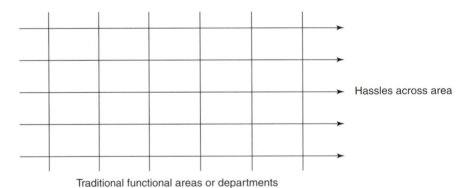

Traditional functional areas or departments

Exhibit 3.3 Process thinking. (*Source: Verne Harnish, Gazelles, Inc. Used with permission.*)

The goal of process thinking is to identify the root cause or causes so the hassle can be eliminated at its source. With process thinking, one immediately sees the value of using cross-functional teams to identify the root cause or causes. The logic is that since the hassle occurs across areas, input from as many affected people as possible from different functional areas, is advantageous in finding a way to eliminate the hassle.

In their book *Reengineering the Corporation*, James Champy and Michael Hammer wrote that a process is a "collection of activities that takes one or more kinds of input and creates an output that is of value to the customer." Thus, the offering of a Sunday brunch for the members of a private club would require a number of activities (e.g., menu planning, purchasing, receiving, storing, issuing, production, serving, and others) that together would add value for the customer (i.e., club member). In *Process Innovation*, Thomas Davenport defines a process as a "structured, measured set of activities designed to produce a specified output for a particular customer or market." The set of activities in place to take and confirm a guest's reservation in a hotel would fit this definition of a process.

In his book, *Business Process Improvement*, James Harrington describes a process as "any activity or group of activities that takes an input, adds value to it, and provides an output to an internal or external customer." In a managed services company providing on-site food services in healthcare, the input may be feedback from the client, the patient, and/or the associate working in food service. The value added is the transformation of this information into quality improvements in the outputs (i.e., products and services) created for and delivered to external customers and associates. In *Juran on Planning for Quality* Joseph M. Juran simply defines a process as a "systematic series of actions directed to the achievement of a goal."

Critical processes directly contribute to the experience that the customer has with the organization. Critical processes would include making hotel reservations via the Internet or telephone, maintaining required temperatures of food in a cafeteria, receiving quality checks of products delivered to a restaurant, maintaining greens at a golf course, filling a vending machine regularly, cleaning a pool at a resort, housekeeping in a shared ownership condominium, the movement of lines of guests at a theme park, and the timing of the details (i.e., registration, program, staging, photography, food and beverage service) at an annual gathering of leaders. All of these processes are designed to add value to the customer experience. In a resort, some guests like to play golf to relax. The process of making the reservation for a tee time, being greeted by the associate upon arrival, playing the 18 holes, and closing the transaction at the end of the experience may be viewed as a process or a number of related processes.

The second fundamental concept in high performance service organizations is **continuous improvement,** in contrast to straight-line linear improvement. Continuous improvement is more likely to occur; it represents a step-like incremental series of better results as presented in Exhibit 3.4. It is a series of planned and monitored outcomes.

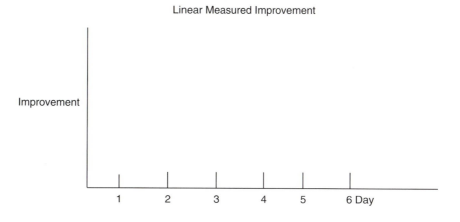

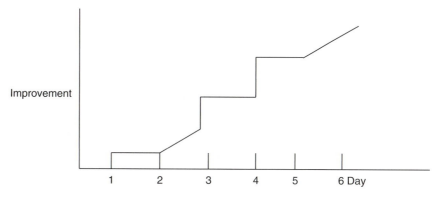

Exhibit 3.4 Linear vs. continuous improvement. *(Source: Verne Harnish, Gazelles, Inc. Used with permission.)*

Functional Teams

Continuous quality improvement in a high performance service organization requires the establishment of several functional teams:

- The **Senior Quality Improvement Team (SQIT)** is the organization's executive team. It is the overseer of quality improvement initiatives.
- The **Quality Improvement Team (QIT)** is composed of managers/workgroup leaders. This team's primary responsibility is to make decisions and monitor quality activities (Exhibit 3.5).

Exhibit 3.5 A Quality Improvement Team (QIT) in a healthcare services company is composed of managers/workgroup leaders. This team's primary responsibility is to make decisions and monitor quality activities. *(Source: HDS Services. Used with permission.)*

- A **Work Group Team (WGT)** is a group of associates based in the functional area in which they work. The goal is to have members of this team become more self-directed by self-managing.
- An **Action Group Team (AGT)** is a team set up to work on a specific hassle or opportunity for improvement and includes representatives from multiple departments.

Every staff member is a member of a Work Group Team (WGT) and each WGT has a leader. The WGT leaders meet with their area managers as a quality team to ensure that ideas are being implemented and improvements are being made. Each area manager is also a member of a quality team; the goal of these teams is to share information and report progress.

The Senior Quality Improvement Team (SQIT) oversees and guides the process. One of the primary responsibilities of the Senior Quality Improvement Team is to appoint to Action Group Teams (AGT) members who represent a number of different perspectives in the organization. These different perspectives focus on specific hassles that cut across areas. Members of AGTs also come from every area directly affected by the hassle. An example of cross-functional AGTs is presented in Exhibit 3.6. Each of these AGTs is permanent and self-managed.

The organizational model for a high performance service organization is presented in Exhibit 3.7. The overarching strategy is to recreate the organization continuously through managing and improving quality via teams. This quality results from high intentions, integrity, sincere effort, customer service, customer-driven direction, and skillful execution on the part of all the teams collectively and the members individually. As an outcome, the organization changes into a high performance service organization.

Action Group Team	Focus
Accounting and Operations	Accounting and operations improvements
Balanced Scorecard	Improvement of results
Client Satisfaction	Client satisfaction improvements
Clinical	Clinical staff development
Financial	Financial improvements
Food is Fashion and Fun	Retail operations improvements
Golden Service	Retirement facilities
Grand Class	Hospitals
Hourly Training	Training for associates
Performance Evaluations	Performance evaluations for associates
Purchasing	Purchasing improvements
Recruitment	Recruitment of associates
Preferred Place to Work	Retention of associates
Recognition	Recognition of associates
Safety	Safety improvements
Technology	Technology improvements
Triplett University	Management development

Exhibit 3.6 Cross-functional Action Group Teams at HDS Services. *(Source: HDS Services. Used with permission.)*

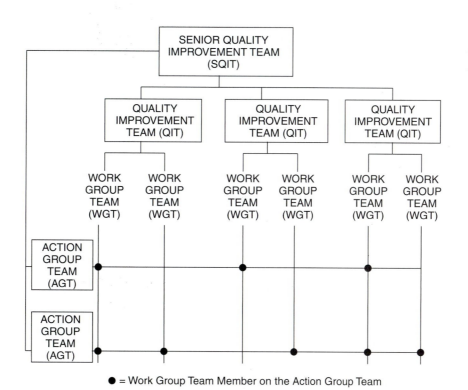

● = Work Group Team Member on the Action Group Team

Exhibit 3.7 Organizational model for a high performance service organization. *(Source: Verne Harnish, Gazelles, Inc. Used with permission.)*

Members of the QITs prioritize the hassles and issues, then they assign the hassle/issue to a WGT for analysis. The WGT studies the hassle or issue and recommends a solution to correct the process. If a hassle or issue affects more than one functional area in the organization, an AGT is formed to bring a cross-functional focus. The AGT analyzes the situation and makes a recommendation for correcting the process. The role of the AGT is to view the situation from the perspective of several organizational areas; this makes it is less likely that the recommended solution will create another (perhaps larger) hassle in a different area of the organization.

The AGT from the theme park pictured in Exhibit 3.8, for example, is shown working on the issue of inadequate guest parking close to the park at peak times. This AGT is composed of representatives from reservations, traffic, security, and marketing/sales.

Exhibit 3.8   AGT from a theme park working on the hassle of not enough guest parking close to the park at peak times. *(Source: Stock Boston. Used with permission.)*

At HDS Services there is a process that guides associates and Action Groups in systematically taking an idea or issue from discovery to approval/rejection and implementation. This process is outlined in Exhibit 3.9.

Core Principles of Quality

The **core principles of quality** in an organization require the top management to be visibly committed to improving quality. Continuous improvement is one of these core principles. This improvement should be focused on the processes that make a difference to the customers. Realistically, it is impossible to simultaneously improve many areas or processes; therefore, it is better to focus on achieving improvement in a few critical areas. For example, a focus on improving the check-in experience for large groups at a convention hotel is a process that would make a difference with group guests. Another specific focus may be adding fresh food choices to a vending machine to improve the variety of selections for customers.

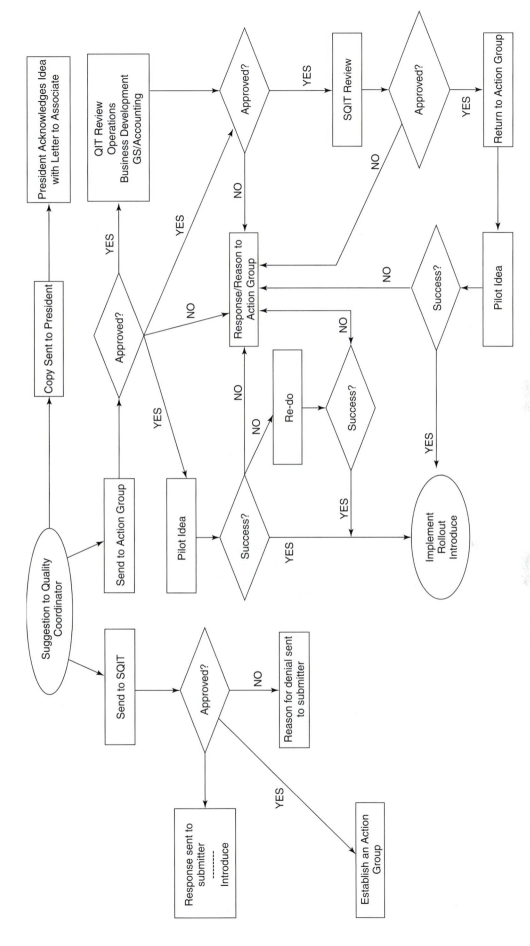

Exhibit 3.9 Idea/suggestion path to approval/rejection. (*Source: HDS Services. Used with permission.*)

45

A **customer-first orientation** is a second core principle. Everything we do should be focused on the customer. A restaurant's menu selections, including daily specials, are driven by the customers' likes, needs, wants, and expectations, for instance. **Trust** is another core principle; we must trust our internal customers to perform the quality work we have empowered them to do.

Teamwork is a fourth core principle. We use the strengths of individuals and the synergy of teams to serve our customers. Teamwork in the assisted living health care organization pictured in Exhibit 3.10 must take place between the administrators, physicians and nurses, maintenance staff, and food service staff in order for the customer to receive the best products and services. A fifth core principle of high-performance organizations is **management by fact.** Decisions are made based on facts, not feelings or emotions. Information is required to make fact-based decisions, and **customer feedback** from both internal and external customers is essential. Feedback from members (external customers) in a private fitness club can be obtained through surveys, one-on-one conversations, and focus groups, for example. The sixth core principle is **preventing hassles** or errors or defects. This is achieved by doing things right the first time. The final core principle of high performance service organizations is **celebration of success.** When we achieve success, we celebrate and recognize associates who have participated and contributed. For example, the recognition of the contributions of seasonal internal customers, both individually and as teams, at a summer resort helps show appreciation as well as build loyalty between the individual and the resort.

Exhibit 3.10 Teamwork in an assisted living health care organization is a core principle of quality. *(Source: HDS Services. Used with permission.)*

Needs and Expectations = Requirements

Needs and expectations of customers are translated into requirements. The requirements are simply valid specifications set between you and the customers. The specifications must be current (not yesterday's), based on expectations (meaning that minimally we meet, but optimally we exceed, expectations), and based on the organization's responsibilities (that is, making a profit, staying in business, growing the business over time).

We learn what customers require through communication and negotiation. The key to communication is asking the right questions and active listening. Consider these three questions:

1. What problems do you have with the present way things are done?
2. How well do we serve you with what we presently provide?
3. What would you like that you are not getting?

Question 3 is best asked by reviewing a list of current products and services with the customers and asking for reactions to each item on the list. This will help define valid needs and expectations and reveal ways that you can meet or exceed these. If the person is not a current customer, in other words he or she is being served by others, you can ask the customer how well others are serving the customer's needs and expectations, and you can ask what is missing.

Customers First

Leaders must become a catalyst of change, by becoming active listeners with an open attitude. Leaders should constantly ask and answer two questions:

- Who is the customer?
- What are the requirements (i.e., needs, expectations) of the customer?

The better way of management rediscovers the answers to these questions regularly, since the answers change over time. The answers provide direction for what needs to be done by all in the organization. The managers/leaders of the high performance service organizations realize that the primary role of the organization is service of external customers, internal customers, and the financial objectives and goals of the organization.

For example, the customer base of the golf clubhouse pictured in Exhibit 3.11 is the membership of the private country club. Guests of these members are also external customers. These distinct customer types will have similar as well as different requirements. The members and their guests both require outstanding service and well-prepared products, which result in a positively memorable experience. However, members may require the club's internal customers to use their

Exhibit 3.11 Members and their guests purchase the products and services in this golf clubhouse at a private country club. *(Source: HDS Services. Used with permission.)*

name when addressing them and to remember their favorite choices (e.g., cocktail preference, table location preference in the main dining room); the guests are not likely to have these same requirements.

All products, services, and experiences provided must be based on taking care of the customer in a way that the customer wants and expects. A big part of a customer-first mentality is to genuinely care how the customers experience what we offer. This mentality becomes an integral part of the organization's culture. It requires initial and ongoing training to start and keep the culture of service. It transforms the organization into one driven by needs and expectations of customers, not one that is a formal, traditional, top-down structure.

Service

Quality management focuses on the importance of service. The level of service quality created and delivered becomes *the* competitive advantage in the organization. The core belief is that if you are not serving the customer, you ought to be serving someone who is. The level of service quality is a combination of the activities of customer-contact staff and support staff. A customer-contact staff member in a five-diamond resort dining room is pictured in Exhibit 3.12, as an example.

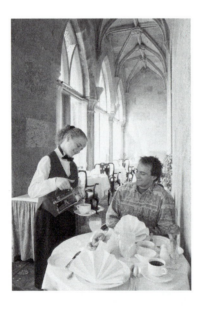

Exhibit 3.12 A customer-contact staff member in a five-diamond resort dining room. *(Source: Dorling Kindersley Media Library. Used with permission.)*

Customer-contact associates are those who regularly interact with external customers. Examples are servers in restaurants, front desk staff in hotels, sales staff for an office coffee service/vending company, service staff in car dealerships, and tellers in a bank. Support staff examples include chefs and cooks in restaurants, staff in a hotel laundry, route drivers for the vending/office coffee service company, mechanics and technicians in a car dealership, and controllers in a bank. The total quality of the services experienced in these organizations is a function of how well these two groups work in concert.

Culture

The better way views quality as an overriding principle in the organization's culture. As a strategic objective, quality is a common thread that runs through the organization's strategic business plan. All of this is driven by a process that measures and continuously improves how those that buy products and services from the organization have their needs met and their expectations exceeded. The senior management of the Detroit Athletic Club, for example, believes that the secret to a successful club is a full and loyal membership that is served by a talented and loyal staff. The relationship between internal customers and members is at the heart of the service commitment. Members who trust and respect the staff draw out of the staff a level of loyalty that is unique to the culture of private clubs.

The culture of a quality-driven organization utilizes teamwork, specifically cross-functional teams. That is, representatives from different departments and areas of the organization come together to identify hassles and ways to reduce or eliminate those hassles. The culture embraces empowerment. Associates share the power of the organization and make decisions in service of the organization's customers. The associates are an essential part of the organization. Leaders create more leaders who are also empowered, not just followers. Leaders at all levels of the organization are empowered to create the memorable service experiences. In other words, after training, people in the organization are given the responsibility for quality; they are not just simply informed of what is expected. Rewards in these organizations link compensation for associates and managers directly to both results achieved in customer satisfaction as well as financial results achieved for the organization.

Kinds of Customers

After investing in customer research, this information must be communicated within the organization. In this way, internal customers can act to meet needs and exceed expectations. Information technology assists in both research and categorizing the findings. Databases can target individual customers to be contacted regarding specific products and services that fit their needs. Customer-contact staff must have an easy way to input the information that they discover, categorize it, and widely disseminate it to those who can use it.

Think back to the two questions we asked when we developed a definition of quality. These were:

- Who are our customers?
- What are their requirements?

Broadly speaking, customers fit into one of two categories. External customers are those who give their time and money for our organization's products and services and experiences. Expanding that definition, external customers are anyone outside the organization. For example, using this definition, external customers would include guests in a hotel, suppliers to that hotel, and governmental agencies who regulate some of the functions in the hotel (e.g., food inspectors for the food service operations in the hotel). Internal customers in that hotel are the associates. For example, the food and beverage outlets in the hotel are customers of the hotel's purchasing department. The front office in the hotel is a customer of the accounting office. Restaurant servers are customers of cooks and chefs in the kitchen.

It may be helpful to picture the customer focus of a high performance service organization as in the model in Exhibit 3.13.

Notice in this simplified diagram that suppliers provide the inputs to the organization. These inputs (supplies, information, and data) are transformed in the

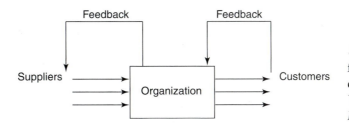

Exhibit 3.13 Customer-focused service organization. *(Source: Verne Harnish, Gazelles, Inc. Used with permission.)*

organization into products and services. These products and services become the outputs from the organization to the customers. Sometimes the products and services are combined into a unique and memorable experience for the external customers of the organization. Information flows from the customers to the organization and information flows from the organization to suppliers. The ultimate goal of this feedback is to improve quality and services/products available to the customers, resulting in enhanced customer satisfaction.

The role of the supplier is critical in the company's provision of products and services to its customers. As Dr. Deming believed, it is best to utilize a limited number of suppliers and avoid purchasing for price alone. He was a proponent of developing true partnerships with suppliers. Just what is meant by "partnership"? In the case of HDS Services, the primary distributor is a national full-line distributor of food service products. The distributor agrees to stock or slot many proprietary items for HDS and ship these items to all HDS units of operation across the country.

As a partner, the distributor works with the food manufacturers that HDS has selected as "preferred" so the HDS can fulfill its obligation to the manufacturer regarding volume commitments. The distributor also involves themselves in special merchandising services, layout and design work, philanthropy, account start up assistance, client education, temporary storage during disasters, and computer networking.

Most organizations that are committed to managing quality prefer exclusively dealing with other companies with similar commitments. This is the preferred relationship because the corporate cultures of the two organizations will more easily blend. The supplier becomes HDS's external customer in the case of a true partnership. By the same token, HDS is the supplier's external customer. Indirectly, the HDS client is also an external customer of the suppliers.

A high performance service organization must focus first and foremost on its internal customers, since it is these associates who carry the culture of service to the external customers. In spite of the important roles that management plays in the creation and delivery of products and services, it is the associates who make the process come to life. This is true with a buffet on a cruise ship (Exhibit 3.14) as

Exhibit 3.14 Associates create the experience on a buffet on a cruise ship for external customers. (*Source: The Viesti Collection, Inc. Used with permission.*)

much as when a family dines out at a family restaurant featuring video games and pizza for a child's birthday celebration. The associates are in direct contact with the external customers, and moment-by-moment they contribute greatly to the service experience. For this reason, the importance of the internal customers cannot be stated with too much vigor or volume. Without the associates, there would be no external customers, no need for managers, and no way to meet the financial obligations of the organization, regardless of whether the organization is privately held or publicly owned. So what do these most important, prime customers of an organization want and expect?

Associates want to be involved in the planning of the work that affects them. They do not want to be blamed if there is an ongoing problem with a process that cannot be fixed by them. Most, if not all associates, want to contribute to planning the effort to continuously improve the levels of quality. Associates also appreciate being involved in working on quality improvement teams. If they are encouraged to improve and innovate, and are trained in quality improvement skills and knowledge, they can be recognized for contributing to the overall improvement efforts.

Most associates are eager to learn and willing to provide external customers with an experience, not just the mundane products or mediocre service. To achieve this, associates need mentors who will help train, coach, and build the necessary knowledge, skills, and attitudes. A mentor assists with the sailing of uncharted waters. For some, this is the adjustment from school to work. For others it is a better understanding of the organization's culture. For still others it is help with aligning the person's expectations with the expectations of the company.

External customers are not unlike internal customers; they too have needs and expectations. External customers pay for experiences (i.e., combinations of products, services, and the total feeling related to the total interaction with the organization). External customers want to know that the associates in the organization have the needs and expectations of the external customers first and foremost in their minds. They want to know that the associates will do anything within reason to satisfy the needs and meet the expectations. External customers want to be understood and satisfied. They want to know that their concerns are the concerns of the associates and that the service provided by the associates will be for the benefit of the external customers.

External customers expect that the decisions and plans made and executed are all in service of the person who is paying the bill. External customers want consistency. If a hassle occurs, they want it fixed quickly and to their satisfaction.

It may be useful to think about both internal and external customers in the following six categories:

1. Existing customers—These are the current users of the organization's processes. They are why we create products and services. In some hospitality organizations these customers are called guests; in private clubs, they are referred to as members. In a managed services or vending company, they may be called clients.
2. Former customers—These customers used to use the products and services of the organization. It is important to learn why they stopped, since that information may help convince them to return if the hassles that drove them away can be eliminated.
3. Indirect customers—This group does not directly use the organization's products and services, but they have an effect on these customers. Indirect customers may include government regulators and advocacy groups.
4. Potential customers—These have never tried the organization's products and services but may be convinced to do so. Identify their needs and expectations, create products and services that meet and exceed, and this

group will become existing customers. Potential customers could be the guests of members at a private athletic club.

5. Suppliers—This group provides products, services, and information to the organization. They share in the quality creation and value determination when they are treated as strategic allies and partners.

6. Ultimate customers— If an organization is part of a distribution network, these are the customers who ultimately receive the products or services.

All of the customer categories are important to consider as we build customer satisfaction within a high performance service organization. Although these categories are a way to sort customers into groups, it must be remembered that individuals within a group may have varying needs and expectations.

Summary

Each of us has paradigms that help us interpret the many kinds of information we are exposed to each day. Our paradigms may shift or stay the same, depending on whether we are change makers or change fighters. In quality management there has been a paradigm shift to the more successful high performance service organization. These organizations use various critical processes to meet and exceed customer needs and expectations. In contrast to a traditional company, a high performance service organization is driven by the needs of its customers, both internal and external.

Key Terms

Action Group Team (AGT)—A team set up to work on a specific hassle or opportunity for improvement and includes representatives from multiple departments.

Celebration of Success—Upon achieving success, we celebrate and recognize associates who have participated and contributed.

Continuous Improvement—Represents a step-like incremental series of better results; it is a series of planned and monitored outcomes.

Core Principles of Quality—Require that top management be visibly committed to improving quality.

Critical Processes—Directly contribute to the experience that the customer has with the organization.

Customer-First Orientation—Everything done should be focused on the customer.

Customer Feedback—May be obtained through surveys, one-on-one conversations, and focus groups.

Empowerment—Each person is given the responsibility for quality, not just simply informed of what is expected.

High Performance Service Organizations—Views quality as a strategic objective that is part of the organization's overall strategic business plan.

Machiavellian Managers—The needs and expectations of their companies, and the managers drove all actions.

Management by Fact—Decisions are based on facts, not feelings or emotions.

Preventing Hassles—Achieved by doing things right the first time.

Quality Improvement Team (QIT)—Composed of managers/workgroup leaders, this team's primary responsibility is to make decisions and monitor quality activities.

Senior Quality Improvement Team (SQIT)—The organization's executive team. It is the overseer of quality improvement initiatives.

Teamwork—Using the strengths of individuals and the synergy of teams to serve customers.

The Better Way—A manager sees change happening and wants to help make it happen.

Traditional Organizations—The organization operated with a culture of fear and hostility. Associates were afraid that when problems occurred they would be blamed, so they waited for precise directions by top management before acting.

Work Group Team (WGT)—A group of associates based in the functional area in which they work. The goal is to have members of this team become more self-directed by self-managing.

Review Questions

1. Discuss a paradigm shift that occurred to you personally. Why did it happen? What change resulted from the paradigm shift?
2. Think about your current or a previous work experience in a traditional organization. Using Exhibit 3.2, describe the experience. How would you alter the components of the experience to transform it to a high performance service organization?
3. Using a current process that you are familiar with at work, name three ways that you could continuously improve the quality in the process.
4. Reflect on the core principles of quality based on your last service experience. How could these principles have been better addressed?
5. Why are internal customers the most important customers of a service business?

Activities in Your Organization

Listed below are some activities you can do in your organization. These are designed to reinforce the key chapter concepts. If you are a student and not currently working in the industry, interview an industry leader about one of these topics.

1. Observe a situation that requires you and other leaders to manage change in your organization. State clearly what change is required. How and why do people resist the change? What are some ways that you and the other leaders can overcome this resistance in your organization? What strategies will you use to become change makers in your organization?
2. Using the questions outlined in this section of the chapter, think of an instance where you were required to struggle with many choices and answer the questions honestly. What did you learn from the experience? How will you use this information to lead more effectively in the future?
3. Use the core principles of quality to analyze your organization. What core principles are being used well in your organization? What core principles need more attention in your organization? How can you use the core princi-

ples to address the needs and expectations of your organization's customers? Will the emphasis on certain principles change based on the kind of customer's (e.g., internal customer vs. external customer) needs and expectations that you are addressing?

References

Capezio, Peter and Debra Morehouse. *Total Quality Management—The Road of Continuous Improvement.* Shawnee Mission, Kansas: National Press Publications, Division of Rockhurst College, Verne Harnish, Gazelles, Inc.

Champy, James and Michael Hammer, *Reengineering the Corporation,* New York: HarperCollins Publishers, Inc., 1993.

Davenport, Thomas, *Process Innovation,* Harvard Business School Press, 1993.

Harnish, Verne and Kathleen Harnish. *Implementing Total Quality Management.* Boulder, Colorado: Career Track, 1994.

Harrington, James, *Business Process Improvement,* New York: McGraw-Hill, 1997.

Juran, Joseph M., *Juran on Planning for Quality,* New York: Free Press, 1988.

Relevant Web Sites

Basic Requirements for High Performance Organizations:
http://www.jboyett.com/high.htm
High Performance Balance (Technology, Management, and Leadership) (by Jim Clemmer):
http://www.clemmer-group.com/models/hperflship.shtml
Quality Management Principles:
http://www.iso.ch/iso/en/iso9000-14000/iso9000/qmp.html

Chapter 4

Tapping the Organization's Hidden Strengths

The most important customer in any organization is the internal customer . . . the associate. Without a selected, trained, and empowered associate, the external customers' needs will not be met and the expectations will not be exceeded. Those organizations that invest in their internal customers add tremendous value to the experiences of external customers, as well as to the bottom line of the organization.

Jerry A. McVety
President, McVety & Associates
A division of HDS Services
Farmington Hills, MI

Learning Objectives

1. Understand why we identify our associates as internal customers, what management must do to create a positive working environment, and how to achieve quality through the organization's associates.
2. Explain how to instill values in our associates.
3. What are the three key components in empowering associates? Cite examples from your work experiences that reflect the opposite approach and results.
4. Explain how using barriers enhances the effectiveness of empowerment.
5. Cite examples of associate diversity and how you would create synergy by managing this diversity.
6. What are the seven steps in the human resource process model? Explain their value in the provision of quality products and services.

Satisfied associates (internal customers) are loyal and unwilling to leave the organization for little more than higher compensation at another organization. When management takes the time and extra steps to build loyalty among associates, their level of satisfaction improves and there is an automatic improvement in external customer satisfaction. Our goal in this chapter is to explore the importance of focusing on the internal customer. If we take care of their needs, they will, in turn, exceed the expectations of the external customer. We also will discuss how to manage a diverse group of associates and how to use this diversity as an advantage. Finally, we offer steps to successfully empower your associates.

Internal Customer Focus

How do we position the organization at a level separate and higher than that of the growing list of competitors? As leaders, we must recognize that the organization's success is not simply a direct result of effective leadership. Rather, it is the combined efforts of all associates and managers. Management and associates become interdependent because of this.

Initially, we must maintain an **associates-first orientation.** Everything we do is based on satisfying the needs of our internal customers. We need to communicate with them and listen to their concerns and ideas. As Patrick Mene from The Ritz-Carlton Hotel Company said, "Involve associates in the planning of the work that affects them, to increase the pride and joy they derive from their work." The goal is to develop a strategic alliance between the organization and its associate team. Eileen Evans, Vice President of Operations at Advanced Office Systems in Sharonville, Ohio, states this goal as follows: "My employees are not employees, they are my customers. Calling them a customer, that is good, (to them) that means you are serving me."

The more we know about our associates' needs, the better able we are to give them the support, tools, ideas, and recognition. In turn, the more successful our associates are, the more successful our external customer satisfaction levels become, and the more successful the organization is. Exhibit 4.1 shows an associate's face, body movements, and unspoken communication. The associates use all of these to create a memorable experience for the customer. Note that the picture of a food and beverage server in a formal dining room shows the associate's dedication, commitment, and need to provide superior service that leaves guests with very positive memories and feelings toward the associate and the organization.

Exhibit 4.1 A food and beverage server in a formal dining room. *(Source: Getty Images, Inc.— Photodisc. Used with permission.)*

We also need to *gain insight into how and what our associates think and value.* Knowing this enables management to tailor its support and communication to be more effective. All associates are different and the level of support needed will vary from one to another. If we base our level of support on associate input, our value will increase in their eyes.

In a survey of teens and young adults, over 90 percent said that being treated fairly by their boss was an important factor in their decision to stay with the organization. Over 90 percent of this same group said that the second most important factor was "a boss who treats others as he or she would like to be treated." When describing characteristics of a "good boss," this same group of respondents said good bosses are managers who can demonstrate how to do the particular task they are asking the staff to do and help the staff when necessary. Younger associates also want to see that there are opportunities for advancement if they do a good job. The organization's leaders must create a work environment that not only attracts talented associates, but also maintains associate stability through organized recruitment efforts.

As an experiment in obtaining feedback from a group of "potential" management trainees, during one of our meetings in our class, Managing Quality in Hospitality Business, we surveyed our students and asked: "What would make a career in a contract management organization more attractive than a career in a hotel restaurant, club, resort, self-operated college or self-operated healthcare facility?" Their unprioritized responses were as follows:

- Shorter work hours
- Weekends/holidays off
- Increased growth opportunities
- Better support staff
- Better corporate structure
- Increased involvement with internal customers
- Increased stability
- Better benefits
- More family time
- Better career opportunities
- Increased networking
- Enhanced diversity
- Enhanced personal and professional growth

This information gives us an insight into how potential managers think and what benefits would attract and retain these individuals. This information may also be used to recruit and retain associates.

We also *need to know how satisfied our associates are.* Feedback surveys must be conducted, and we need to maintain open communication within the entire team. This is why we are proponents of **managing by walking around (MBWA).** Managers must create communication opportunities and MBWA helps achieve these opportunities. Managers should never go directly to their office upon arrival at work; they should tour the operation or part of the operation and greet as many associates as possible. Building trust and removing fear from the relationship between management and associates is of primary importance.

The **recognition of associate success** is also very effective in recruiting and retaining because it reinforces the contribution of the associate. Recognition does not have to wait for awards banquets and the annual evaluation. It can be done almost on a daily basis, and it is particularly effective when it takes place in front of the associate's peers.

Associates who are committed to the organization's vision, mission, and core values can be a powerful source of energy, customer service, organization growth, and profit. Most people would rather stay in the hotel where they are greeted by the doorman's offer to help with their luggage and holds the door open, a front desk agent who is friendly and efficient, and a helpful and courteous bell staff. Service is key and service is created and delivered by your associates. This is the basic premise for treating associates as customers.

Associates as Creators and Deliverers of Service

Associates are customers in the sense that they have needs to be identified and satisfied, and expectations to be met or exceeded. The associates in a lounge are considered customers who combine the beverage products and deliver service to the guests. While these beverage servers (Exhibit 4.2) are associates who serve the external customers, they are, at the same time, internal customers of the management of the organization. Understanding and addressing this simple fact will do more to improve service to external customers, and result in positive financial performance, than any other action by management in a service organization.

Exhibit 4.2 Beverage servers are internal customers of the management of the organization. *(Source: HDS Services. Used with permission.)*

When asked what helps associates view their organizations in a positive light, the item that tops the list often includes "management listens to staff suggestions." Companies recognized as preferred employers by associates frequently have a number of associate recognition programs to immediately acknowledge performance.

Associates regularly must be given the opportunity to openly communicate their concerns and suggestions for improvement. Specifically, management should ask the associates for the following:

- Suggestions that would help do the job better
- Suggestions for improving customer service
- What they like most about the job
- What they like least about the job
- Suggestions for improving those tasks liked least
- Suggestions for reducing costs or increasing revenues

This assessment of associates must be done at regularly scheduled intervals in writing, as well as more frequently in informal ways (e.g., conversation). The goal is continuous feedback to continuously improve. Management must listen to the voices of the associates, and then take action based on the comments, suggestions, and ideas.

Synergism, Diversity, and Empowerment

Life Without Synergism and Empowerment

During the last half of the twentieth century, CEOs and other senior managers have talked exhaustively about **synergism** and empowerment. The key to synergism rests in management's ability to manage diversity, which is often perceived as more of an issue than an untapped strength of the organization. The word "empowerment" has been used so frequently that it is seen as an overplayed principle of management that never worked in the long run because of a dwindling level of associate skill and loyalty to the organization. Managing diversity and empowering people are both powerful hidden strengths of the organization, however, and when properly employed, create an entirely different and more successful organization.

At the Detroit Athletic Club, internal customers are empowered to make good decisions. The senior management believes that the more someone knows about what is right in their part of the organization, the more it gives internal customers the confidence to make the right decisions.

The hostess at a family restaurant pictured in Exhibit 4.3 shows by her smile that she has been treated well by the management and other internal customers of the organization. She is sharing this same genuine hospitality with the two external customers and she is taking responsibility to individually identify creative ways to respond to the challenges of improving quality service for external customers. In short, she is empowered.

Exhibit 4.3 A hostess at a family restaurant. *(Source: PhotoEdit. Used with permission.)*

The need for immediacy of information drives some managers toward what they refer to as **follow up.** Their associates, however, identify follow up as micromanaging, mistrust, suffocation, badgering, and a lack of delegation. This management style was prevalent with executives and line managers in the pre-Deming years. Initially, this habitual follow up forms a shell or barrier around the associate. Thus, there is little freedom to manage, build, and develop into a more effective and empowered manager or associate. Inevitably the associate or manager becomes less communicative with the executives of the firm, and teamwork and collaboration become virtually nonexistent. Follow-up can play a key role with recognition, however, offering support to associates, and answering questions, as well as mentoring to help the associate develop necessary skills.

Common sense tells us that anything less than full, open communication leads to eventual gridlock, inferior service and products, and mistrust. The inevitable result is the associate or manager's separation and transition to another organization with the appropriate management practice and principles. Since the management of quality requires continuous improvement, it follows that empowering the internal customers to participate in important business decisions is key to quality improvements.

Many people may think the main underlying cause of staff dissension is gossip in the work place, lack of performance, lack of respect for the executive team, or poor financial results. However, the primary root cause of dissension is a focus on and exaggeration of differences due to **diversity.** This includes race, religion, personality, personal objectives, and financial/cultural background. Some companies and their executives succumb to the negative aspects of diversity. The most successful companies, however, use diversity as an organization's strength.

Transforming Diversity to Synergism

Dr. Stephen R. Covey, a noted author and educator, addresses the amazing ability of certain groups of people to transform diversity into synergetic teams. He presents his key points for transformation in his video, *Mauritius: Celebrating Differences.* Mauritius is a very small island off the coast of Africa; its environmental and social circumstances seem to give its people little chance of long-term survival and sustainability. For example, the island is densely populated and there is a shortage of locally produced food. (In 1965 Mauritius was totally dependent on a single export product—sugar cane.) In addition, the island is located 6,000 miles from the closest major market. Ethnically, the island consists of 20,000 Caucasians, 750,000 Indians, 300,000 Creoles, and 30,000 Chinese, and four different religious beliefs are actively practiced. Typically, the prognosis for the success of these groups as a nation would be quite grim. However, what has transpired in the last several decades is just the opposite. Because of its diversity, the country is a model for harmony, peace, financial stability, and spirit of synergy.

In the video, Dr. Covey explains how the presence of a common **value system** united the people of this small country. Everyone on Mauritius places top priority on the value system; in fact, they hold it above their personal needs.

Today in Mauritius:

- poverty does not exist
- the literacy rate is 98 percent
- police do not carry guns
- associates are imported to fill positions
- they have one of only a few democracies in Africa, and
- everyone celebrates all inter-religious holidays

Associates' Values

So how do we help associates develop their values? First, the CEO and the executive team must develop a broad **common purpose and vision.** The vision must mirror the goals of the organization, but it also must be able to be adopted by all of the diverse groups in the organization. Everyone must enroll in the vision and mission, and all associates need to know their roles in the organization's future. When associates enroll, the organization's purpose automatically must become personal agendas.

Second, every associate must be convinced that "it is not I or me, it's us." The voice of the whole group must take precedence over any individual's voice because what can be achieved as a group far surpasses individual accomplishment. Your organization's associates must realize that they have to cooperate to make anything work. Management must bring the associates together, give everyone the opportunity to express their view, and, based on the values of the organization, help empowered associates make the right decisions. These decisions will produce services and products no single individual would have been able to achieve. The result of this synergism will be delighted customers whose expectations have been exceeded.

Management must *build positive relationships* among individual associates and associate groups. The two internal customers who work in a hotel's IT department pictured in Exhibit 4.4 have positive synergy due to the positive relationship they have built between themselves in the organization. The most effective teams are those with differences in associate talents, perceptions, titles, and roles, but one purpose and vision based on the foundation of a strong value system. Obviously, the organization's value system must include **cooperation** as one of its key components. When associates use compromise in dealing with other members of the group, there will be synergistic gain, but it will be less than the synergism gained from placing the organization ahead of personal agenda. For example, if members of the team challenge each other and offer differences of opinion, there will be better results than if differences are not discussed.

Exhibit 4.4   Positive synergy due to the positive relationship. *(HDS Services. Used with permission.)*

Respect is another important part of the value system's foundation. At HDS Services we value "walking in the associates shoes" and have experienced what the associates are experiencing. We do not ask an associate to do something that we as management would not do. At The Ritz-Carlton Hotel Company, all internal customers say that "We are ladies and gentlemen serving ladies and gentlemen." That philosophy not only applies to internal customers serving external customers, it also defines the ways that internal customers interact and communicate with each other.

For the most part, respect should be earned. This is accomplished more easily among associates who work closely together. In situations where work groups and cross-functional teams are established, individuals assigned to a team will be working with associates whom they do not know very well. Some level of respect is required for success and synergistic gain in these situations. (Remember, the greater the focus on organization values over personal agendas, the greater the synergy and the greater the team results.) So, how does management develop a high level of mutual associate respect?

Management and associates need to measure their level of mutual respect and ability to value the differences in people. If everyone valued the differences in their fellow associates, respect, cooperation, and synergism would abound. Associates should ask themselves how they react when someone disagrees with their point of view. Do they always listen to what the other person is saying, especially if there is a different opinion? Does another person's gender, race, religious beliefs, or position ever influence them?

If people value the differences in others, work with them, respect their opinions, listen to them, and encourage synergistic activity, the results will be unmatched. Certain groups or teams have been more successful than others in our company. The primary reasons for success seem to be the ability to get along with others, strong communication skills, respect for differences, and **confidence** in the vision, values, and processes of the organization. A team of associates cannot improve the working environment of the organization if they cannot work together. No organization is hassle free; all organizations and teams face challenges. Successful teams and organizations face challenges differently because they work together synergistically. A note of caution, however—do not think that synergism can be achieved more easily if all members of the group resemble each other or were hand-picked for their similarities. Diversity has tremendous value. Some leaders tend to want to work in an environment of total associate harmony. This will not contribute to the diversity and resulting synergism necessary for the organization's success.

Another important ingredient in a value system is **trust.** An environment of trust within the team brings about openness, effective communication, and creativity. Low trust levels breed territorialism, defensiveness, protectiveness, and ultimately legalese and the need for abundant documentation. A middle-of-the-road position results in polite dialogue versus open communication, fewer results, and less synergism. For example, HDS Services has an Operating Committee that determines corporate policy and directs the executive team of the organization. The meetings of this committee are very spirited because we promoted open confrontation and disagreement as long as respect for one another is maintained. This open environment also requires a high level of trust among the members of the committee.

Economic objectives are a part of most organization value systems as well. These drive managers to achieve success from diversity and the different talents of associates. For example, our corporate objectives include double digit growth in gross profit dollars each year, and, as previously stated, we achieve this goal through success in managing the differences in each department within the organization.

Dr. Covey summed up the value of differences with the following statements. "Strength truly does lie in difference. These aren't just nice words. These are moral imperatives for those who really want to solve problems in entirely new ways. Go for synergy. The moment someone disagrees with you, say to them, 'Good. You see it differently.' As we come to transcending purpose, common vision, and shared mission in our relationships, then we can afford to have many differences, and they'll become strengths. We actually want them, because if we don't have them, then we'll be limited by incomplete data and partial perspective." Most of us are limited in our knowledge and experience, so working with diverse groups gives us more balance.

The Tale of the Mentor comes from Homer's *Odyssey*. When Odysseus, King of Ithaca, went to fight in the Trojan War, he entrusted the care of his kingdom to Mentor who served as the teacher and overseer of Odysseus's son, Telemachus. After the war and many years later, Telemachus, now grown, went in search of his father. Telemachus was accompanied in his search by Athena, Goddess of War and patroness of the arts and industry, who assumed the role of Mentor. Father and son were reunited and together they cast down those desiring Odysseus's throne and Telemachus's birthright. Athena's role as Mentor for Telemachus was not only to raise him, but to develop him for responsibilities he was to assume in his lifetime. In time, the word Mentor became synonymous with trusted friend, advisor, teacher, and wise person.

Empowerment

Often referred to as the "E" word, the principles of this management tool are quite simple in theory, but much more difficult to implement and practice. Empowerment minimizes follow up by management because it helps make associates more responsible for their actions. Empowerment is simply providing direction for what needs to be done, the tools to do it, and then getting out of the way so people can achieve the results.

When associates have the power to fix problems, there is no need for management to "fix the blame." Whether an organization uses associate teams to improve quality or not, empowerment is essential. When teams are being formed, those who are actually doing the job must be included on the teams. They know the challenges with quality better than anyone else in the organization and can suggest meaningful ways to improve quality. In addition, those associates who are treated well are more likely to treat external customers well by delivering the expected levels of quality.

If all organization associates believe in and adopt the organization's vision and mission statements (Exhibits 4.5 and 4.6), they will be empowered to make well-informed decisions. An excellent tool to evaluate the extent to which associates are empowered is to ask key associates to list the 10 most important items they are responsible for accomplishing. Then ask management the same question. Empowered associates and management will give very similar responses to this question because they are in tune with each other and the corporate vision and mission.

At HDS we knew we needed to strengthen the teamwork in the organization, and in order to bring everyone closer together, we developed a corporate vision and mission statement. We wanted the key management associates of the organization to be involved because they would take ownership of projects and would be more likely to focus on the statements down the road. The development of the statements was relatively simple; it required only two or three meetings and brainstorming sessions. The vision statement of HDS is:

> We will be the **Preferred Partner** in providing management and consulting in the dining service and hospitality industries.

The HDS Services mission statement reads:

> HDS Services is dedicated to providing hospitality based dining services management at a level which exceeds our customers' expectations.

VISION STATEMENT

We will be the
PREFERRED PARTNER
in Providing Management and
Consulting in the Dining Service
and Hospitality Industries.

HDS®

S E R V I C E S

Exhibit 4.5 Vision statement. *(Source: HDS Services. Used with permission.)*

HDS MISSION STATEMENT
SERVICES

HDS Services
is dedicated to providing
hospitality based
dining services management
at a level which exceeds
our customers' expectations.

Exhibit 4.6 Mission statement. *(Source: HDS Services. Used with permission.)*

The mission statement describes what the organization has to do to achieve the vision for the organization. The objective is to have all associates focus on the mission and enroll in its application.

Associates must be able to make decisions without fear of failure because upper management supports learning from mistakes in the work environment. They also must have total freedom to expand their experience, not at the organization's expense, but at the organization's direction and with its support. This concept forces management to mentor associates in order to reduce the number of **"red beads"** (known as hassles or barriers or obstacles) and failures.

Perhaps the most well-known story that describes empowerment in the workplace involves a well-known department store chain that specializes in high-end clothes and has a reputation for excellence in customer relations and satisfaction. An elderly man walked into the store carrying two recently purchased automobile tires and approached the cashier in the men's suit department. He placed the tires on the counter, informed the clerk that the tires he purchased made the front end of his car wobble, and insisted on a refund of $150. Upon seeing the receipt, which identified the date of purchase, the clerk filled out a credit slip for the customer without hesitation. (Nordstrom associates are empowered to take action under a stated financial cap. Ritz-Carlton associates have an empowerment spending cap of $2,000.) Another clerk, having witnessed the transaction, was totally bewildered and made a derogatory comment of disbelief. Word spread throughout the department, but everyone soon changed their thinking when they saw the man purchasing several thousand dollars in men's clothing. Suddenly everyone had changed their attitude to one of congratulatory recognition, and the associate was chosen associate of the month. This example has been used by many Baldrige Award winning companies in their training and development programs to reflect excellence in customer service and satisfaction.

Associates should be empowered to think and act "outside the box," because it is the unusual aspects of service excellence that take customer satisfaction to its highest level. The organization will keep satisfied customers in the short term, but it will keep loyal customers for a lifetime.

Another story tells of a sales executive staying at The Ritz-Carlton Hotel in Dearborn, Michigan, after spending the day and evening at Ford World Headquarters. He was from the East Coast and was flying from Detroit to Honolulu the next morning to join his wife. He was running a little late the next morning but easily managed to get to the airport which was a short distance away. Soon after his arrival he boarded a 747 but suddenly realized he had left his briefcase at the hotel. He immediately used his cell phone to phone the hotel.

He told the customer service agent about his dilemma. The agent took the necessary information about where to send his briefcase and assured him that it would be at the hotel in Hawaii that evening. The agent contacted housekeeping and a supervisor went directly to the guest's room only to find that the briefcase was not there. The supervisor then tried to locate the housekeeper assigned to clean the room. She was nowhere to be found. Following multiple pages, a cursory search of the hotel, and a non-productive phone call to her home, the search ended. The assumption was that they had an associate theft on their hands.

The next day the hotel learned that the guest had received his briefcase and that it had been delivered by the housekeeper from Dearborn.

Although the retail store and hotel incidents are highly unusual, they emphasize how an empowered associate can make the right decision when given the opportunity and the proper environment. The bottom line is that upper management wants all their associates to make the decisions that they would make. So, how do we as managers create a team of empowered associates? There are three key components in associate empowerment.

Sharing Information

In traditional companies information trickles down from the top. This includes historical information, current information, and information concerning strategic business planning, both present and long term. Other important information includes the organization's core principles, the vision, the corporate mission, and product-related facts. By sharing information, the decision making takes place as close to the point of service as possible, so the organization can best respond to the customers.

To have all associates enrolled in the vision, mission, and core values of the organization, management must teach and share as much information as possible. One core feature we find in most successful companies is the relentless development of skills in associates and managers. Most organizations make this commitment because they recognize the close relationship between positive financial performance and the number of talented, well-trained people on staff. Associates that are truly mentored throughout their careers will maximize their potential, and contribute greatly to the corporate effort. Just think what your organization could achieve if all associates reached their maximum potential! So, how do we get managers to become great coaches or mentors? They need three attributes: 1) the ability to teach, 2) the desire to teach without fear of the associate taking their job, and 3) the ability to recognize and reward for success. These skills must be supported by the CEO in order to create a learning environment within the organization. In today's competitive market, intellectual capital is as important to success as traditional financial worth or capital.

Another example of information's role in associates' and the organization's success is the sharing of financial information. In the past this information was thought of as highly confidential and off limits. Executives now realize how important it is to share financial data with associates. Pre-Deming managers feared that their "secret" financial performance would leak out to the competition. Today, the most successful leaders share a myriad of financial information. Not only does this enhance making informed decisions, it also breeds trust within the organization. Trust leads to high levels of associate morale, and this leads to the most important goal of all, excellence in customer satisfaction. Associates who have financial information are better able to handle customer questions, comments, and complaints.

Empowered service associates provided with information regarding menu pricing can respond to customers' questions. Service staff that are knowledgeable of the menu's content, how food is prepared, and the factors involved in menu pricing can improve the level of customer confidence and satisfaction. These servers can answer any questions or complaints at the point of service and virtually eliminate the overused response "let me call the manager." If a customer queries an associate about the price of a menu item and this associate can respond intelligently with factual information about ingredient cost, labor intensity of production, or product supply and demand, you will have satisfied customers. Imagine a customer in a restaurant asking about the price of Maryland Crab Cakes and receiving an answer about the change in the quality of waters for crab growth and proliferation and the resultant shortage of raw product. A 25 percent increase in the cost of the menu item is easier to understand with this information. Even if the customer did not order the crab cakes, he or she would gain an immediate respect for the associate, the management, and the restaurant as a whole. Customer loyalty is difficult to gain, and what could have turned out to be a large negative for the restaurant developed a good impression and stronger customer relationship.

Autonomy

There seems to be a paradox between team building and management's desire to train associates to be independent and not fear making mistakes or failure. Independence and team principles don't conflict at all. Teamwork simply enhances one's ability to make the proper decisions. Teamwork also leads to a higher degree of communication between associates. Independence, on the other hand, leads to an associate's willingness to take a position on an issue and make a decision that is right but not always popular. The downside of too much independence is an attitude of arrogance. This attitude can breed disrespect, destroy teamwork, and lead associates away from focusing on the important aspects of the business.

Autonomy, the second key to empowerment, is most effective if associates have **functional limits.** Functional limits are not barriers; they are principles that allow associates to concentrate on important and clearly defined areas of responsibility. This enhances the decision-making process so that decisions are made at the point of service in the organization. There are many different types of functional limits including niche, values, corporate perception, goals, casting, and organizational systems.

Niche defines and delineates the identity of the business. Pre-Deming managers believed that if a person could manage, he or she could be successful in any business. Not true! In companies without a clear delineation of services and products, associates are unable to make good decisions because in many areas they lack the knowledge and information required. In companies where they do only what they do best, success is more easily achieved because associates are members of a strong team and are more knowledgeable, more informed, better able to make sound decisions, more highly motivated, and able to function more independently.

At HDS Services the executive team has established clearly defined service markets in which to operate and sell. These service markets include food services in business and industry, education, health care, and private clubs, and consulting to the hospitality industry. There are many other service markets such as corrections, public schools, sports and recreation, environmental, and plant operations. HDS limits its services to markets where they have the expertise. We do only what we do best and continually strive to do it better.

Value limits are contained in operational guidelines such as the organization's core principles of management. At HDS Services the core principles are to:

- Provide services of the highest quality to the client and its customers and use integrity as the foundation. (Integrity is defined as rigidly following a code of ethics in all business dealings.)
- Practice the highest level of business ethics, avoid petty politics and gossip, and keep associates focused on their own jobs rather than those of others.
- Achieve a level of profit that will support corporate growth and provide the resources necessary to achieve all corporate objectives. During the 1990s HDS Services achieved its targeted level of growth and profit 8 of the 10 years and this trend continues into the twenty-first century. Many of these profits have been reinvested in the organization in the form of people, programs, support services, and retail packages.
- Maintain an external orientation focusing on customer requirements and the quest to fulfill these requirements better than any other provider. We are guided by a deep and shared understanding of customers' needs and behavior and competitors' capabilities and intentions. Continuous improvement toward "world class" quality will provide corporate growth.
- Develop a "partnership" with our customers, creating long-term relationships built on trust and ensuring the respect, confidence, and loyalty of our associates and clients. For example, HDS has been the food and nutrition services provider at Providence Hospital in Southfield, Michigan, for almost four decades. Our relationship with this prestigious client has been built on trust and it is a mutually beneficial relationship. We call it a "partnership."

- Develop a strong sense of loyalty with suppliers to gain a significant marketing edge through shared information, product enhancement, and technological leadership. Our primary distributor not only sells HDS its food and supplies, they also provide retail merchandising expertise, product information, philanthropic assistance, and marketing information to enhance our sales performance and market penetration.
- Develop the personnel of the organization to their maximum potential in a climate that fosters a high degree of associate trust and involvement and rewards associates for market-driven behavior and a "customer always comes first" philosophy. Personal and corporate performance will be judged by quantitative measures related to potential and relative to that of the competition and market share.
- Grow at a rate equal to human resource development and availability—a rate that assures vertical mobility for highly talented, aspiring personnel and is conducive to achieving maximum profitability. (Both executive vice presidents of HDS joined the organization in 1970 after graduating from Michigan State University as management trainees. Today, they coordinate sales and operations activities for a $300 million organization.)
- Align strategy, organizational structure, people, and programs in a way that assures an external market orientation, avoids isolation from the market, and is responsive to customer requirements and proactive in all management functions.
- Foster creativity and initiative through management freedom and delegation and promote the use of management objectives rather than management directives. Position in the organization should not determine the value of an idea. For example, HDS has an hourly associate recognition program which presents the highest performing associate in each operating unit with the recognition they deserve. The program is called the Silver Performance Program. All Silver Award winners are eligible for the Gold Performance Award which is an organization wide award. This idea was submitted to the Senior Quality Improvement Team by an associate.
- Encourage open communication and the permeation of corporate objectives, philosophies, and concepts through the entire organization. This enables all associates to know what is expected of them. Let people do what they were selected to do by giving them the resources and getting out of their way.

All of these guidelines establish limits or a framework within which to manage and operate. Associates focus on these principles, practice them, and, with these values totally internalized, are better able to make the proper decision. Associates at HDS Services have Pictures Quality (Exhibit 4.7) and a code that they freely choose to enroll in (Exhibit 4.8). Both further reinforce the shared core values of the individuals in the organization; they are used to keep everyone focused on the organization's values, mission, and vision.

Corporate perception defines the future of the organization. Associates who know where they and the organization are going have a clear picture of what the organization's future is and are the best decision makers. These decisions could move the organization ahead in the industry because they tend to have a greater and magnified effect on the business. Innovative hotel/restaurant service, products, and ambience, such as the member service received at a private club, the cleanliness and efficiencies seen at the theme park, or any other number of exceptional service experiences are examples of this.

Clearly defined **goals** also establish limits because they provide the what, when, where, and how of doing business. Concentrating on the goals keeps everyone working within a framework and gives associates the autonomy to be empowered. Throughout the year it is important for management to conduct

OUR **HDS** SERVICES TEAM:

Partnership
Integrity
Creativity
Trust
QUALITY
Recognition
Education/Empowerment
Strong Financial Growth

Exhibit 4.7 PICTURES QUAL-ITY core values. *(Source: HDS Services. Used with permission.)*

meetings in which objectives are revisited and reinforced because associates tend to wander from the original goals as time passes. At a recent meeting the HDS Services marketing team decided to make a significant change in the business plan. This change involved different identification of their signature programs, which affects advertising and marketing pieces used throughout the year. Since

HDS Services
ASSOCIATE CODE

To serve all customers with respect, honesty, and sincerity. Customers will be greeted with a name, a smile, friendliness, and a commitment to quality.

Exhibit 4.8 Associate code. *(Source: HDS Services. Used with permission.)*

these changes would negatively affect the organization's current financial plan and goals, we had to suggest the marketing department hold these plans until the following year.

Casting limits define who does what in the organization. Defined responsibilities assure management that certain functions will be delegated to specific individuals within the organization. Similar to other limits, casting allows associates the opportunity to concentrate on their own responsibilities, and they become more specialized and knowledgeable in their field of expertise.

The final limit is the use of **organizational systems.** These systems define how things are done based on experience, organization standards, and customer expectations. Organizational systems also explain who is involved and why. High tech companies and manufacturers use a myriad of detailed processes that are documented in the form of flow charts. These systems are meant to give the associate "the how" of getting the job done. These systems simplify the associate's responsibilities; therefore, the overall job becomes very clear and the organizational system enables the associate to have a high degree of expertise.

In summary, all of these limits enhance the associates' ability to concentrate on their field of expertise, realize their individual potential, and become better decision makers. Empowered decisions are made at the best possible level within the organization—the point of products and services creation and delivery.

Self-Directed Groups

The third key to successfully empowering associates is the use of **self-directed groups.** These are teams that work with little oversight or direction from management. The pre-Deming manager and associate would always wait to get direction from the corporate hierarchy before taking action. Later in the twentieth century problems were taken to work groups and cross-functional teams for intervention and associate direction. The major difference between the use of self-directed groups and hierarchical direction is that associates, not management, make up the self-directed groups. These groups are empowered to resolve issues and decide on the best course of action. For example, one of our clients was experiencing a deterioration of qualitative results from patient surveys and the root causes were determined to involve improper food temperatures. After our self-directed group brainstormed possible interventions, they decided to review the process of tray distribution by nursing services. Ultimately, the result was to change the responsibility for tray distribution to the food services department. The result was an immediate increase in survey scores. Associates who are members of self-directed groups take ownership of the problem and recommended solution because the solution was authored by peers rather than the organization executives.

Another example of a self-directed group is a cross-functional team of restaurant service and production professionals who regularly meet to plan seasonal menus for the organization's guests. In this case, the direction comes from the requirements of the customers rather than a dictate from senior management. The senior leadership of the Detroit Athletic Club believes that empowered internal customers consistently do their best to do what is right each day, 100 percent of the time. This is a goal all share and pursue each day. Associates understand when senior managers explain that all should "be content where you are . . . work with what you have and NEVER be satisfied."

In summary, empowerment works when the person giving up the power and the people sharing the power have a mutual vision of where the organization is going, what it wants to create, and what the goals are. The person releasing the power to others must demonstrate high personal and business standards and ethics, and they must believe that there is more than one way to effectively achieve the goal. The people sharing the power must trust the leader and the leader must trust them. The person who empowers others also must give them the permission to make mistakes and learn from those mistakes.

Human Resources Process Model

The most valuable resource in a high performance service organization is the human resource; the human resources process allows these organizations to hire and develop strong associates. Care in selecting the right individual is essential, especially in times of relatively low unemployment in the economy and fewer applicants. If the human resources process model is followed, the result will be an improvement in the quality of products, services, and experiences created and delivered for customers. This model is presented in Exhibit 4.9.

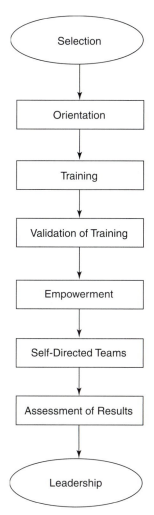

Exhibit 4.9   Human resources process model.

The service industry faces challenges with the human resources process on a daily basis. When the unemployment rate is low, the labor market is tight and it is difficult to recruit qualified associates. Pressures to increase wages typically accelerate under such conditions. In times of higher unemployment rates, there may be more candidates for a position, but the individuals may not possess the necessary qualifications. The goal is to have associates join the organization by choice, not by chance.

It may be useful to categorize associates based on the need or desire to retain them. One classification scheme suggested by Bernadette Kenny, Chief Operating Officer of global career services organization Lee Hecht Harrison follows:

- Gold medal contenders—fit in and are positioned correctly within the organization
- Olympic qualifiers—fit in the organization but need to be repositioned
- Olympic hopefuls—potentially fit within the organization somewhere
- Non-qualifiers—either don't fit or don't want to fit

A gold medal contender beverage server is pictured in Exhibit 4.10. This contender has been trained, empowered, and developed so that she can create and deliver memorable experiences that build external customer loyalty.

Exhibit 4.10 Gold medal contender beverage server in a lounge. *(Source: Getty Images, Inc.— Image Bank. Used with permission.)*

Effective organization team members may be asked to help recruit new members. Schools can be a good source of team members, if associates and managers are encouraged to participate in career days and career fairs at those schools. A presentation such as "Life After 12th Grade" could be just the thing to get someone interested in applying at the organization. Civic organizations, such as rotary clubs, may also be a source of heightened visibility for the company if managers are active members. Another idea is to contact former associates and ask if they are happy at their new places of employment. Some may decide to return to the organization. Some organizations pay current associates a finder's fee if they help to recruit new associates who join the organization and stay a specified amount of time. Typically, companies pay half of the finder's fee after three months and the remainder after six months of the new associate's tenure. Applicants for open positions should be asked if they know others they would be willing to refer to the organization.

The best reference for new associates may be from those current associates who have made a positive contribution to the organization. Other aids to or sources for recruiting applicants include the following:

- Signs inviting external customers to join the team
- Radio ads using the demographic information of the radio station (e.g., who listens at what times to which radio shows) to target the right audiences of potential associates

- Partnering with high school-to-work programs
- Retired people who want to work part time and typically have a strong work ethic
- Special needs populations (e.g., people with disabilities)
- Immigrant groups
- Working with community leaders to fill positions
- Churches and groups that encourage women to re-enter the workforce

It is most important to not let hard-to-fill vacancies lead to the hiring of just anyone. Nevertheless, once recruitment is completed the first step in the process is **selection.** The goal is to screen applicants and identify people who share the organization's vision, mission, and values. First the vision, mission, and values must be identified; then they can be used to screen applicants during selection. For example, the application cover could read as follows:

> "At HDS Services, we believe in anticipating, understanding, and ful-filling our customers' expectations. We also believe in continuous quality improvement of all we do." *If* this sounds like the kind of place that you would like to contribute your talents and skills to, please complete the attached application and return it as soon as possible to set up an interview.

In high performance service organizations, associates are selected; we do not simply "hire the help" as is the case in other organizations. Selection is based on defined criteria. Perhaps the most important criterion is the attitude of the applicant, followed closely by the talents and skills of the individual. In a service organization, a service attitude is essential to meeting the needs and exceeding the expectations of customers. How do we assess attitude? One way is by asking particular questions during the selection interview:

- Think about one word that best describes you. What is it? Why?
- If you could choose whatever you wanted as a career position, what would you choose? Why?
- Describe a situation that made you laugh. Why did it make you laugh?
- Talk about a positive service experience you recently had.
- Tell me about a time when you were on a team that achieved a desired result. What did you achieve? How did it happen?

In the process of selection, attempts are made to evaluate the compatibility of the applicant's goals and vision with the goals and vision of the organization. When personal visions are aligned with the vision of the organization, there is a strong potential for enrollment. Using the application and the selection interviews, the applicant is assessed in relation to how well the individual "fits" with the organization's needs and how the organization could assist the individual in achieving personal goals. Perhaps the organization values trust, flexibility, and the ability to change, as well as caring and commitment, support for associates, fun, and accountability. These values should be raised during the selection process through questions, role plays, what-if scenarios, and other techniques that assess how good the fit is between the applicant and the organization. Finally, the individual's experience is assessed.

Notice the difference in this first step of the process compared to a traditional organization. Traditionally, the applicant's experience is the primary criterion; in this model it is the last. The individual is required to "buy into" the organization's goals and vision; in this model, we are seeking alignment of personal and organizational goals and visions. In the traditional organization, hiring decisions usually are made by a human resources associate or the manager of the department in which the vacancy exists. In the high performance model, internal customers participate in the decision to extend an offer to the applicant during the series of selection interviews. This process is more time consuming, but the goal is to select an individual able and willing to fully engage in exceeding customer expectations while contributing to the process of continuous improvement.

Orientation is the next step in the human resources process model. This step is more than a quick review of associate policies and procedures typical in a traditional organization. Orientation, like selection, begins with the organization's vision and mission. These two statements are brought to life when presented by a senior manager during orientation. Stories of identity, often called campfire stories, about specific ways the vision and mission have been brought to life are an important part of this phase of orientation. People must understand how to make the vision and mission real if they are to make contributions in positive ways. They must understand their role and how it contributes to the success of the organization as it exceeds the expectations of customers.

Orientation also includes discussions of the philosophies and standards of the organization. When these are presented by other managers, as well as associates, they become more than words on a piece of paper. These presenters have the opportunity to model the vision, mission, and values of the organization during orientation for the new recruits. This leadership behavior sends a strong message to the new person. During this step in the process, active listening skills can be used and an overview of the processes (i.e., continuous improvement) and team building exercises should be included. The various functional areas of the organization also should be explained by representatives from those areas so that the new associate has a big picture view of the organization.

The next step is **training.** The requirements for training are fundamentally the same for all new associates, but they will differ somewhat based on the associate's specific functional area. The constant is a review and deeper exploration of the organization's vision, mission, principles, and standards. Training should begin with a discussion of these then move the focus to the functional area and the specific role of the new associate. It is not possible to overcommunicate these messages since they form the core of meeting customer needs and exceeding customer expectations.

Training also includes specific knowledge, skills, and attitudes so that the new associate may understand and successfully contribute to the mission and needs of the functional area. Training in a hotel banquet kitchen (Exhibit 4.11) includes teaching the knowledge, skills, and attitudes needed to make the products the external customers require and serve those who are in guest-contact positions delivering the products and services. Together, the products and services and guest-contact and support associates create the experience for the external customers.

Training must reinforce the techniques of active listening and it should show the trainee how to provide personal feedback as well as input from external customers. Training is also part of a set of strategies to reduce associate turnover. The effects of high associate turnover are presented in Exhibit 4.12. Some suggested ways to reduce associate turnover are presented in Exhibit 4.13.

Training is not exclusively provided by a human resources staff specialist in a high performance service organization. It is actively presented by the same individuals who participated in the selection process from the functional area—managers and associates. Training is everyone's responsibility; it is the most important activity following customer service. Training includes the basics of quality improvement, dehassling, problem-solving processes, and team participation and should be ongoing, occurring during pre-shift meetings, meetings, one-on-one discussions, in written communications, and at other opportunities. All must be trained to realize the fact that all have a voice in the improvement of

Exhibit 4.11 Training includes knowledge, skills, and attitudes. *(Source: Getty Images, Inc.—Liaison. Used with permission.)*

Reduced quality
Less knowledgeable associates
Management cannot focus on primary tasks
Service to external customers can suffer
Negative impact on the financials
Reduced associate morale
Reduced trust
Increased errors and waste
Relationships with external customers are interrupted
Increased associate stress levels
Increased associate fear
Higher expenses
Increased anxiety to external customers
Decreased self-esteem in associates that remain
Reduced teamwork
Reduced productivity

Exhibit 4.12 Effects of associate turnover.

quality. In some meetings, leaders will ask questions and expect to listen more than they speak.

Training starts with the desired result in mind: a customer whose needs are satisfied and whose expectations are met or exceeded. These questions can be asked and answered once this desired result is communicated: What are the necessary skills, knowledge, and behaviors that we all should exhibit for this desired result to happen? What training is necessary to instill these skills, knowledge, and behaviors in the qualified persons being selected?

Validation of training is the next step in the process. Unless the results of training are assessed, there is no way to know whether the training has been ef-

Detail expectations during selection
Make associates believe that you care through your actions
Improve training
Quality one-on-one conversations
Mentor associates
Associate peers assist with selection interviews
Empower associates
Provide incentives and recognition
Provide improved orientation
Be flexible in work hours
Be honest during conversations
Train managers
Walk the talk

Exhibit 4.13   Some suggested ways to reduce associate turnover.

fective. Validation of training provides a way to compare. Training validation includes technical skills and knowledge, as well as attitudes. Training is validated by associates and managers in each functional area. Additional validation is provided by customers, both internal and external.

Empowerment, a concept discussed at length earlier in this chapter, is the next step in the process. It is only possible if associates have been selected, properly oriented, carefully trained, and training has been validated. Empowered associates know that they are important contributors to the process of dehassling the organization. When an empowered associate receives a complaint from a customer, the associate "owns" the complaint. In other words, an empowered associate would never pass a complaining customer off to another in the organization or send the complainer off without resolving the complaint to the customer's full satisfaction. When a hassle is identified, an empowered associate often will simply ask the customer experiencing the hassle: "What will it take for me to correct this situation to your satisfaction?" The customer's response will indicate the solution. That is a prime example of exceeding customer expectations and creating customer loyalty. Exhibit 4.14 presents some additional strategies for empowerment.

Believe that the feedback associates provide represents reality
View information sharing as a two-way communication
Accept that information is power
Help others see how their piece fits into the whole
Communicate a work ethic through teamwork
Assist others in learning from mistakes
Add power through one-on-one meetings with associates
Share financial information
Conduct quarterly "town hall" meetings with all associates
Display data and show measurements in understandable ways
Trust others to make appropriate decisions
Rely on the areas of expertise of others

Exhibit 4.14   Strategies for empowerment.

The empowered associate is responsible for following up with the customer to determine that the problem or hassle has been addressed to the customer's satisfaction. This follow-up could be in the form of a conversation in person, a telephone call, or written communication. In the spirit of continuous improvement of quality, an incident form is completed to describe the problem or hassle and how it was solved. Incident forms are rich resources for the identification of process hassles by the quality teams. Once identified, these hassles can be eliminated so other customers will not be plagued with the same problems.

Self-directed teams are the goal in the next step of the human resources process model. (Team effectiveness will be discussed in more detail in the next chapter.) In order to achieve regular improvements in quality, teams must be utilized to dehassle the organization. In some high performance organizations, the priorities for problem resolution are defined by members of the quality improvement teams. In other cases, the teams working to fix the process prioritize the problems and work on them from top priority on down. In either case, the top priority hassles are those that are chronic, severe, and have a dramatic negative impact on the level of quality in the products or services created and delivered.

Once an associate has been selected, oriented, and trained, we need to **assess** the results. Broadly speaking, this assessment occurs in three different, yet related, areas: internal customers, external customers, and financial assessments. Internal and external customers provide verbal and written feedback regularly for assessment. The goal of assessing each customer group is to obtain a realistic insight into the level of quality delivered and the need for process improvements. Financial assessments are essential and might include the various financial statements (e.g., cash flow, income statement, and balance sheet) as well as a series of ratio analyses. This set of assessments determines how the organization is doing relative to the needs and expectations of the owners. In combination, these three assessment areas provide a fairly complete picture of how effective and efficient the organization is in meeting the needs and exceeding the expectations of its three broad groups of customers. By tracking these assessment results over time, trends in continuous improvement as well as areas that need to be improved can be observed.

Leadership is the final step in the human resources process. This step refers to more than just top management in the organization. High performance service organizations require leadership at all levels. The expectation is that internal customers will take the lead in training new associates, assisting with the validation of training, leading through empowerment by "owning" problems, leading by actively participating in and contributing to effective teams, and continuously assessing the results of processes over which they have control.

In addition to the need for development in task-oriented skills and competencies, there is an acute need to develop leadership skills, competencies, and capabilities. Leadership is possible in any position in an organization. When internal customers use leadership skills to make their decisions, they put the core values, vision, and mission into action, making them come alive as part of the experience for themselves, other associates, and external customers. Associates who have effective leadership skills are not afraid to take action to meet customer requirements. This level of internal customer effectiveness requires a culture with a high level of trust and information sharing. This culture is created and nurtured through the direct actions of the senior leaders of the organization.

Summary

All of the steps in the human resources process are necessary for retention of associates. Today it is essential to retain people who are good in service organizations. This starts with selecting those who can be and are willing to be trained and then helping them improve. One of the best ways to improve retention is to give associates opportunities to develop their skills and knowledge. The obvious benefit to the associates is that with the improved skills and knowledge, they can move to the next level of the service organization. The commitment from the organization is that we will help associates develop.

If you empower your associates, involve them in the development of any changes that would ultimately involve their duties, and treat them as customers, they will take care of the external customers. This is management's ultimate goal. In addition, there are strategies available that can assure success in managing diverse groups of associates. Diversity should be viewed and used as a strength rather than a weakness and a challenge.

Key Terms

Associates-first Orientation—Everything is based on satisfying the needs of internal customers. The company needs to communicate with them and listen to their concerns and ideas.

Autonomy—Associates with functional limits who are independent and do not fear failure or making mistakes .

Casting Limits—Defines who does what in the organization.

Common Purpose and Vision—This must mirror the goals of the organization, but it also must be able to be adopted by all of the diverse groups in the organization.

Confidence—Confidence of associates is needed for vision, values, and processes of the organization to be successful.

Cooperation—When associates use compromise in dealing with other members of the group.

Corporate Perception—Defines the future of the organization.

Diversity—Includes race, religion, personality, personal objectives, and financial/cultural background.

Economic Objectives—These drive managers to achieve success from diversity and the different talents of associates.

Empowerment—Providing direction for what needs to be done, the tools to do it, and then getting out of the way so people can achieve the results.

Follow Up—The manager's need for immediacy of information from an associate.

Functional Limits—Principles that allow associates to concentrate on important and clearly defined areas of responsibility.

Goals—Provide the what, when, where, and how of doing business.

Managing by Walking Around (MBWA)—Managers should never go directly to their office upon arrival at work; they should tour the organization or part of the organization and interact with as many associates as possible.

Niche—Defines and delineates the identity of the business.

Organizational Systems—Define how things are done based on experience, organization standards, and customer expectations. Organizational systems also explain who is involved and why.

Orientation—Where people understand how to make the vision and mission real if they are to make contributions in positive ways. They must understand their role and how it contributes to the success of the organization as it exceeds the expectations of customers; also includes discussions of the philosophies and standards of the organization.

Preferred Partner—A vision for providing management and consulting services.

Recognition of Associate Success—Recognition does not have to wait for awards banquets and the annual evaluation. It can be done almost on a daily basis, and it is particularly effective when it takes place in front of the associate's peers.

Red Beads—Hassles, barriers, obstacles, or failures.

Respect—Respect should be earned; some level of respect is required for success and synergetic gain.

Self-Directed Groups—Teams that work with little oversight or direction from management.

Selection—The goal is to screen applicants and identify people who share the organization's vision, mission, and values.

Sharing Information—To have all associates enroll in the vision, mission, and core values of the organization, management must teach and share as much information as possible.

Synergism—Decisions that produce services and products that no individual alone would have been able to achieve.

Trust—An environment of trust within the team brings about openness, effective communication, and creativity.

Validation of Training—Training is validated by associates and managers in each functional area. Additional validation is provided by customers, both internal and external.

Value Limits—These are contained in operational guidelines such as the organization's core principles of management; establish limits or a framework within which to manage and operate.

Value System—In an organization, helps empowered associates make the right decisions.

Training—Includes specific knowledge, skills, and attitudes so that the new associate may understand and successfully contribute to the mission and needs of the functional area.

Review Questions

1. Why should we focus on the internal customer?
2. What do we need to know about our associates?
3. What is MBWA?
4. What is wrong with tenacious follow-up?
5. Why are the people of Mauritius successful in their efforts to achieve synergy and how does this example apply to your organization?
6. What are the three keys to making associate empowerment successful?
7. What are the functional limits of empowerment?
8. What is the difference between hiring associates and selecting them?
9. What is the ultimate goal in the human resource model?

Activities in Your Organization

Listed below are some activities you can do in your organization. These are designed to reinforce the key chapter concepts. If you are a student and not currently working in the industry, interview an industry leader about one of these topics.

1. Think about your organization from the point of view of your associates. What would make a position/career with your organization more attractive than a position/career with a different organization? Develop a list and then ask your associates this same question. Compare the responses.
2. Since associates in your organization are the creators and deliverers of service, it is essential that you ask for and listen to their suggestions for improvement. Meet with a group of four to six associates and ask them several questions:

- What would help them do their jobs better?
- How can they improve customer service?
- What do they like most about their jobs?
- What do they like least about their jobs?
- What are their suggestions for improving what they like least?
- What are their suggestions for reducing costs or increasing revenues?
- What did you discover that would help you as a leader improve quality in your organization?

3. Review the three keys to empowerment relative to your organization. How are the keys *not* currently being addressed/used in your organization? This analysis will pinpoint barriers to managing and improving quality by empowering people. How are these keys currently being addressed/used in your organization? This analysis will identify strategies that need to be reinforced to empower people to manage and improve quality.

Reference

Covey, Stephen R. *Mauritius, Celebrating Differences.* Provo, Utah: Covey Leadership Center, 1996.

Relevant Web Sites

Human Resource Management as a Process (by Figen Cakar and Umit Bititci):
   http://www.dmem.strath.ac.uk/CSM/Research/hrmproc.htm
Human Resources Learning Center:
   http://www.human-resources.org/Default.htm
Mauritius Training Video and Covey:
   http://www.employeeuniversity.com/corporatevideotraining/catalog/mauritius_2946602.htm
Self-Directed and Self-Managed Teams (by Mark Chatfield):
   http://irism.com/selfteam.htm
Self-Directed and Self-Managed Work Teams Assembled (by Carter McNamara):
   http://www.mapnp.org/library/grp_skll/slf_drct/slf_drct.htm
Ten Tips to Keep Motivated Employees (by Joyce Weiss):
   http://www.ecustomerserviceworld.com/earticlesstore_articles.asp?type=article&id=613

Chapter
5   *Team Effectiveness*

It takes a team to produce a quality guest experience at the Hitching Post. Quality is not just good. Quality stands out because it is visible in the services and products that our guests experience. When the team has provided quality, the guests feel special, important, different than the ordinary, and on top of the world because of the extraordinary Hitching Post team effort. And our team members catch this same extraordinary feeling by providing these experiences.

Paul A. Smith
Owner
Hitching Post Inn Resort & Conference Center
Cheyenne, WY

Learning Objectives

1. Understand the definition and operation of a team.
2. Define what it means to "do right" when it comes to teams.
3. Describe the role of collaborative thinking in the process of building team effectiveness.
4. Detail the characteristics of self-directed work teams and total customer satisfaction teams.
5. Know how to use the high performance teams process model to define team formation, framework, management, participation, monitoring, and evaluation.

Effective teams are the heart of managing and improving quality because they add tremendous value and power to the efforts of their members. Teams help focus a diverse set of skills and views when addressing complex challenges. The diverse cross-functional team in Exhibit 5.1 meets regularly to identify problems in customer service in their casino gaming operation and come up with ways to dehassle the process.

Exhibit 5.1   A diverse cross-functional team in a casino gaming operation meets regularly to identify hassles in customer service and dehassle the process. *(Source: Getty Images, Inc.—Taxi. Used with permission.)*

Teams also enroll the members by giving members ownership of challenges and the responsibility to solve problems by making decisions. The process and quality of decision making is improved by using teams, and people are energized when they have a say in the decision-making process. That energy level has been described as passion, endurance, competition, persistence, perseverance, motivation, and unity. Call it *esprit de corps,* team spirit, or simply the excitement and fun of being part of something greater than yourself, most people like the atmosphere of a team and are moved to share ideas and information in such an environment.

In his video presentation, *Do Right,* Lou Holtz, the former head football coach at Notre Dame and a legend among college football coaches, discusses several aspects of teamwork that apply to both sports teams and business organizations. He indicates that everyone has problems in life, but those individuals who are successful in life are the ones who overcome adversity. The team approach enhances our ability to overcome problems.

People *do* have the power to choose to be successful or to fail. When we react positively to a crisis or to adversity, we become stronger and certainly more capable of achieving success. This positive attitude permeates down from the top of the organization, and those at the top of any company have the ability to set the pace for all of their associates. When executives set high goals for themselves, associates recognize them as a benchmark, and tend to follow the example.

Lou Holtz said there are three basic rules to live by:

1. Do right.
2. Do the best you can.
3. Treat others as you want to be treated.

His definition of teamwork is "everyone being committed to the success of each other." If there is a central objective or sense of purpose, the team will do well; if they are simply trying to get through the day, however, nothing will improve.

So, how do leaders assemble and manage a successful team?

- Identify the central objective and mission statement.
- Clarify all elements of the goals.
- Identify leadership and facilitator responsibilities.
- Identify all members with their location and area of expertise.
- Communicate openly and honestly, showing mutual respect.
- Assign tasks fairly and in keeping with skills.
- Establish meeting time, place, and agenda.
- Promote collaboration of team members.
- Celebrate success.

If you are a team member, here are some helpful hints that will enhance your ability and the team's ability to succeed:

- Be prepared for meetings.
- Be committed to the central objective.
- Assist other members.
- Never judge other members.
- Understand differences in team members.
- Understand cultural variances.
- Tolerate disagreements and avoid defensiveness.
- Share information.
- Hold others accountable.
- Treat members as equals.
- Celebrate success; seek opportunity from defeat.
- Encourage each other and commit to team decisions.
- Remember to use the quality tools in the process of continuous improvement.

Before we explore some examples of teams, consider the requirements necessary for teams to form, function, and thrive. The organization, in general, and the team, in particular, must have a culture that is open to ideas and honest in approach. Members must be stimulated and encouraged to participate and cooperate. This stems in part from the commitment each member has to the shared vision of the team and to solving the problem or addressing the challenge facing them. Team members must understand the direction and desired result for the team through clearly stated goals and objectives, and when conflicts arise, members must be willing to compromise for the good of the team and/or the organization. This social responsibility is sometimes made more difficult when team members are strong-willed and firm in their opinions; however, the good of the whole must take precedence over the good of the individual.

Teams and team members also must be recognized for their commitment and acknowledged for their achievements. At HDS Services, there is a **"Team Wall"** located adjacent to the corporate boardroom. This wall contains photographs of teams from HDS operations across the country. There is a statement indicating what each particular team accomplished. At the entrance to the Team Wall corridor, a brass plate reads: **T**ogether **E**veryone **A**chieves **M**ore. This is the underlying principle behind teamwork, and when combined with diversity of team members the principle allows us to reach maximum effectiveness and accomplishment.

What Is a Team?

What is the difference between a **work group** and a **team?** At HDS work groups are formed on a temporary basis. They are given an issue or issues to resolve and when resolution is achieved, the group is dissolved. The tenure of the work group is measured by the complexity of the issue and the time required for successful resolution.

Sometimes work groups are called **Idea Teams (IT)**. Every associate is a member of an Idea Team or work group, and all Idea Teams have leaders. The teams meet with area managers as a Quality Improvement Team (QIT) to ensure ideas are being implemented and improvements are being made. As discussed in Chapter 3, continuous improvement is the major objective of the QIT. Each area manager is a member of a QIT, which shares information and reports progress in the improvement of quality. The Senior Quality Improvement Team (SQIT) guides the overall process and also appoints members to cross-functional Action Teams (AT) to work on specific quality improvement targets. The members of the Action Teams are Idea Team members from every area directly involved with the problem. The responsibilities of each team are summarized in Exhibit 5.2

Team	Characteristics and Responsibilities
Action Group Team	- Cross-functional from every affected area
	- Work on specific quality improvement targets
Idea Team or Work Group	- Group of associates according to function
	- Permanent part of departmental organization
	- Associate involvement in decision making and goal setting
Quality Improvement Team	- Includes area managers, lead associates, Idea Team leaders
	- Reviews Idea Team recommendations
	- Approves Idea Team ideas and projects within empowerment guidelines
	- Monitors quality improvements
	- Reports quality improvements to senior management
	- Recognizes and rewards achievements and success
	- May appoint Action Teams to address a quality improvement challenge
Senior Quality Improvement Team	- Defines policies and procedures for the management of quality in daily operations
	- Directs, coordinates, refines, and approves recommendations in the process of continuous quality improvement

Exhibit 5.2 Team characteristics and responsibilities. *(Source: HDS Services. Used with permission.)*

The board of directors is considered a team, and in smaller organizations a department is considered a team. At HDS Services we have a Sales Team, an Operations Team, an Administrative Services Team, an Operating Committee Team (executives), and a Directors Team. In the operating units there are also many teams comprised of supervisors and associates. These are all tenured teams that are committed to the journey of continuous quality improvement.

During the implementation phases of the quality effort, a **Steering Team** is formed to get everyone involved and acclimated to managing quality improvements, removing barriers to quality, and identifying all the company's primary processes. This team includes senior management. The primary processes identified by the Steering Team are reviewed, modified, and eventually improved by **Process Analysis Teams.**

Most companies have aggressive plans for growth, and in order to be successful, they need to beat the competition. It is this competition that drives us to be better players; we can accomplish more by working together. Through the use of teamwork, each member of the team becomes more confident, not only in the team, but as an individual as well.

Not everything about teamwork is perceived as being positive, however. There is a downside to the team process. *Decisions are made by committee,* which sometimes slows down the decision-making process. This is particularly aggravating in an environment where speed and efficiency are key to the process. This does not have to always be the case, however. For example, a committee from an independent casual restaurant (Exhibit 5.3) may meet regularly to brainstorm ways that sanitation, including safe food handling, can be improved in the organization.

Exhibit 5.3 A committee from an independent casual restaurant brainstorming ways that sanitation can be improved. *(HDS Services. Used with permission.)*

Quick decision making is essential in organizations with today's rapid pace. Customers expect it, as do investors. Sometimes, decisions may be delayed in the hope of not making a mistake; this strategy is more detrimental to the team and the organization than making a decision, evaluating the results of the decision, and then modifying the decision later. In other words, make mistakes faster so the process (not the blame) can be fixed and improved faster. Effective teams encourage differences of opinion, but seldom run into a situation where a vote is required to make a decision. Consensus is arrived at through discussion. It is important for team members to compromise for the good of the team and/or the organization.

Associate conflicts also can develop as a result of team arrogance. This arrogance can even lead to finger pointing as one team suggests the other is not performing up to expectations. Other conflicts can result from one or more team members not pulling their weight.

Participative Management

Once the barriers to effective team communication and **participative management** are removed, the level of stress in the organization is reduced because individuals can receive more information. Getting input and creative ideas from all team members is a painstaking process, but it is important to the success of the company.

The bottom-up approach to the decision-making process creates an acceleration in the number of creative ideas that are put to use and improves company performance. That is, associates are the prime generators of ideas for improvement since they are closest to the point of creation and delivery of products, services, and experiences for external customers.

Associates of participative managers are highly motivated because they have a stronger sense of ownership in the company. They truly have a voice in the company's decision-making process and an opportunity to plan the work processes that affect their job. The partnership between associates and senior management also enhances the confidence the associates have in corporate leadership. Because of this high level of performance, future targets will be established at higher levels, and future improvements will be generated in larger increments.

Organizations that practice a participative management style follow a new paradigm for teams within the organization. These teams participate in activities that were once reserved for specialists in the organization. Teams in a participative management environment may be asked to help interview applicants and involve themselves in the actual selection process. Teams also may be asked to help in any vendor-related bid process, and they actually approve suppliers and their products, including the development of specifications. They also may be responsible for collaboratively reviewing and evaluating the performance of their managers and the company's strengths and weaknesses. Finally, these teams may be involved in the selection and purchase of capital equipment. All of these areas of involvement are off limits to associates who work for more traditional organizations.

Collaborative Thinking

Transforming individual-thinking associates into **collaborative-thinking teams** has its challenges. In addition to the added responsibilities of team participation, associates will have to learn how to handle customer feedback, both positive and negative. Once they understand not to "shoot the messenger," and learn to use the information to improve products and services, they should be recognized for their efforts.

Elements of collaboration include cooperation, symbiosis, and synergism. **Cooperation** means working together toward a common quality improvement goal. **Symbiosis** refers to helping each other. **Synergism** refers to increased effectiveness, which is a result of working together. The organization becomes more competitive as a result of collaboration and increases its growth rate, market share, and profitability. One example of collaboration is the relationship between suppliers and hospitality service organizations. This collaboration involves the exchange of information, ideas, and processes. The sharing of ideas and information could evolve into sharing of assets and a strategy based on a shared vision.

Collaboration results from partnering and strategic alliances. For example, HDS Services has a strategic partnership with HHA Services, a contract maintenance and environmental services provider. Together, the synergy of this team offers potential clients a full-service line of contract services and the level of quality offered by the partnership improves along the way. Collaboration also can take place within an organization such as an assisted living organization when there is sharing of ideas and information between the dietitian and the unit director (Exhibit 5.4).

Exhibit 5.4 Collaboration is sharing of ideas and information. *(HDS Services. Used with permission.)*

Examples of Teams

Self-Directed Teams

Unlike traditional companies that were driven by the hierarchy of the organization, companies that will be successful in the future will utilize **self-directed teams** to drive change and improve performance. The primary challenge for developing effective self-directed teams is successfully transitioning associates from the traditional, hierarchical management principles to teams practicing **Trifecta** management, that is, changing cultures. Changing cultures is a major educational undertaking that requires time, patience, and financial commitment.

All members of teams must first understand and accept the new role of executive management. It will change from giving direction, dictating orders, and driving the organization to coordinating the actions of the many and various self-directed teams. There could be, given the size of the organization, over a thousand different teams taking action simultaneously. Each team's responsibility is to use these interventions in the process of continuous improvement.

The largest hurdle in the team management style conversion is staff trusting executive management to relinquish power and delegate authority. At the same time, executive management must make the commitment to trust their teams and individual associates. All changes or interventions must meet the basic requirements of external customers, internal customers, and the financial objectives of the company.

Newly formed self-directed teams will need assistance during the initial stages of formation and development. A facilitator and coach may be used at this point in the team building process. For the initial three to six team meetings, the coach will teach and promote the 10 key factors leading to team success (Exhibit 5.5) and increase the confidence of team members so they can maximize their effectiveness.

1. Schedule team meetings at appropriate times.
2. Circulate minutes from action group meetings.
3. Define the goals, priorities, agenda, and membership of the team.
4. Solicit additional volunteers who are interested.
5. Be certain that the team has the support of executives including directors and stakeholders.
6. Empower the group to act and make decisions.
7. Distribute the team meeting agenda in advance.
8. Define responsibilities of the individual members and the team as a whole.
9. Set obtainable goals and select an opportunity for a quick success.
10. Coach team members.

Exhibit 5.5 Ways to make self-directed action groups more effective.

Obviously, selecting team members is an important part of having successful self-directed teams. First, make certain that egocentric, selfish individuals are not selected. The preferred team is made up of individuals who genuinely want to work together and help each other achieve their goals (Exhibit 5.6). Make sure all teams contain at least one member that is connected in some way to the company's executives. This gives the team members additional confidence that their decisions will receive support. The team will need balance, so make sure members have various skills and use diversity as a strength. Be certain to involve all affected individuals or departments when making teams; if you fail to include everyone, making an effective change in one area of the company can result in a negative affect on

Exhibit 5.6 Two internal customers making a salad bar in a university residence hall ready for the luncheon rush. *(HDS Services. Used with permission.)*

another area of the company. Also remember to concentrate on the "what" of the issue and not the "who." Remember the **85/15 Rule of Quality,** which indicates that 85 percent of the company's problems are process-based, not people-related.

A tool that effective self-directed teams frequently use is the **PDCA Cycle.** A graphical representation of the PDCA Cycle is presented in Exhibit 5.7. **PDCA** stands for **P**lan, **D**o, **C**heck, and **A**ct. An example of the work of a self-directed team is the product development process at The Ritz-Carlton Hotel Company. The process is presented in Exhibit 5.8.

The first step in the **product development process** is to identify customers. These customers can be categorized as external or internal customers and can be further divided into existing customers, former customers, indirect customers, potential customers, suppliers, and ultimate customers, using the categories described in Chapter 3. These customers may be listed in priority order based on sales or sales potential, contribution to the profitability of the organization, ability to influence others or some other set of criteria. Discovering customer requirements is the next step in the process. The requirements may be discovered through one-on-one conversations with customers, feedback from associates based on customer complaints or suggestions for improvement, legal actions against the organization, or industry trends that apply to the organization's customers. Once determined, the requirements must be prioritized. The next step is to develop the product/service. This step requires looking at a product/service concept including:

- Problem or need of the customer
- Product and/or service specifically needed by the customer
- Promises—what can the product/service do for the customer?
- Personal advantage—what can the customers do because of the product/service that our organization is creating and delivering?
- Positioning—what is the benefit of our product/service vs. that of the competition's product/service?
- Price/Value—what must the customer give up in time and/or money to get the product or service?

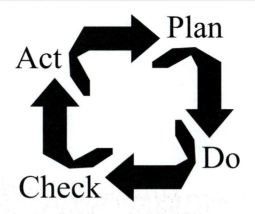

P = Planning - Get things started.
- Present the issue(s).
- Describe the symptoms.
- Identify the root causes.
- Express all feelings on the issue and debate pros/cons.
- Seek compromise and summarize.

D = Doing - Initiate solutions or interventions on a test basis.
- Assign tasks.

C = Checking - Evaluate the results.
- Do not measure against compliance.
- Use the CQI process.
- Review team performance.

A = Acting - Monitor the results and present to the team.
- Adopt the solution that works.
- Reward team members for achievement.
- Document.

Exhibit 5.7 PDCA cycle. A graphical representation of the PDCA Cycle. *(HDS Services. Used with permission.)*

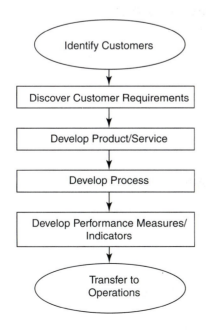

Exhibit 5.8 The product development process at The Ritz-Carlton Hotel Company using a self-directed team.

The fourth step is to develop the process to create the desired product/service for the customer. The process includes selecting and training people and getting equipment, facilities, raw materials, and information needed to create and deliver the product/service.

Next, performance measures/indicators must be developed. These are used to categorize information so that plans and decisions can be made and variations from the planned outcomes can be identified and fixed. If there is a negative variation, the process is fixed; if the variation is positive, there is cause for celebration and congratulations for those involved. Some of these indicators are monitored monthly (e.g., profitability). Others are monitored weekly (e.g., customer counts) or daily (e.g., revenues). Often, the outcomes are compared to data from the last period or last year. Additionally, other organizations are used to provide benchmark data, such as performance indicators that can assist the organization in the establishment of relevant standards. At this step in the process, however, it is most important to measure the organization's progress relative to the priorities it has established for its customers based on the requirements of those same customers.

The final process step is to transfer the responsibility for the process to operations. The associates in operations can use the documented information to implement the process and improve it over time. Before the process is transferred to operations, however, the associates who will be responsible for it must be trained. They also must know how to monitor and measure the process, and the reward system must be determined.

Total Customer Satisfaction Teams

Motorola has adapted a team concept from the Japanese called **Total Customer Satisfaction (TCS) Teams.** TCS teams fundamentally encourage associates to shape their work environment through problem solving and goal accomplishment. Each TCS team is made up of 3 to 12 members from various departments, areas, and backgrounds. The team addresses key issues and initiatives in the company, such as reduction in cycle times (the time it takes for a process), quality improvements, improvement in profitability, environmental issues, and overall process improvements.

Teamwork

The team is the lifeblood of a high performance service organization. The roles of the Senior Quality Improvement Team (SQIT), Quality Improvement Teams (QIT), Action Group Teams (AGT), and Idea or Work Group Teams (IT or WGT) have been outlined earlier in this chapter. Now we will delve deeper into the concept of teamwork to find out what makes teams work in a high performance service organization.

There is a difference between a team and a group. A team is two or more individuals who work together as a cohesive unit to achieve a specific and shared goal that requires interdependent action and collaboration. A group, on the other hand, is any number of individuals who have a common goal but work without collaboration. Sometimes the two are combined, as in an AGT, which is a cross-functional assembly of internal customers. Once formed, an AGT establishes the foundation, manages the process, and achieves continuous improvement. Review Exhibit 5.9 and visualize how an AGT might work in a resort hotel, a vending company, and an organization that provides services in a healthcare organization.

While teams and groups have similarities, high performance teams generally go through a process known as the **high performance teams process model** (Exhibit 5.10). This model takes inputs and creates outputs.

CONTINUOUS IMPROVEMENT
- Launch initiatives (follow the implementation process)
- Measure AGT progress
- Evaluate AGT effectiveness
- Improve effectiveness through action
- Interchange AGT members

BUILDING THE TEAM
- List possible initiatives
- Determine size of AGT
- Assign a group leader
- Gather volunteers
- Commit to self-direction

MANAGING THE PROCESS
- Get team member input to prepare for meeting
- Have everyone participate
- Facilitate member communication
- Use the appropriate decision-making process
- Promote trust and listening skills

LAYING THE FOUNDATION
- Establish processes for communication
- Set team and individual goals
- Define types of issues and ideas the group will address
- Identify individual team member roles and responsibilities

Exhibit 5.9   How Action Group Teams (AGTs) work.

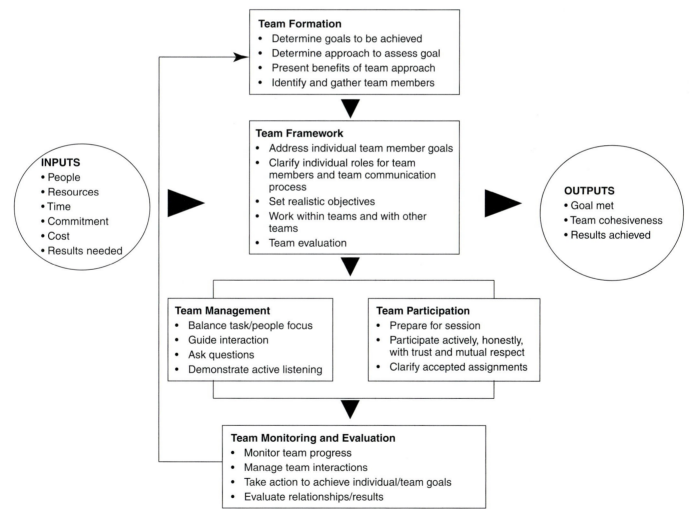

Team Formation
- Determine goals to be achieved
- Determine approach to assess goal
- Present benefits of team approach
- Identify and gather team members

Team Framework
- Address individual team member goals
- Clarify individual roles for team members and team communication process
- Set realistic objectives
- Work within teams and with other teams
- Team evaluation

INPUTS
- People
- Resources
- Time
- Commitment
- Cost
- Results needed

OUTPUTS
- Goal met
- Team cohesiveness
- Results achieved

Team Management
- Balance task/people focus
- Guide interaction
- Ask questions
- Demonstrate active listening

Team Participation
- Prepare for session
- Participate actively, honestly, with trust and mutual respect
- Clarify accepted assignments

Team Monitoring and Evaluation
- Monitor team progress
- Manage team interactions
- Take action to achieve individual/team goals
- Evaluate relationships/results

Exhibit 5.10   High performance teams process model.

The goal of a high performance team must be determined before the team can be formed. The goal is determined after identifying the results that are needed (e.g., elimination of a hassle that is negatively affecting customer service). Goals for different teams (contrast the goals for a hotel sales team to those of a vending services team of route drivers) will vary based on the results needed, which are based on the requirements of the customers. The team's goal should be stated, clarified, and put into writing. Next, it must be determined how to assess the goal. To do this, the team must eventually know the criteria for success and how to assess goal needs. The assessment is based on the results needed; the nature of the task; people, time, and cost estimates; and resources available. These factors are shown as inputs in Exhibit 5.10. Once the assessment is completed, an appropriate method can be selected.

Next, the goal, goal needs, and plan for achievement can be presented to the Senior Quality Improvement Team. These factors should always be framed in the context of the customers' requirements, such as the groups who purchase what the hotel sales team has to offer or the clients who contract with the vending company. Next, team members are identified. The structure of the team needs to be defined because team members need to know the "rules" for how the team will function. Team members also must be informed as to the expectations for participation and interaction within the team. Above all, members must be expected to contribute in positive ways to the team.

After a team is formed, its framework must be developed. The framework step begins by addressing individual team member goals. The two AGT members from a theme park in Exhibit 5.11 are meeting to discuss individual goals and concerns. The framework covers the relationships between these individual goals and the team goals identified during team formation. The team also must develop consensus on the team mission statement. This statement should state who/what the team is, its purpose, and in what interest the team functions or operates. At the Detroit Athletic Club this is called the Statement of Purpose and it documents why the department exists from the club members' perspective. Team missions must be in harmony with the organization's overriding mission and in alignment with the organization's upper management's mission.

Exhibit 5.11 Two AGT members from a theme park meet to discuss individual goals and concerns. *(HDS Services. Used with permission.)*

The second task in this step is to clarify individual roles for team members, as well as the communication process that will be used. Members' roles are based on the individual's expertise and characteristics. One member of a vending services client development team may have customer relationship service expertise, while another team member may have a strong understanding of the applications of information technology to the customer service process.

Communication is the lifeblood of the team and is needed for team coordination. Communication builds trust; when quality information is not available, gossip and rumors take the place of facts. Communication within the team also has the power to enhance the process of improving quality. When members of the hotel sales team communicate, they can build on the expertise of individuals and present a more well-rounded sales strategy to the potential groups interested in booking meetings and conventions. Effective communication results in synergy that benefits both the internal customer team members and the external customers.

Team members must be courageous to play "devil's advocate" and present the other side of an issue while questioning the way we have always done things in the organization. There is a potential danger to team effectiveness when communication is not effective. Consider the example from the NASA Challenger incident in 1986. The space shuttle exploded despite the highly developed NASA team. The external pressures on the team leader changed the normal team process of communication. As a result, communication became limited and important information was dismissed as lower priority. It was later discovered that the explosion of the Challenger was directly related to suppressed information on safety and performance of the "O" rings.

The next step in the product development process is to set realistic objectives. These objectives describe what the team is going to do. They must be achievable, observable, and measurable. For example, an automatic merchandising company may have objectives that include 10 percent growth each year, and they can easily be measured. The conditions of the objectives determine the action required and the expectations are defined by the organization's standards. The result of combining action and expectations is the objective:

$$ACTION + EXPECTATION = OBJECTIVE$$

The fourth component of developing a team framework is to work with other teams. The hotel sales staff will likely have to ask for the assistance of the reservations department and the front office department if they are going to be able to upsell during the reservations process and the arrival/check-in process. This is particularly important when the problem or hassle being addressed is a major issue or it spans a number of areas in the organization. Finally, the method(s) for team evaluation must be determined at this stage. Questions that help with this determination include the following:

- Why should the team be evaluated?
- What should we evaluate?
- How should we develop an evaluation plan?

Answers to these questions (with input by all team members) will help formulate the plan for team evaluation. The objective is to have those involved on the team determine the evaluation criteria and understand these criteria in advance. The criteria may be categorized as results (i.e., tasks) or relationships (i.e., people). The list in Exhibit 5.12 can be used to evaluate the extent that synergy takes place on an AGT.

Before we leave the topic of team evaluation, consider why teams should be evaluated. Evaluation helps identify accomplishments and whether the leadership is shared and effective. The analysis also helps pinpoint the team's strengths and weaknesses. In the spirit of continuous improvement of the team process, evaluation helps identify points of team decline, group dissatisfaction, low morale, drop in individual participation, drop in productivity, reduced standards of quality, confusion about the team's purpose and roles of individuals, and stagnation and ineffectiveness. Without evaluation, there is no way to determine if the team is successful. For example, there is no way a hotel sales team can

Use this form to assess AGT member synergy.

Description	Synergy Yes	Synergy No	Suggestions
Members openly expressed views, and reached consensus			
Members are enrolled in the team outcomes			
Members provided peers with all pertinent information			
Members treated peers with respect			
Members practice professionalism in peer interaction			

Exhibit 5.12 Action Group Team (AGT) member synergy.

determine its effectiveness without regular evaluation. Some suggested criteria to evaluate team results are presented in Exhibit 5.13.

Team management is the next step in forming successful high performance teams. There must be a balance between the task focus and the people focus. A task-focused team emphasizes well-documented data, deadlines, a systematic structure, shared expertise, strong leadership, and quality results. A people-focused team is sensitive to member needs such as availability, workload in and out of the team, comfort levels (with assignments and with other team members),

Use this form to evaluate the results of your team efforts (tasks).

Description	Goals Achieved	Goals Not Achieved	Suggestions
All options were discussed in depth			
Everyone was involved			
Goals were totally supported by ALL members			
Criticism and conflict were well managed			
Goals were met after considering external customer, internal customer, and financial expectations			

Exhibit 5.13 Evaluating team results.

and social relationships. The vending organization's tasks are to sell to new clients, retain present clients, and obtain more sales from the existing clients. Effective high performance teams seek to balance both tasks and people.

It is important that team members clearly understand the team's purpose. This can be achieved when terminology is clarified, stakeholders (those who have a keen interest in the team's results) are identified, expectations are clear, related issues (support or obstacles) are addressed, and results are anticipated and visualized.

Successful teams are driven by the **enrollment** of members. Enrollment is different than the typical "buy-in." Enrollment is encouraged when members see a link between personal goals and team goals, then freely choose to enroll. Enrollment flourishes when concerns of members are addressed and expectations are heard. It is enhanced when individual team tasks are directly connected to a person's abilities and expertise, and enrollment is encouraged when responsibility and accountability are present.

The next three parts of team management are related: guiding interaction, asking questions, and active listening. Interaction is guided by the team's leader. Rather than dominate the brainstorming and discussion about building group business in the hotel, the team leader should encourage the ideas of others and participation by all. Discussion must occur and everyone should be encouraged to participate. Team members should feel free to express their opinions about the tasks as well as the team's operation. Hidden agendas should be eliminated; everyone should have the opportunity to ask questions and make contributions. An informal, comfortable, and relaxed climate in team meetings reduces signs of boredom and tension. There will be disagreements, but they are civilized. The team is comfortable with the disagreements and doesn't avoid, smooth over, or suppress conflict. Unresolved conflict should be dealt with by the team leader and the individual team members most involved with the conflict.

Active listening is effective because it utilizes techniques such as questioning, paraphrasing, and summarizing to generate and clarify ideas. After all voices have been heard, consensus decisions can take place. Consensus decisions are those that have substantial, but not necessarily unanimous, agreement. They are reached through open discussion of and listening to everyone's ideas and avoiding formal voting or easy compromises. For example, it may be the consensus of the team that new client solicitation for a vending company should be concentrated in a particular geographic area to build on the organization's existing business base in that area. If a member of the team does not agree with this strategy, he or she owes it to the other team members to state the reasons why in as compelling a way as possible. However, if the team decides by consensus to concentrate in this area, then the dissenting team member owes it to the team to support the consensus decision. That is known as social responsibility: doing something for the good of the organization rather than the good of an individual.

Team participation is as important as team management in the process. Team participation is stimulated when the team leader and members prepare for the meeting. Preparation has four components: contact, decide, network, and research. As a team member, it is a good idea to contact the team leader or another member of the team to familiarize oneself with the purpose, objective, and structure of team meetings. That familiarity will help a team member determine his or her role, the role of others, and expectations (both time and contribution). Then the individual should ask for an agenda so he or she can review the issues and determine where to contribute to the meeting's agenda topics. The person also should ask about the expertise of others to determine both how his or her expertise complements and supports that of others. Active participation from all will permit the team to capitalize on a broad spectrum of team-player types and styles. Everyone has a contribution to make; diversity of input adds to the strength of the team.

Indicate "Yes" or "No" for the following	Yes	No
1. Is the AGT improving?		
2. Are completion timelines met?		
3. Do we avoid re-work?		
4. Is AGT leadership effective?		
5. Are meetings effective?		
6. Are there enough initiatives?		
7. Can launches be improved?		
8. Do Team meetings stay on track?		
9. Are meeting minutes published?		
10. Is there sufficient talent on the team?		
11. Does the AGT meet frequently enough?		
Other:		
Other:		
Other:		
Other:		
Other:		

Exhibit 5.14   Measuring effectiveness and improvement.

Team monitoring and evaluation is the final step in the successful high performance teams process model. Following each meeting, or on a less frequent basis, team members should assess progress. A checklist for this is found in Exhibit 5.14.

The checklist will help monitor AGT progress as well as the progress of other teams. If any of the answers are "no," action must be taken by team members on the team to improve and change the answers to "yes."

In summary, the team approach feeds the improvement process with a wide range of expertise and many points of view. This results in a variety of resources that can lead to improvement.

- The team approach presents more opportunities for enrollment by individuals.
- Because tasks can be shared, a team generates more information sooner.
- Both risks and opportunities for success are shared among team members.
- For those who disagree, a team environment provides numerous opportunities for channeling disagreement into productive communication.
- Teams offer an opportunity to view the big picture or the whole process, particularly when they are cross-functional teams working on a hassle that cuts across functional areas in the organization.

Exhibit 5.15 presents a list of ways to make teams of associates more effective.

A team gives individuals the opportunity to demonstrate their commitment and share growth and learning among team members. Oftentimes this growth and learning takes place one-on-one, as cruise ship passenger service improvement team members interact with each other (Exhibit 5.16) outside of team meetings.

There are many important factors that directly affect the success of teams, but we believe the following 10 drive success.

1. Teams must respond as quickly, directly, and positively as possible. Successful teams live by the **24/72 Rule:** ideas need to be acknowledged

Be certain that the team has the support of top management.
Define the purpose and structure of the team (focus, agenda, goals, scope, and assignment).
Define roles of the individual members and the team as a whole.
Solicit qualified volunteers who are interested and committed to the team's purpose.
Set obtainable goals and provide an opportunity for a quick success.
Train team members.
Send the team meeting agenda in advance.
Give the team the authority to act and make decisions.
Schedule team meetings at convenient times.
Establish open, honest communication.
Circulate minutes from team meetings.
Set a timeline for the team.

Exhibit 5.15   Ways to make associate teams more effective.

Exhibit 5.16   Cruise ship passenger service improvement team members interact. *(HDS Services. Used with permission.)*

within 24 hours and decisions completed within 72 hours. At HDS, every written suggestion is acknowledged with a letter from the president of the company. In the letter, the process for reviewing the idea is described, and the recipient informed about who and what team will review the suggestion and get back to them with a decision.

2. Teams must have a passion for meeting and exceeding customer expectations. They also must understand the principles behind "doing things right the first time." However, the fear of failure or making a mistake must not slow or stop action.

3. Team members must be committed to supporting other team members, but they also must recognize that conformity is not the most important ingredient. Creativity is the key. Members are encouraged to differ, argue, and discuss matters and key issues. Then, they must make a unified decision on what action is to be taken.

4. Teams must practice the principle that no suggestion is too small to consider, and they should avoid individual member competition.

5. Teams must be process oriented. In order to comply with this, members must understand all processes involved in the functioning of the company. This includes the complete cycle from vendor to company to customer.

6. Teams must measure their own performance and progress. This is a key to continuous improvement.

7. Team members must set aside all personal agendas in favor of what is important and best for the company. They must stress the value of each associate's ideas to the organization.
8. Teams must adopt all the principles of continuous quality improvement, including the following steps:
   - Brainstorming the issues
   - Identification of the root causes
   - Prioritizing the interventions
   - Taking action
   - Monitoring the results
9. Team members must not only share responsibilities, they must also share leadership. Teamwork is a collaborative effort and the entire team must understand the power of synergism.

    Newspaper editor Bob Stromberg once described the fascination he felt as a boy, when lying on his back in an open field. He saw "the 'head goose,' the leader of the V formation, suddenly swerve out, leaving a vacancy which was immediately filled by a goose from behind. The former leader flew along side and took a position at the back of the line, and they never missed a beat."

    Flocks are never leaderless. Leadership comes from anyone at any time, and it goes to anyone at any time.
10. "Everyone must be involved," as stated by Dr. Deming in his fourteen points. Total involvement is critical to the success of the team.

Summary

Effective teams are the heart of managing and improving quality because they add value and power to the efforts of their members. High performance teams have various goals depending on the issue being addressed, and they go through a process of formation and framework, management, participation, monitoring, and evaluating criteria development. Teams use collaborative thinking to enhance effectiveness through symbiosis and synergism. Self-directed work teams and total customer satisfaction teams are further ways to enhance the effectiveness and contributions of teams.

Key Terms

24/72 Rule—Ideas need to be acknowledged within 24 hours, and decisions completed within 72 hours.

85/15 Rule of Quality—85 percent of the company's problems are process-based, not people-related.

Action Group Team (AGT)—Cross functional from every affected area and work on specific quality improvement targets.

Associate Conflicts—Can develop as a result of team arrogance and other conflicts can result from one or more team members not pulling their weight.

Collaborative-Thinking Teams—Associates learning to use the information to improve products and services; they should be recognized for their efforts.

Cooperation—Working together toward a common quality improvement goal.

Enrollment—Flourishes when concerns of members are addressed and expectations are heard. It is enhanced when individual team tasks are directly connected to a person's abilities and expertise. Enrollment is encouraged when responsibility and accountability are present.

High Performance Team Process Model—Team Formation, Team Framework, Team Management, Team Participation, Team Monitoring and Evaluation, inputs and outputs.

Idea Teams (IT)—The teams meet with area managers as a Quality Improvement Team (QIT) to ensure ideas are being implemented and improvements are being made.

Participative Management—Getting input and creative ideas from all team members; once removed, the level of stress in the organization is reduced because individuals can receive more information.

PDCA Cycle—Plan, Do, Check, and Act.

Product Development Process—Used to identify the customers.

Process Analysis Teams—The primary processes identified by the Steering Team are reviewed, modified, and eventually improved by this team.

Quality Improvement Team (QIT)—Reviews Idea Team recommendations, approves Idea Team ideas and projects within empowerment guidelines, monitors quality improvements, reports quality improvements to senior management, recognizes and awards achievement success, may appoint action teams to address a quality improvement challenge.

Self-Directed Teams—Utilized to drive change and improve performance.

Senior Quality Improvement Team (SQIT)—Defines policies and procedures for the management of quality in daily operations; directs, coordinates, refines, and approves recommendations in the process of continuous quality improvement.

Steering Team—This team is formed to get everyone involved and acclimated to managing quality improvements, removing barriers to quality, and identifying all the company's primary processes. This team includes senior management.

Symbiosis—Helping each other and increased effectiveness, which is a result of working together.

Team—A team is two or more individuals who work together as a cohesive unit to achieve a specific and shared goal that requires interdependent action and collaboration.

Total Customer Satisfaction (TCS) Teams—Encourages associates to shape their work environment through problem solving and goal accomplishment.

Trifecta—Changing management cultures.

Work Group—Work groups are formed on a temporary basis. They are given an issue or issues to resolve and, when resolution is achieved, the group is dissolved. The tenure of the work group is measured by the complexity of the issue and the time required for successful resolution.

Review Questions

1. What is the definition of a team? Describe a team that you are a part of. Why is this team effective or not effective?
2. How will you apply the philosophy of "Do Right" to your organizational team? Does it also apply to your team of family members and/or friends? If so, how?
3. How can you utilize collaborative thinking as a team member to make the team more effective? Give an example from a team that you have had experience with recently.
4. How could you transform your work team into a self-directed team?
5. Why would you want to be a member of a total customer satisfaction team? What are the advantages for you? For the external customers? For the organization?

6. Using one of the elements of the high performance teams process model (please see page 91), how you would alter an ineffective team that you were a part of to make it more effective?

Activities in Your Organization

Listed below are some activities designed to reinforce the key chapter concepts in your organization. If you are a student and not currently working in the industry, interview an industry leader about one of these topics.

1. Think about your organization and the teams that are at work within it. How would you characterize these teams using Exhibit 5.2 in this chapter? Do you have action teams? If so, what are their particular quality improvement targets? How do the action teams interact with the idea teams or work groups? Using the evaluation criteria, are there specific ways that the results (tasks) and relationships (people) of these teams can be improved in your organization?

2. Use the Product Development Process in Exhibit 5.8 to identify the customers for whom you intend to develop a new product or service offered by your organization. Categorize the customers using the groups described in Chapter 3. Then, list the customers in priority order based on sales or sales potential, contribution to the profitability of the organization, ability to influence others (e.g., to become a customer of the organization), or some other set of criteria. Discover and prioritize the customers' requirements and develop the product by translating the requirements into a product concept. Develop the process to create the desired product/service for the customers and performance measures/indicators. Finally, outline how the process will be transferred to operations. Review this with another team member and ask for feedback on how the overall process might be improved.

3. Consider a team that you are a member of in your organization. Evaluate the team member synergy using Exhibit 5.12 in this chapter. What areas could be improved? What actions will you take as a team member? Now evaluate the team results using Exhibit 5.13. What results are being achieved? Which still need work and what will you do to improve the results? Evaluate the team's effectiveness and improvement using Exhibit 5.14. How will you continue to improve? What will you do to improve the results that are not being achieved?

References

William I. Gorden, Erica Nagel, Scott A. Myers, and Carole A. Barbato. *The Team Trainer*. New York: McGraw Hill, 1996.

Holtz, Lou. *Do Right*. Video. Alexandria, VA: Washington Speakers Bureau, 1988.

Holtz, Lou. *Do Right II*. Video. Alexandria, VA: Washington Speakers Bureau, 1991.

Relevant Web Sites

Achieving Total Customer Satisfaction Through Six Sigma (by Jane Erwin):
http://elsmar.com/pdf_files/Six_Sigma.pdf

Creating Total Customer Satisfaction:
http://www.imtc3.com/servicequality.html

Empowered Employees—A New Team Concept for Total Customer Satisfaction (by Mary Hellinghausen and Jim Myers):
http://www.masetllc.com/pdfs/129.pdf

Hitching Post Inn Resort & Conference Center Website:
http://www.hitchingpostinn.com/

How to Build a Successful Team:
http://www.altika.com/leadership/teambld.htm

Importance of Building a Team:
http://www.teamtechnology.co.uk/tt/h-articl/tb-basic.htm

PDCA Cycle:
http://www.hci.com.au/hcisite2/toolkit/pdcacycl.htm

Team Effectiveness and High Performance Organization:
http://www.eagle.ca/~mikehick/teams.html

Chapter

6 *Serving External Customers*

Quality in fact and quality in perception must be managed in any quality improvement effort. Quality in fact relates to our internal standards. We get what we expect, so set high expectations. Quality in perception is how our service is perceived by our customers.

Don Fletcher
President and Chief Executive Officer
Port Huron Hospital
Port Huron, MI
(Winner of the 1998 Michigan Quality Leadership Award)

The secret of a successful club is a full and loyal membership that is served by talented and loyal staff. The relationship between the staff and members is at the heart of service commitment. Members who trust and respect the staff draw out of the staff a level of loyalty that is unique to clubs.

J. G. Ted Gillary
Executive Manager, Detroit Athletic Club
Detroit, MI
(Winner of the 2003 Michigan Quality Council
Quality Leadership Lighthouse Award)

Learning Objectives

1. Understand quality from the perspective of external customers, including the quality perceived, and quality and service.
2. Describe the customer satisfaction challenge from a customer-first viewpoint.
3. Define the characteristics of loyal customers and detail how to build customer loyalty.
4. Describe the differences between fact and perception when it comes to customer satisfaction.
5. Define how to use customer information to improve quality.
6. Understand the various ways to solicit feedback from customers so that quality can be improved.
7. Describe the value of customer complaints, how to generate more, and how to use the information to improve quality.

Focus on External Customers

Jerry McVety, president of McVety & Associates and vice president of HDS Services, has aptly observed that "If you don't know why customers are satisfied, you will not stay in business." Customer assessment goes hand-in-hand with customer service because assessment helps determine the effectiveness of the service delivery as perceived by the external customer. Before we discuss assessments, however, we must understand the needs and expectations of external customers.

We have already established that the internal customers are the most important people in a service business because they create and deliver the service experience. This is true in a public business (such as a hotel company), a privately held company (such as an independent restaurant), and a non-profit organization (such as an association of vending operators and suppliers). In fact, this is why internal customers often are thought of as stakeholders in the organization. If internal customers are treated well (i.e., their needs are identified and satisfied and their expectations are understood and met), they will create pleasant experiences for external customers. As Chairman of the Board and Chief Executive Officer of Marriott International, Inc., J. W. "Bill" Marriott, Jr. says, "Take good care of your associates and they will take good care of your customers."

Basically the keys to internal and external customer satisfaction are the same: 1) knowing who the customers are and 2) knowing what they need, want, and expect. Management should exceed what is wanted or expected and add extras. These extras might include anticipatory service—service before the customer asks for it. Extras could be product features that the customer did not expect initially or experiences that make the encounter with the associate memorable. For example, the genuine, friendly, and helpful greeting in a cafeteria from the chef during the luncheon meal in a corporate business and industry dining facility (Exhibit 6.1) could boost tired spirits, help stressed attitudes, and improve productivity for the rest of the business day. Extras could also be the part of an experience that convinces the customer to return.

Exhibit 6.1 A genuine, friendly, and helpful greeting in a cafeteria by the chef during the luncheon meal in a corporate business and industry dining facility. *(Source: HDS Services. Used with permission.)*

All of these transform **customer service** into **customer satisfaction.** With more organizations advertising their high quality products and services, the concept of quality has been blurred in the minds of customers. Products or services now fall into the same class; televisions, oil changes, dry cleaning procedures, and computers often are perceived to have similar or equal quality by customers. These products are sometimes referred to as **commodities.** What differentiates these commodities is not their price or quality; it is the service the organization provides.

Today, many organizations proclaim and deliver good, better, or superior customer service. In fact, with the progressive expectations of today's increasingly sophisticated customer, the minimum levels of service expected have been increasing steadily over time. Additionally, today's customer is more attuned to price and believes that the lower the price, the better the value. All of these factors impact customer satisfaction.

Increasingly, customers view products as indistinguishable commodities. The CD player that you purchase at one retailer is identical to the player available at the other retailer. It is the same brand with the same model number, but the player has a lower price at the high volume discount retailer. If you expect a higher level of service, you may decide to purchase the player with the higher price. If not, the lower price will deliver more value for the same player. Remember that higher levels of service add value. Service is *the* added value for today's customers.

Quality Perceived

Some characterize **quality perceived** as the difference between the products and services of one organization compared to similar products and services available to customers from other organizations. Others characterize quality perceived as the value added when a product or service is created and delivered. Both definitions are right; customer-driven organizations realize that there is a difference between quality that meets expectations and quality that exceeds expectations.

Today, **intangible aspects** of customer service are growing more important than the **tangible aspects.** Tangible aspects of quality relate to technical elements, such as cleaning and pressing a shirt at a laundry or the act of changing the oil and filling all the fluids in an automobile. The technical parts of service are relatively easy; they are largely mechanical.

The intangible parts of service are more difficult to create, deliver, and measure. A smile by the person working behind the counter in a laundry is an intangible service element. A friendly greeting and genuine "thank you" by the person changing a customer's oil is another example of an intangible service element. These intangibles make the service experience memorable; they transform the customer from a simple user of a product or service into an advocate for the organization. The delighted customer will share positive testimonials about the organization with friends and encourage them to experience customer satisfaction first-hand.

Fact versus Perception

Customers who are totally satisfied by both the tangible and intangible parts of service truly love the organization and are more likely to become loyal customers. When a customer simply likes an organization's products or services, there is little emotional connection based on a mutually beneficial relationship. This customer may leave the organization quickly if a lower price is found elsewhere or another organization provides better service. In contrast, those who love a product or service, and consequently the organization, have a vested interest in building the relationship. They are not likely to defect on price alone; they have too much invested to let price alone drive the change.

In a relationship trust is based on dependability. When we tell a customer that we will be there between 2:00 and 3:00, they are looking for and expect us at

2:00 p.m. If we arrive any time after, we are late. Customers, like everyone, filter what they hear through their own unique paradigms. Be certain that there is a clear understanding between what was said and what was heard. Remember that the customer's (both external and internal) perceptions are all that matters—that is the customer's reality.

In a private club, when members sponsor family, friends, and business colleagues to join their club, the club has moved beyond its purpose of simply the utilitarian use of the facilities *as perceived by the members.* The club has become the members' home-away-from-home and a place of hospitality that successfully melds family, community, friendships, and business together. The quality of the club is defined as perceived by the members.

Customer Satisfaction Challenge

External customers expect customer service as part of the product or service offered for sale. Customer satisfaction, on the other hand, is what transforms regular customers to loyal customers. These loyal customers provide a component of marketing that one cannot purchase: positive word-of-mouth advertising.

Some have said that the growth and success of a high performance service organization lies in customer satisfaction resulting from superior, outstanding, and valued customer service. Everything we do in a high performance service organization is related to satisfying the customers' requirements. When a business traveler who has suffered delayed and cancelled flights since early in the morning arrives at the front desk of a hotel (Exhibit 6.2), the guest wants to be listened to, cared for, and checked into a clean and comfortable room where he can relax and refresh following the travails of business travel.

Exhibit 6.2 Business traveler at the front desk of a hotel. *(Source: Getty Images, Inc.— Photodisc. Used with permission.)*

To provide customer satisfaction, we must identify customer needs. This requires an understanding of the customer's business and/or the customer's individuality so that we can suggest ideas, products, and services. The goal is to create a strategic alliance that results from a mutually beneficial partnership between our business and the business of our customer. The more successful the customer and the customer's business becomes, the more successful our business will be. We must gain insight into what customers think so we can tailor products and services to their needs. Not all aspects of service are equally important to all customers and customers will develop ideas for improving processes in which they are involved in the organization. When organizations adapt these processes, based on customer input, they add value in the eyes of the customer.

Organizations also must know what their customers feel. If we want to meet expectations, the level of service provided should be the level that the customers feel is important, no more and no less. If we want to exceed expectations, the level of service should be higher than what is expected. Customers' feelings are influenced by their interactions with the organization and its competition. When customers spend time interacting with our organization, we want their experience to be positive.

Finally, organizations must know whether or not their customers will return. While some customers return because they find it easier to do business with the organization or know the organization's products or services are the least expensive, many returning customers are simply loyal customers. They are loyal because they perceive greater quality, and therefore value, from the organization. For example, an office supervisor (Exhibit 6.3) who enjoys the coffee provided by an office coffee service company (the product), the pleasant interaction with the company's representative, and the way problems are solved by that representative (the service) will be loyal because of the experience (the combination of the two).

Exhibit 6.3   The experience is a combination of the coffee (the product) and the service. *(HDS Services. Used with permission.)*

We cannot assume that we know customer needs and expectations without regularly asking, so we must stay in touch with customers. One of the common goals in high performance service organizations is to have all associates regularly probe customers to identify changing needs and expectations. It is important that customers are not simply asked: How was everything? A better question for customers is: What is the one thing that we can do to provide you with even more superior service? Other times, you might simply ask customers: Is our service hassle-free? If not, what can we do to make it hassle free for you? Digging deeper to determine perceptions of quality and value by the customers will lead to insights into what will satisfy them.

It is important to measure customer satisfaction levels regularly. While there are a number of tools presented later to do so, the primary measure is **customer retention.** If we can prevent customers from leaving the organization, we have the opportunity to build loyal customers.

At Motorola, the teams of associates that address the continuous improvement of quality are called the **"Top Box" teams.** The term "Top Box" refers to the top rating on a scale of 1 to 5, where 1 = very dissatisfied and 5 = very satisfied. The top box is 5 in this example and the goal is to convert customers from the lower scores to the higher scores for customer satisfaction. Motorola has identified indicators of customer loyalty as the following:

- The overall satisfaction in working with the company
- The choice to do business again with the company
- The recommendation to others to do business with the company

At Motorola, in the spirit of continuous quality improvement, the Top Box teams target the areas where customers have not rated the company as 5, since there is a huge correlation between intent to return and a score of 5.

Loyal Customers

External customers come to our organization to spend their money and their time, hoping that their needs will be met and their expectations exceeded. This meeting and exceeding occurs because of the products and services that we create and deliver. Sometimes a satisfied customer is not necessarily a loyal customer. Customers are more likely to be loyal when the organization continuously improves the quality of the products, services, and experiences. **Customer loyalty** comes from the customers' perceptions of value. If customers do not perceive that they receive value, even though their needs have been met and their expectations exceeded, they are always on the verge of switching to another organization if a better deal comes along. A better deal may mean a lower price, friendlier service, more convenience, more choices, or more for the same price. One of the keys to customer loyalty is to understand what customers value and then determine whether the organization meets, falls short of, or exceeds those expectations. Once the expectations are understood and the organization's performance is compared to those expectations, we can determine the gaps that need to be filled to meet the requirements of the customers.

Loyalty is essential because it adds repeat sales and new customers through word-of-mouth advertising. These two outcomes lead to increased market share for the organization. A restaurant guest who has decided to return with her friends before she has left the restaurant is a loyal guest who will tell others about her positive experience and bring people to share it. High performance service organizations view customer service as a revenue generator rather than a cost center and they know loyal customers can reduce costs. As customer retention rises, less will have to be spent finding new customers to replace those who have defected.

An additional benefit from creating loyal customers is that associates tend to experience higher satisfaction in their work. The pride of being part of an organization with loyal customers leads to increased staff retention. Because these internal customers work in the organization longer, they make more positive contributions and are more productive.

One of the greatest barriers or obstacles to building external customer loyalty is high internal customer turnover. In general, organizations with the highest staff turnover have the worst customer retention. (These organizations also experience rising costs in human resources, including recruitment, selection, orientation, and training.) When staff turnover is reduced, it is more likely that internal customers understand the needs of the external customers and can at least meet, and will usually exceed, the expectations.

Customer loyalty is directly affected by the relationship of the associate with the customer, but service organizations also are likely to have a complex array of technical, operational, and financial issues that impact customer satisfaction and customer loyalty. Loyalty is strengthened in the relationship when customers are asked to provide input on how products and services can be improved. It also is enhanced when service providers visit customers' businesses to understand first-hand the needs, wants, and expectations of the customers.

Customer loyalty frequently results in repeat sales and referrals from those satisfied customers to others. Loyalty is based on the price paid for a service, but it is largely driven by the value, that is, the price in relation to the quality received. Loyal customers are easier to serve since they understand the way that your organization operates and generally make fewer demands on the time of associates. Loyalty leading to customer retention also impacts associate retention positively. And as associates increase their tenure with the organization, the result is usually higher productivity. In that regard, customer loyalty leading to associate loyalty affects the bond in the shared vision that all have for the organization.

As we said, one way to measure customer loyalty is to look at the rate of customer retention. Thus, if you are a managed services company or hotel management company that provides these services to clients under contract, the number and percentage of contract renewals would be a key indicator of customer loyalty. To build loyalty, an organization has to sell more than a commodity or product. The product or service must be differentiated in the eyes of the customer and positively perceived by that customer. In other words, the customer has to believe that there is value in the product or service. In the process of building relationships with customers, if the organization's service helps solve a problem for that customer, there is a shift from a commodity focus to one that is based on a relationship. The development of the relationship leads to the perception by the external customer that the service organization is a partner, not simply a supplier, and a partner is one with whom a relationship is entered into rather than a transaction.

Partners share strategies. They work together to collaborate and co-evolve. If there are issues, barriers, or obstacles that have been identified, the partners work together to solve them since it is in the best interest of both to reduce or eliminate hassles. To strengthen the customer relationship, it is important to work together to achieve a common agreement on common goals. When problems surface, it is important to work together to solve them. Most customers will be more loyal to service providers who have helped them solve problems than those who have not. Since some customers do not have a rational understanding of what quality is, personalized service can lead to increased feelings of value and enhanced customer loyalty. The building of customer loyalty is the responsibility of everyone in the organization. As Peter Drucker has said, "when people are held responsible, they act responsibly."

Using Customer Information

The primary use for information gathered from customers is to better define needs and expectations or improve the processes in the organization. The end result is satisfied and more loyal customers. The information needs to be sufficiently detailed so that it can be interpreted and categorized to permit those involved to act upon the data. Carefully defining what information is needed in advance of collecting it will result in usable, specific information.

It is important to ask and answer the following questions before collecting information:

• How effectively are the current customers analyzed to determine the differing requirements of each segment?

- How effectively are potential customers analyzed to determine the differing requirements of each segment?
- How effectively are the product and service features identified for each customer segment?
- How effectively are the experience expectations identified for each customer segment?
- How effectively is customer focus attitude promoted throughout the organization?
- How effectively are customer relationships managed in terms of access, follow up, training of customer-contact associates, solicitation and analysis, and resolution of complaints?
- How comprehensive and well defined are standards for customer contact in terms of responsiveness, accuracy of information, and solicitation and resolution of complaints?
- How effective are the methods for determining customer satisfaction?
- To what extent are trends tracked in customer satisfaction indicators?
- To what extent are favorable trends being achieved in customer satisfaction?
- To what extent is customer satisfaction regarded as the prime strategic objective?

Selecting the right questions to ask loyal dinner customers in a fine dining restaurant located in a metropolitan downtown office building (Exhibit 6.4) will help determine the value perceived in staying in the city after work to enjoy a relaxing dinner in the restaurant. The questions must be selected based on what information the organization wants to gather. This may sound simplistic, but if the right questions are not asked, most likely the necessary information will not be obtained.

Exhibit 6.4 Loyal dinner customers in a fine dining restaurant located in a metropolitan downtown office building. *(Source: Photo Researchers, Inc. Used with permission.)*

It is also important to keep questions and surveys short so customers will take the time to answer them. Regardless of the type of system utilized to obtain information about customer satisfaction, it is important to widely distribute the information, particularly to associates. Providing feedback to those customers who have taken the time to give you their feedback is equally important. Data should be gathered frequently, each month at a minimum, and should involve all associates since it helps all get closer to the customer.

After answering the preceding questions, determine how to measure progress using either time measurements, cost metrics, or by tallying. Data should be measured in ways that make sense and help improve quality and dehassle processes. When analyzing data, ensure that the information being gathered is tied back to the strategic objectives. Continuous progress in achieving the strategic objectives of an organization should be a large part of the data metrics. Those who assemble and analyze data also frequently must ask if the time to do so is worthwhile. If a theme park is monitoring an area of service (e.g., the length of lines at food concessions during lunch) that consistently has high levels of performance, as validated by park guests, then perhaps attention and the metrics should be focused in a different area. Finally, always keep the customer's perspective in mind. It is important to try, as much as possible, to see the world through the customer's eyes. Try to ensure the organization and the customer both have a vested interest in assisting with the collection of customer information.

Hearing the Customers' Voices

Having established the need for accurate, timely, and reliable customer feedback, we now will explore ways to obtain it. In all cases, the goal is to hear the voices of the customers. The process of determining what the customer wants, needs, and expects is one of asking, listening, and using tools. Customer feedback may be obtained either informally or formally. Be aware, however, that sometimes **informal feedback** or hearsay clouds the more accurate data from formal methods of feedback. Nevertheless, there is value in observing the guest's experience with a service. It can serve as another method of surveying the level of customer satisfaction with the service. The Walt Disney organization trains cast members to use observation as an assessment tool. That is how the Disney organization learned that ice cream sold from kiosk booths was too cold and park guests could not eat the frozen products when purchased. This Disney example also shows how teamwork is necessary to define the customer's requirements and then deliver them.

Informal Feedback Methods

Informal methods are numerous and include feedback from customer-contact associates, comment cards, focus groups, sampling of products by customers, secret shoppers, management contact with customers, and shopping the competition. Informal methods are usually qualitative, ongoing, and involve more direct customer contact than formal methods. Those who are in direct contact with customers on a daily basis are a rich source of information; during their exchanges, customer needs and expectations surface. The goal is to capture, retain, sort, and act on this information. One way to do this is to have associates complete a brief form at the end of the shift that details product comments, service comments, and suggestions/ideas for improvement that were heard.

Comment cards are used in many service businesses ranging from hotels to car dealerships to restaurants. Many customers have little interest in completing comment cards because they simply do not know if or how the information is used. When comment cards and a reply on how the problem was eliminated are posted, however, it is a rich testimony that action was taken.

Comment cards, if returned by mail, should be printed on postage-paid and pre-addressed cards. Both general questions (location of the business if part of a chain and how many times the individual has been a customer) and specific questions (rating telephone skills and friendliness of the service staff) are usually included with additional space for written comments.

Often those who complete comment cards are either very satisfied or extremely upset. A rating scale helps eliminate some of the emotion and is useful in identifying the true causes of satisfaction or dissatisfaction. A sample comment card is presented in Exhibit 6.5. Note the feedback asked for requires the customer to grade the various quality components of the overall experience.

Comment cards must be readily available if their use is to be encouraged. The organization's comment card in Exhibit 6.5 is deposited directly into a box located in

How's The Food?

HDS
S E R V I C E S

Please let us know how
we are satisfying you.

You're important to us!

	ALWAYS	MOST OF THE TIME	SELDOM	HARDLY EVER
The meal looks appetizing.	☐	☐	☐	☐
There is sufficient variety on the menu.	☐	☐	☐	☐
I received what I ordered.	☐	☐	☐	☐
The food tastes good.	☐	☐	☐	☐
The hot food is hot.	☐	☐	☐	☐
The cold food is cold.	☐	☐	☐	☐
The food texture is appropriate (tender, not overcooked).	☐	☐	☐	☐
The staff is courteous.	☐	☐	☐	☐
The meals are on time.	☐	☐	☐	☐
The dishes/glassware are clean and attractive.	☐	☐	☐	☐

Your Name *(Optional)*:_____ Room Number: _____

Diet:_____ Date: _____

Please tell us what would make our food and service even better:

_____

_____

_____

Thank you!

TOGETHER
T4Q
FOR QUALITY

Exhibit 6.5 Sample comment card. *(Source: HDS Service. Used with permission.)*

the business and clearly identified with a "How's the Food?" sign. If the comment card is signed, the unit manager contacts the customer, either verbally or in writing, to follow up on any hassles identified. If comment cards are anonymous, the resulting responses and attempts to resolve the issue could be listed in the company's newsletter. The comment card displayed in Exhibit 6.5 lends itself to graphically tracking results over time. Once collected, comments should be categorized and summarized. The summaries as well as the actual comment cards are given to the Action Group Teams or Work Group Teams so they can begin the process of dehassling.

Focus groups are another informal research technique. These groups provide more than simple "yes" or "no" answers. Focus groups with internal customers may help discover that associates are starved for information about customer feedback. Focus groups also are suited to external customers and are usually made up of frequent as well as infrequent customers. Sometimes participants are asked to complete a brief questionnaire prior to the group discussion. This technique helps center the discussion. When non-customers or ex-customers are invited to join a focus group, additional ideas are generated.

Focus groups with ex-customers can provide valuable insights into problems or hassles that drove them away. If the problems or hassles are still occurring, they are likely to be driving others away as well. Focus group responses are subjective; nevertheless, they provide opportunities to learn about process improvements, levels of quality, valued products and services, missing products and services, and impressions and perceptions of the organization.

Sampling of products by customers sometimes works well in obtaining feedback in a food service organization. This practice can lead to decisions about which items to add to the menu. In a supermarket, product tastings can stimulate sales of those items, particularly when recipes and discount coupons are distributed at the time of the product sampling. In a restaurant, product samples can result in feedback about taste, appeal, preference, possible selling price, and value.

Secret shoppers appeal to some organizations as they attempt to obtain insights into their products and services from the customer's perspective. Individuals are retained by the company to anonymously evaluate the service experience. They may visit the company at different times of the day or week and they usually make purchases with cash to avoid detection. The belief is that the secret/mystery shopper is treated as the average customer would be, so they see the organization through the customer's eyes.

These shoppers complete a critique about the products, services, facilities, and other indicators of the overall service experience. Often, the shopper is paid a wage in addition to being reimbursed for the products and services that the shopper purchased. Data gathered from secret shoppers must be quantitatively presented and compared over time periods and by restaurant outlet or region for chains.

Management contact with customers should take place regularly because the personal interaction can harvest a great deal of useful information. Comments must be recorded so they can be categorized, analyzed, and used for the dehassling process, if necessary.

Shopping the competition is also part of customer service evaluation. One advantage of this technique is that it allows an organization to see how competitors take essentially the same commodities (i.e., products) and add value with their own unique service. We are not suggesting that the goal is to become just like the competition—that strategy rarely works. The goal is to see what distinctive sources of service value the competition is adding and then determine what we can do differently to retain customers (and potentially lure some of the competition's customers to our organization).

Formal Feedback Methods

Methods for obtaining **formal feedback** from customers might include traffic studies, questionnaires sent to randomly selected customers, surveys, personal interviews, and technology-based data mining. **Traffic studies** require visits to the competition two or three times during the same part of the day. An independent researcher uses a set of questions to ask customers the names and locations of their organizations, job titles, whether they are here because of business or pleasure (are they residents or nonresidents), and their zip codes. Additional information may include the customer's gender and an estimate of the customer's age. These data can assist in pinpointing where to direct marketing efforts for the organization.

Questionnaires and surveys can provide useful information for the organization. The external customer survey in Exhibit 6.6 is delivered with each catered event/special function and the person in charge of the function is asked to complete the survey immediately following the event. The survey is collected and results are tallied and graphed. These results are posted for all internal customers to review and the results are sent to action group teams and work group teams for identification and prioritization of the process problems and resolutions.

I.   How would you rate the food quality?

Very Good	Good	Fair	Poor

II.   Were cold food temperatures acceptable?

YES	NO

III.   Were hot food temperatures acceptable?

YES	NO

IV.   Please rate the service:

Very Good	Good	Fair	Poor

V.   What pleased you about this event?

_____

_____

_____

VI.   What would you have liked to see handled differently at this event?

_____

_____

_____

VII.   If there was a problem or concern please note so that we may
        correct it.

_____

_____

_____

As part of our continuous quality improvement process, we would appreciate you taking a few minutes to complete the following questionnaire. Your opinion and comments are important to us.

Thank you,
Manager, Food Service

TOGETHER
T4Q
FOR QUALITY

Exhibit 6.6   Sample external customer survey for a catered event. *(Source: HDS Services. Used with permission.)*

Surveys do not always have to be written. They may be conducted face-to-face, over the telephone, or using technology. A face-to-face external customer survey may be facilitated by the questions presented in Exhibit 6.7. Begin with the general questions and then move to the specific questions.

General Questions
• What would you expect from a high performance service organization regarding products and services and experiences?
• What do we do well? What can we do better?
• What is changing about your needs? What is changing about your expectations?

Specific Questions
• What do you experience when you ask for help in our organization?
• How do you find our courtesy and friendliness?
• What is the quality level of (specify a product or service)?

Exhibit 6.7   Starting a conversation with a customer. *(Source: Verne Harnish, Gazelles, Inc.)*

State-of-the-art point of sale equipment also can collect customer satisfaction information at the time of service. Some organizations are utilizing computer kiosks to make it easier and faster to obtain information. With touch screens, the organization's products, services, and facilities can be evaluated quickly. The system provides instant feedback at both the unit level and the corporate level. A major advantage to technology-driven feedback systems is the ability to rapidly change what is asked and what information is obtained.

Regardless of the type of system utilized to obtain information about customer satisfaction, it is important to widely distribute the information, particularly to associates. Additionally, feedback to those customers who have taken the time to give you their feedback is equally important. It is equally important to gather the data frequently, a minimum of once each month. The data gathering should involve all associates, since it helps all get closer to the customer. You need to gather data in sufficient detail so you can translate what the customers are saying into actions to improve quality. When gathering data, it should be done with a specific purpose in mind so you can gather specific information in advance, determine how to best measure the data in terms of time, cost, count, or other measure. It is also essential to always keep the customer's perspective in mind.

A simpler way is, simply, to ask the customer about a product or service that the customer has experienced from the company. The associate should carefully listen for indicators that the customer is either satisfied or not satisfied with the product, service, or experience. These conversations take place regularly (Exhibit 6.8) in restaurants between external customers and internal customers that care about what their customers experience. Remember, it is the quality that is *perceived by the customer* that is most important in customer satisfaction.

Exhibit 6.8 Conversation between restaurant external customers and internal customers. *(Source: Getty Images Inc.—Stone Allstock. Used with permission.)*

Get More Customers to Complain

Traditional managers were satisfied when they heard no complaints. The assumption was that everything was going right. Now we know that often it is not the case. Customers do not complain either because they do not know who to complain to, they believe what they say will not matter anyway, or they have already decided to never set foot in that business again.

We have to make it easier for customers to complain if we want valuable feedback for improvement. Some of the tools mentioned earlier help make the complaint process easier. The more opportunities given to customers to make suggestions, the more suggestions will be submitted. In the spirit of continuous quality improvement, an incident report, presented in Exhibit 6.9, can be used to record incidents causing hassles. Once the record is distributed, it can be analyzed and the problem can be resolved.

Any negative incident involving your area is to be documented and investigated. Copies of the completed form need to be sent to the area supervisor.

DATE: _____ TIME: _____

LOCATION: _____

INDIVIDUAL INVOLVED: _____

NAME OF PERSON WHO REPORTED INCIDENT: _____

SUPERVISOR/MANAGER OF AFFECTED AREA: _____

DESCRIPTION OF INCIDENT: _____

_____

_____

HOW WAS INCIDENT DISCOVERED? _____

_____

_____

EFFECT OF INCIDENT ON INDIVIDUAL: _____

_____

_____

ACTION TAKEN BY MANAGER OF AFFECTED AREA: _____

_____

_____

COPIES TO: _____

_____

Exhibit 6.9 Incident report.

Customers find it easier to complain when they can contact the organization via a toll free 1-800 number or send a pre-addressed, postage-paid comment card. Electronic kiosks draw curious customers and make it easier for those who are comfortable with computers to use them to complain. Representatives who phone customers and ask about quality levels in products, services, and experiences, as well as satisfaction levels, also make it easier for the customer to complain.

Once complaints surface, focus the resources of the organization on responding in a timely way. Complaints logged on an incident form or in a logbook (Exhibit 6.10) should be accessible soon after they are recorded. Technology makes it easy to track and sort these data. Vow to resolve each complaint quickly and to the satisfaction of the customer. If that can be done immediately by an empowered employee, do it. If it takes someone else in the organization, find that

RECEIPT, REVIEW AND RESOLUTION OF COMPLAINTS					
Date	Name/Address	Nature of Complaint	Possible Causes	Resolved Y-N	Reviewed By

Exhibit 6.10 Customer complaint log.

person, explain the hassle, and ask the person to solve it now. Once the particular complaint has been resolved, the resources of the organization must be focused on changing the process that led to the complaint.

As part of the human resources model (see Chapter 4), take every chance possible to discuss, develop, and reinforce the value of customer complaints to associates. They are treasures waiting to be mined; they hold the key to short-term improvement and long-term staying power for a high performance service organization. In memos and meetings, development sessions and newsletters, private conversations and notes, and any other communication media, trumpet the value of complaints and complainers.

Raise the visibility of complaints by posting them for all to see with an indication of how the hassles were eliminated. Publish information about complaints and their resolution in the company newsletter and talk about them in meetings after the internal customers in the meeting have had the opportunity to hear from the complainer in person. Regularly invite a panel of customers to a meeting to discuss their product and service experiences with the group. (It is best if all of the experiences are not positive, since that transforms a faceless complaint into a real person.)

Shift the paradigm so that complaints are seen as a way to identify high-priority problems or hassles and an opportunity to make the organization better. This strategy depersonalizes complaints and places them in a strategic light.

Complainers should be thanked with handwritten notes, phone calls, certificates, or small gifts. Consider designating a complainer as a "consultant of the week" to emphasize the importance of the information provided. Remember, complainers are honored customers who should be celebrated rather than scorned as troublemakers.

Change the system of quality indicators, performance measurements, and compensation to incorporate customer complaints. Perhaps one or more of the quality indicators discussed earlier should have the number of customer complaints received and how rapidly they were resolved as a component. Managers should regularly report the number of customer complaints that they solicit and what was done to fix the process that caused the complaint. Managers should not be compensated for simply reducing the number of complaints, but they should be rewarded based on the number of complaints they identify and the speed at which the complaint is taken care of, as well as acting to permanently fix the process.

Service Excellence

The **service excellence** philosophy of Dan Mathews Jr., senior vice president and chief operating officer of the National Automatic Merchandising Association (NAMA), is that "service excellence is not something you simply must do to stay in business. This leader, from NAMA—the official trade association of the vending and office coffee industries—also believes that service excellence is something that you must *want* to do and enjoy to truly be successful." This leader also stresses that it is essential to strive to improve a little bit each day. This daily improvement will add up to a huge differential advantage in 30, 60, and 90 days. A core component of this daily improvement is his **Process Improvement for Service Excellence** presented in Exhibit 6.11.

The Service Excellence Process begins and ends with the assessment step. More will be said about assessment in a later chapter of this book; it is sufficient now to understand that both internal and external customers must be assessed regularly (weekly, monthly, or quarterly) at the start of and the end of activities to improve service excellence. The purpose of the assessment is to identify the top concerns facing each category of customers. Some organizations will select the top three hassles and use a process to identify the root causes of these hassles. Think of these hassles as gaps between what is required by customers (the organization's standards) and what is actually taking place. The gap is the difference between what the customers require and what we are creating and delivering in our organization. The gap step requires a "yes" or "no" decision. If there is no gap, the result is associate satisfaction, customer retention, and a positive organization culture. If there is a gap, it is necessary to provide a service excellence overview to all managers and associates.

The **service excellence overview** covers the basics of service excellence. During the overview, it is important to ask and answer the following question: What barriers are standing in your way to providing world class service? Everyone in the organization must have an opportunity to participate in the answer to this question. In addition to the service excellence overview, it is essential to develop the **leadership skills** of those in the organization (see Chapter 12).

The next step in the process is to raise the **awareness** of the organization's **strategic plan** among associates and managers. By doing so, each can determine what he or she is able to contribute to making the plan become a reality. We also need to train those who are in the organization in order to develop the needed skills and behaviors in associates as well as managers. Training best takes place after the **team champions** are identified. These individuals are responsible for ensuring that all are trained properly. Next, identify the **metrics** for tracking the key

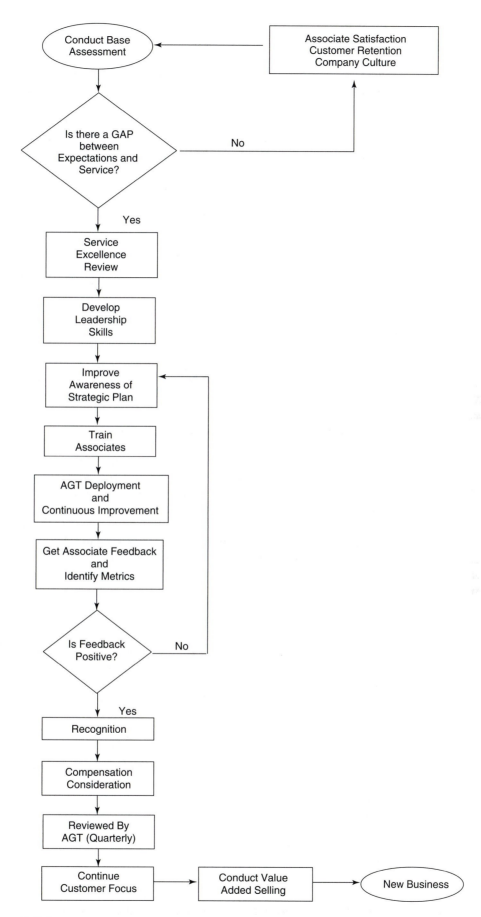

Exhibit 6.11 Process improvement for service excellence. *(Source: Dan Mathews, Jr. Used with permission.)*

indicators of effectiveness for each department in the organization. Think of these metrics as instruments on the dashboard of a vehicle. Like these dashboard instruments, we only look at a few (e.g., the speedometer and the fuel gauge indicator) regularly. These are the critical key metrics to track. The others (e.g., the oil indicator and battery indicator) are less important. After tracking the metrics, they must be analyzed; again, the analysis of fewer is better. A single page recap of key indicators in this period compared to the last period is preferred. There is more on metrics in a later chapter covering the tools of the trade.

The next step is **team deployment** continuous improvement. Team leader responsibilities are assigned to promote continuous quality improvement in this step. Then, **associate feedback** is utilized to provide **recognition** for the efforts. Associate feedback includes regular performance appraisals and completion of training programs. Recognition is based on the performance of the teams and the individuals and consists of rewards for service excellence performance. This recognition is also tied to **compensation,** as a "pay for performance" compensation program. The next step in the process is a review by the AGT (consisting of one representative for each position classification in the organization). The purpose of the AGT is to review service excellence progress in quarterly meetings. **Customer focus,** on the other hand, must be continuously evaluated. This feedback may be obtained by interviewing a number, say three to five percent, of customers each quarter to ensure that the organization's delivery of products and services was more than promised. **Value added selling** ties into the inclusion of value added results in new sales proposals and leads to a key result, **new business.** New business is the lifeblood of an organization that intends to grow.

The Process for Improvement for Service Excellence presents the components of a service excellence strategy in an organization. The steps in the process may need to be modified to apply to a specific organization; however, the primary advantage to thinking of service excellence as a process is the ability to view the whole as well as the parts of the process. In this way, it is possible to see where improvements may be made and measure the effects of these improvements. The process provides a way to present the big picture view to others while focusing on areas that need improvement. In short, the Service Excellence Process leads to the ultimate goal of any organization—customer satisfaction.

Summary

Quality is always defined and understood from the standpoint of the external customers. It is their expectations of quality that dictate the products, services, and experiences provided by a high performance service organization. Customer satisfaction follows from customer service that meets or exceeds expectations. Loyal customers are most valuable to an organization because of their word-of-mouth advertising as well as their long-term economic value. It is essential to continuously gather information from customers so quality can be improved based on their feedback and input. Customer complaints are valuable sources of feedback and complainers should be celebrated as they help us see products, services, and experiences from the customers' perspectives.

Key Terms

Associate Feedback—Includes regular performance appraisals and completion of training programs.

Awareness—Each can determine what he or she is able to contribute to making the plan become a reality.

Comment Cards—When comment cards and a reply on how the problem was eliminated are posted, it is a rich testimony that action was taken. Often those who complete comment cards are either very satisfied or extremely upset.

Commodities—Products or services now fall into the same class; perceived to have similar or equal quality by customers.

Compensation—Pay for performance.

Customer Focus—Must be continuously evaluated. This feedback may be obtained by interviewing a number (say three to five percent) of customers each quarter.

Customer Loyalty—Customers perceive greater quality, and therefore value, from the organization and are therefore loyal. Loyal customers are valuable to an organization because of their word-of-mouth advertising, as well as their long-term economic value.

Customer Retention—Preventing customers from leaving the organization; providing the opportunity to build loyal customers.

Customer Satisfaction—Follows from customer service that meets or exceeds expectations.

Customer Service—Includes both intangible aspects and tangible aspects. Tangible aspects of quality relate to technical elements; intangible parts of customer service quality are more difficult to create, deliver, and measure.

Focus Groups—Focus groups with internal customers may help discover that associates are starved for information about customer feedback. Focus groups also are suited to external customers and are usually made up of frequent, as well as infrequent, customers.

Formal Feedback—Formal methods for obtaining customer feedback include traffic studies, questionnaires sent to randomly selected customers, surveys, personal interviews, and technology-based data mining.

Informal Feedback—The goal is to capture, retain, sort, and act on this information. For example, to have associates complete a brief form at the end of the shift that details product comments, service comments, and suggestions/ideas for improvement.

Intangible Aspects—More difficult to create, deliver, and measure. Examples are a smile by the person working behind the counter, a friendly greeting and genuine thank you by the person changing a customer's oil; makes the service experience memorable.

Leadership Skills—In addition to the service excellence overview, it is essential to develop these in the organization.

Management Contact—Should take place regularly because the personal interaction can harvest a great deal of useful information.

Metrics—These measurements are for tracking the key indicators of effectiveness for each department in the organization. Think of these metrics as instruments on the dashboard of a vehicle. Like these dashboard instruments, we only look at a few (e.g., the speedometer and the fuel gauge indicator) regularly.

New Business—The lifeblood of an organization that intends to grow.

Process Improvement for Service Excellence—To identify the top concerns facing each category of customers.

Quality Perceived—Products and services of one organization compared to similar products and services available from other organizations; and as the value added when a product or service is created and delivered.

Questionnaires and Surveys—Results are posted for all internal customers to review and the results are sent to action group teams and work group teams for identification and prioritization of the process problems and resolutions.

Recognition—Based on the performance of the teams and the individuals and consists of rewards for service excellence performance.

Sampling of Products—Sometimes works well in obtaining feedback in a food-service organization. This practice can lead to decisions about which items to add to the menu.

Secret Shoppers—Attempt to obtain insights into their products and services from the customers perspectives. Individuals are retained by the company to anonymously evaluate the service experiences.

Service Excellence—Something that you must want to do and enjoy to truly be successful. It is essential to strive to improve a little bit each day.

Service Excellence Overview—It's important to ask and answer the following question: What barriers are standing in your way to providing world class service? Everyone in the organization must have an opportunity to participate in the answer to this question.

Shopping the Competition—Allows an organization to see how competitors take essentially the same commodities (i.e., products) and add value with their own unique services.

Strategic Plan—Part of the process to raise the awareness among associates and managers, so each can determine what he or she is able to contribute to making the plan become a reality.

Tangible Aspects—Technical elements, such as pressing a shirt at a laundry or the act of changing the oil and filling all the fluids in an automobile.

Team Champions—Individuals that are responsible for ensuring that all are trained properly.

Team Deployment—Initiating continuous quality improvement.

Top Box Teams—A team that has a goal of converting low customer satisfaction scores to high customer satisfaction scores.

Traffic Studies—Require visits to the competition two or three times during the same part of the day.

Value Added Selling—Value added results in new sales proposals leading to a key result, new business.

Review Questions

1. What is the relationship between quality, service, and satisfaction?
2. Thinking back to the last time you were a customer searching for service, what did a service associate do (or not do) to make your experience memorable (positively or negatively)?
3. Do you consider yourself a loyal customer to a particular product or company? Why?
4. Quality in fact is different than quality in perception. Can you share a recent example from a service experience that you personally encountered that illustrates this?
5. What kinds of customer information would be useful as feedback to improve quality? How would you go about gathering and analyzing this information?
6. Why is it important to solicit customer complaints? What are two new ways that you will use to solicit customer complaints? What will you do with the information?

Activities in Your Organization

Listed below are some activities designed to reinforce the key chapter concepts in your organization. If you are a student and not currently working in the industry, interview an industry leader about one of these topics.

1. Use the "Customer Information" section of this chapter to analyze your organization's information needs regarding customers. Select a category of cus-

tomers (see "Kinds of Customers" in Chapter 3) and utilize the questions in the "Customer Information" section of this chapter to carefully define what information is needed from that category of customer prior to collecting the information. Once you determine the information to collect, decide how you will measure progress in either time measurements, cost metrics, or by tallying. Now review your plan with another leader in your organization and ask for feedback on ways the plan may be improved before beginning to gather the customer information.

2. There are general and specific questions that can be used to start a conversation with a customer. Some examples are given in this chapter. Review these questions and modify them and/or add to them based on a particular customer that you intend to have a conversation with about customer satisfaction. Your goal is to obtain an accurate picture of how satisfied that customer is with the products and services of your organization. Now have the conversation with the customer. What did you discover during the conversation that you did not know before? What did you reinforce during the conversation that you already knew? How will you use the information to improve customer service and customer satisfaction? (This is an example of the continuous improvement process at work.)

3. Customer complaints are not negative; they are positive ways to obtain feedback about what is really happening in your organization's efforts to meet and exceed the needs of customers. Today's quality paradigm requires that you regularly solicit customer complaints and view these as opportunities to improve. Review the chapter section on customer complaints. Determine three to five essential activities that you are currently *not* doing to obtain customer complaints. Try the activities that you selected for one month. What information did you obtain about your customers that you did not previously know? Now let another month go by while tracking this same information. How does the information in the second month compare to the information in the first month? Are there trends starting to develop? How will you use this information to improve customer service and customer satisfaction?

Relevant Web Sites

Effectiveness of TQM:
http://www.dti.gov.uk/mbp/bpgt/m9ja91001/m9ja910017.html
Five Rules to Customer Care:
http://www.sbaonline.sba.gov/gopher/Business-Development/Success-Series/Vol3/Serv/serv6.txt
Improving Customer Satisfaction:
http://busreslab.com/tips/tip11.htm
Marriott International Enhances Customer Loyalty and Boosts Profitability:
http://www.crmadvocate.com/casestudy/siebel/marriott_54.pdf
National Automatic Merchandising Association:
http://www.vending.org/

Chapter

CQI Journey

Strive to improve a little bit every day; it will add up to a huge differential advantage in 30, 60, and 90 days.

Dan H. Mathews, Jr.
Senior Vice President and Chief Operating Officer
National Automatic Merchandising Association
Chicago, IL

Learning Objectives

1. Explain the steps in the decision-making process.
2. Understand the 10 steps in the CQI process.
3. Explain why leaders should focus more on processes and less on individual associate performance.
4. Explain the role of management in high performance service organizations versus that of traditional companies.

This chapter focuses on continuous quality improvement as a journey—a journey that takes years of implementation, action, measurement, and celebration. At HDS Services the journey was a five-year evolution from misdirected attempts to achieve quality to "walking the talk" in meeting or exceeding our customer's expectations. It goes beyond commitment and education; successful transformation requires major changes in the way managers manage. It is a completely new approach to making decisions.

CQI Defined

Continuous quality improvement (CQI) results from process thinking, a barrier-free working environment, recognition that this is a long-term transformation, and patience and focus. CQI is defined as continuously making small incremental improvements in the processes that generate the company's products and services. The majority of these improvements are generated from associates' ideas and process thinking. For example, an automatic merchandising company that sells vended products to a Big Ten university would have a better understanding of which particular vended products were most popular if they asked the route drivers which products sell fastest. These same route drivers should be asked why, from their perspectives, the vending machines in the business college building are more frequently in need of restocking (due to the large numbers of business students, the large classrooms in the business building used by business students and other university students) compared to other buildings (e.g., food science and chemistry) on campus. The CQI process is as follows:

1. information goes to management
2. information is reviewed by management and disseminated to determine the root cause (issue) or best approach for implementation (innovative idea)
3. a plan of action is developed and activated by a team, and
4. progress is measured periodically for improvement

These steps are illustrated in the Process Outline in Exhibit 7.1 and the CQI Graph in Exhibit 7.2.

Everyone must be involved in the effort to improve, and they must recognize that this is a journey or long-term venture. The most challenging piece of the process is remaining focused on the issues and applying **interventions** properly.

What is an intervention? It is the action taken after the root causes of the problem are identified and prioritized and solutions are developed. These solutions become the actions or interventions. The chart in Exhibit 7.2 shows a slight downturn in improvement immediately following intervention. This is caused by associates adjusting to the new process. This is a tradeoff in the short-term for improved quality in the long-term.

The Performance Excellence Program (PEP) used at the Detroit Athletic Club is a process designed to achieve CQI, and it encompasses all principal criteria necessary for achieving organizational excellence. Looking for a platform to articulate and organize their quality initiatives, the club adopted the *Criteria for Performance Excellence* identified in the Baldrige National Quality Program. Further, the DAC's strategic plan addresses the performance objectives with actionable goals. These goals are communicated to the individual worker through the Consistent Performance Process (CPP). The CPP can be repeated through all departments and service centers, building on a common vocabulary necessary to achieve understanding by the staff at large. Through a series of steps that became increasingly refined after each iteration, management is able to effectively introduce PEP to all

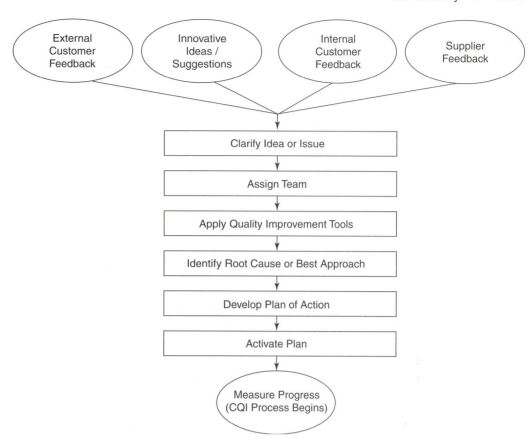

Exhibit 7.1 Process outline. *(Source: HDS Services. Used with permission.)*

departments in understandable terms. The first step is to flesh-out the full scope of a department's services through the use of cross-functional teams and the role clarification process. Armed with a better understanding of the value of their departments, leadership is equipped to define performance excellence for their service group. It begins with a statement of purpose, articulating why each department exists from the club member's perspective. It also includes **service**

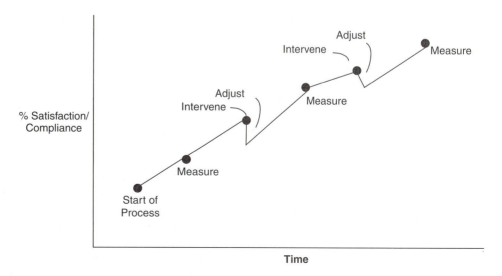

Exhibit 7.2 CQI graph. *(Source: HDS Services. Used with permission.)*

guarantees for each department: what we have to do 100 percent of the time for club members to be highly satisfied. The third component is the Consistent Performance Process (CPP). This allows the department to fully develop its standards, procedures, policies, and practices required for the department's training manual(s). The PEP concludes with training for each internal customer, certification of each internal customer, and measurement and/or feedback (Exhibit 7.3).

<u>**Cross-Functional (Interdepartmental) Teams**</u>
• identify and prioritize areas of focus
• identify current successes
• identify areas of improvement/challenge
• determine solutions and/or action plans

<u>**Role Clarification Process**</u>
• identify current problems/concerns
• identify expectations
• develop task list
• identify action items

<u>**Table of Contents—Training Manual**</u>
• standards and procedures
• policies, practices, and processes
• job descriptions—focused on delivering the guarantees

Exhibit 7.3 Consistent Performance Process (CPP) in use at the Detroit Athletic Club. *(Source: Detroit Athletic Club. Used with permission.)*

Steps in the Process for Quality Improvement

Continuous quality improvement in a high performance service organization is a 10-step process. Each step builds on the previous one and adds strength to the overall CQI process.

Step 1—Assign Responsibility
The leaders of the high performance service organization are responsible for overseeing the CQI effort. These leaders begin the process for quality improvement by assigning responsibility (Exhibit 7.4). They establish responsibilities for quality improvement and set priorities, based on the results of assessments, to improve the quality of products, services, and experiences.

Step 2—Delineate Scope of Service
The goal of this step is to identify key functions of each department. **Key functions** are described as those that have the greatest impact on the quality of products, services, and experiences ultimately created for and delivered to the customers. These functions are embedded on the Detroit Athletic Club's statement of purpose and service guarantees for each department in the club. The focus of quality improvement efforts then becomes understanding and improving these key functions.

Step 3—Identify Important Aspects of Products and Services
In this step, the priorities and subjects for ongoing monitoring are chosen. The aspects to be monitored may include key functions, procedures, core processes, products, or other activities that affect customer satisfaction. These aspects may occur frequently or affect large numbers of customers,

Exhibit 7.4 Leaders of a high performance service organization begin the process for quality improvement by assigning responsibility. *(Source: HDS Services. Used with permission.)*

put customers at risk or reduce their satisfaction if not delivered, and/or cause hassles for internal or external customers.

Step 4—Identify Indicators

Indicators are used to measure the quality of products and services. They may relate to the process, the products, the services, or the experiences. These measurements help monitor and provide information about the quality of products, services, and experiences compared to an established threshold or standard. The Detroit Athletic Club's Personal Progress Interview helps identify indicators by asking the following questions:

- What did you do last month and how did it go?
- How are you doing on your service guarantees?
- Is there anything that we can do to help you achieve your goals?
- Is there anything getting in the way of your personal success?
- What are your goals and ideas for the coming month?

Step 5—Establish Thresholds for Evaluation

A **threshold** or standard for evaluation helps associates answer the question: Based on these data, must we launch an intensive evaluation of this aspect of the product, service, or experience? Each threshold is specifically related to an indicator and may be thought of as a "yard stick" of what is an acceptable level of performance.

Step 6—Collect and Organize Data

Data from the monitoring efforts need to be collected and analyzed. Data may be collected from a variety of sources including customer records, department logs, incident reports, and direct measurements, among other ways. At the Detroit Athletic Club, the Role Clarification Process is used to collect data. The process is used at cross-functional meetings and begins with an overview of the Performance Excellence Process (PEP) and the Consistent Performance Process (CPP). The process continues by identifying the concerns/problems currently existing in each department and conducting a discussion about the expectations of each department. Where the current state does not meet the ideal, action items are developed and prioritized. The action items are implemented to close the gap between the existing and the ideal.

To make the data collection process most efficient, answer the following questions:

- Who will collect the data?
- Will collection be concurrent (i.e., while the operation is taking place) or retrospective (i.e., after the operation has taken place)?
- Will sampling be appropriate?
- Is data collection designed with computer support in mind?
- How often will data be organized, analyzed, and compared with thresholds?
- Who will organize the data?
- How will data be presented?
- Who will apply the thresholds for evaluation?

Step 7—Initiate the Evaluation
The department must apply the thresholds for evaluation at regular intervals. An Action Group Team may be assembled to evaluate the processes involved and determine whether there is an opportunity for improvement. Tools (e.g., cause and effect diagrams, flow charts, standards, policies) are used to evaluate the processes with the focus on improving the process (i.e., systems, equipment, and associates).

Step 8—Take Actions to Improve Products and/or Services
These actions are directed toward identifying the root causes of problems and toward overall improvement in products and services. Consider these possible actions:

- for systems hassles—changes in communication channels, adjustments in staffing, changes in equipment, or changes in products
- for knowledge hassles—associate training, making data or reports accessible, and circulating and reviewing information
- for behavior hassles—coaching, counseling, changes in assignments, and disciplinary action

Associates are critical resources in the development of improvement ideas. Implementation is more likely to succeed when we are putting our associates, rather than their management's, ideas into play. Training at the Detroit Athletic Club includes property knowledge, department knowledge, product knowledge, service knowledge, process knowledge, follow up/feedback, and certification.

Step 9—Assess the Effectiveness of Actions and Maintain the Gain
It is essential to identify areas for improvement and then take action to improve. It is equally important to determine if the actions taken produced the desired effect and if this effect can be maintained. This step determines whether indicators should be revised or priorities should be changed.

Step 10—Communicate Results to Relevant Individuals and Groups
Reports should include the results of the monitoring process—the conclusions, recommendations, actions, and follow up.

Quality in a high performance service organization can be improved most effectively by focusing on all key activities and coordinating the efforts throughout the organization. Effective performance measurements are utilized to collect reliable data. These data may be posted on a Quality Board for all to view (Exhibit 7.5) and decide where he or she may contribute to the continuous improvement of quality. Processes that have important direct or indirect effects on products, services, and/or experiences, including those that impact cross-functional areas in the organization, must be addressed. Once the processes are identified, the focus changes to the improvement of these processes.

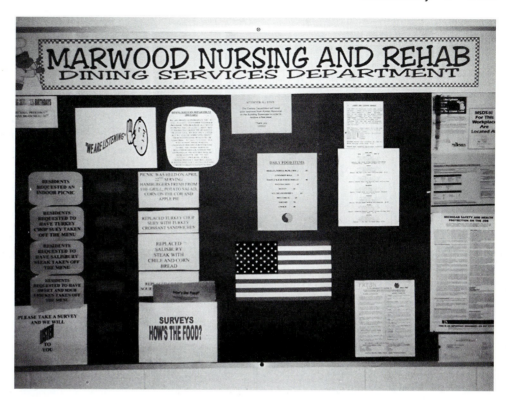

Exhibit 7.5 Quality board. *(Source: HDS Services. Used with permission.)*

Leadership is essential in the improvement of quality in high performance service organizations. Assessment and improvement activities are supplemented by other sources of feedback. Assessment and improvement are organized around the flow, as well as the creation and delivery, of products, services, and experiences, rather than compartmentalizing activities within individual departments. The focus is always on the processes first rather than on the performance of individuals. The ultimate goal is to achieve continuous improvement rather than simply minimizing or eliminating the immediate hassle. (Of course, the improvement must be maintained and ramped up over time.) Improvements must be based on a detailed understanding of the requirements of the customers. For example, both children and their parents in a school foodservice program are the customers (Exhibit 7.6) whose requirements drive the CQI process.

Exhibit 7.6 Children and their parents in a school foodservice program are the customers whose requirements drive the CQI process. *(Source: SuperStock, Inc. Used with permission.)*

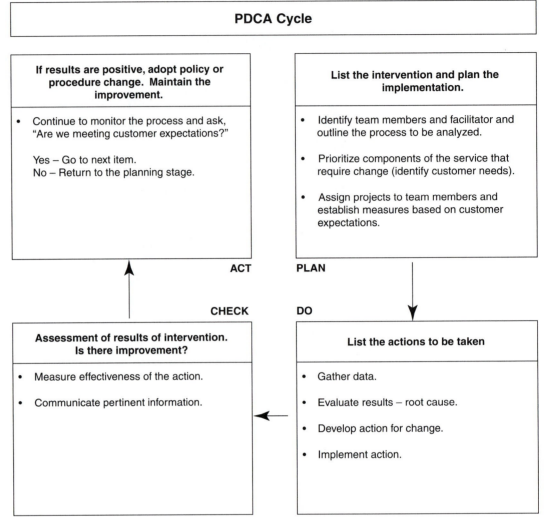

Exhibit 7.7   PDCA Cycle for the 10-step process.

CQI Process Tools

Exhibit 7.7 presents a PDCA (Plan-Do-Check-Act) Cycle for the 10-step process. It begins with assigning responsibility, step 1 in the plan box. In this PDCA Cycle, steps 1 through 3 are "Plan" activities. The next four steps are "Do" activities; steps 8 and 9 are "Check" activities, and step 10 is an "Act" activity. If the answer to the question in step 10 is "no," the next action is to return to step 3 in the plan box. If it is "yes," the next item for improvement is selected and the PDCA Cycle begins for that item.

The 10-step CQI process also may be illustrated in the form of a flow chart (Exhibit 7.8). In this flow chart the first step is indicated as an oval shape. Following steps are presented in rectangles. Questions, or decision points, are noted in diamond shapes and the arrows indicate the direction of the flow of the process.

Each cycle of the PDCA is designed to identify and eliminate the most apparent root cause of the hassle. It is a loop because it returns to the plan box to try still another intervention to further reduce the hassle. Therefore, as the PDCA continues to cycle, more and more of the root causes of the hassle are eliminated.

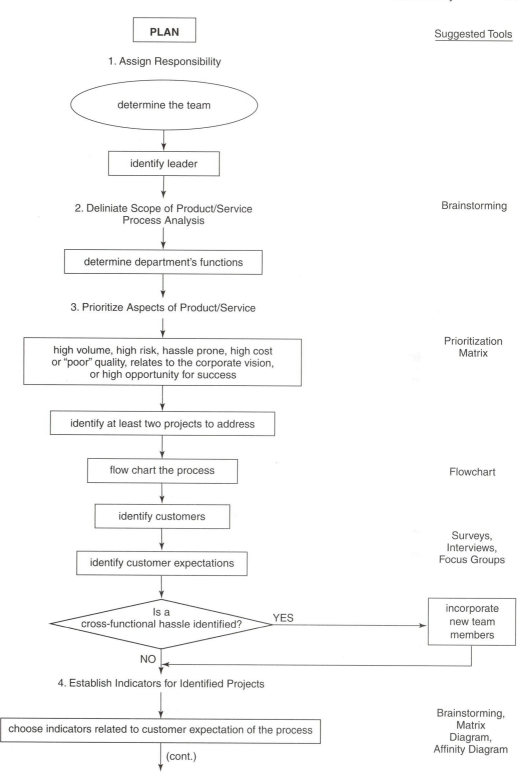

Exhibit 7.8 Flow chart of the PDCA Cycle.

Management's Role

The role of managers and supervisors in a high performance service organization is different than in traditional companies. In a high performance service organization, management is responsible for organizational planning which includes

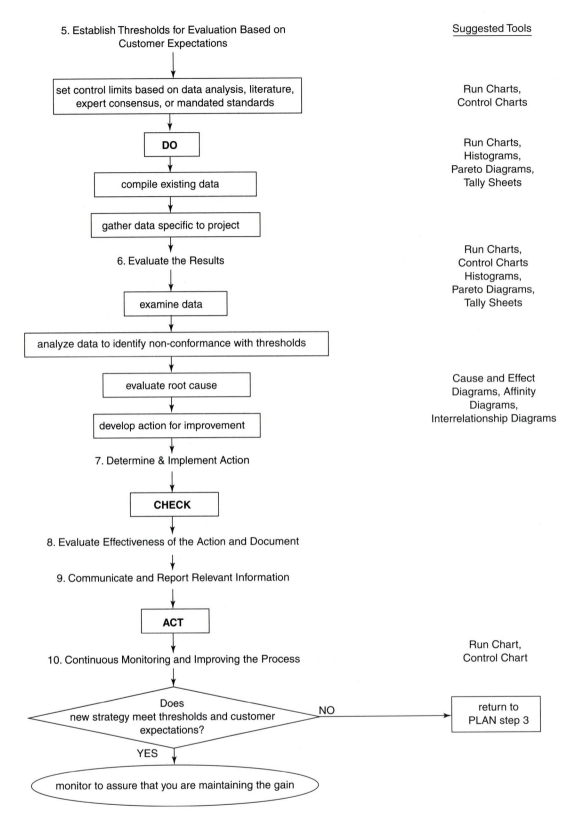

Exhibit 7.8 continued

both the short-term as well as the long-term strategic planning activities. Management must drive the process and regularly evaluate organizational practices and policies in the spirit of continuous improvement. Evaluation of the process by management and internal customers will lead to an identification of hassles and issues that can then be eliminated or improved. For example, the retention of clients is essential for a managed services organization (e.g., contract foodservice business); a loss of these clients is a hassle or problem. The management of a private club is held accountable for the service guarantees made to members and the hassles that take place when they are not delivered. The management of an automatic merchandising company must continuously evaluate the satisfaction levels of both the clients who have contracted for the company's products and services as well as the ultimate customers who purchase the vended products. While everyone in the organization has to think about and act on what they will personally do to help retain clients, to deliver on service guarantees, and to satisfy customers, it is the responsibility of management to drive the process.

Management is responsible for ensuring that what gets done is measured at intervals that permit the comparison between actual results and planned outcomes. Furthermore, management must determine what is important to measure. Without measuring the right factors using the right metrics, it will not be possible to improve. For example, continuous quality improvement at the Detroit Athletic Club for the various departments and services and for the club as a whole means increasing the number of members, both club members (i.e., external customers) and staff members (internal customers), who are "highly satisfied." The focus is to continually move members from the "satisfied" category to the "highly satisfied" category on assessments. These metrics indicate whether or not improvement is taking place. The documentation and the regimen required by the CPP are valuable because it keeps the CQI process moving forward. Client retention, customer satisfaction, and sanitation would be important metrics to track in a contract food service business.

Management also helps drive the recognition of internal and external customers who contribute to the improvements in the process. While the old axiom "what gets rewarded gets done" holds true, it is also true to say that "what is rewarding gets done." Both the external reward system and what the individual finds internally rewarding should be in harmony.

Management must set the pace for communication and ongoing education for improvements to continue to take place. The key to communication is to actively listen. By actively listening to internal customers (Exhibit 7.9) and external customers, powerful insights for problem solving will be gained. Education and training must be both initial and ongoing. This training becomes a retention strategy and helps develop future managers for the organization. Assessment is the final role of management in the CQI process; this objective evaluation of process and people must lead to improvement.

Exhibit 7.9 By actively listening to internal customers, management gains powerful insights. *(Source: HDS Services. Used with permission.)*

The improvement of quality requires an understanding of processes. Action Group Teams (AGTs) created by management are critical here because they are the team charged with the primary responsibility for the ongoing improvement of quality. These teams take the hassle, obstacle, or barrier and develop, implement, and evaluate ideas for improvement of the process. In other cases, management drives the improvements, and the responsibility for making the process changes on a daily basis never gets to the associates. While management is well-intentioned, as we have stated before, it is the associates that must take the responsibility for improving quality since they are the direct creators and deliverers of quality for external customers. The people that are doing the work know best about improvement opportunities and changes to be made.

Generally, it takes time to realize the effects of improvements, but associates are more likely to commit to CQI if they can see a direct benefit. In other words, associates must perceive that their improvement efforts are making a positive difference. Expectations must be realistic but **stretch goals** are frequently the way that improvements get started. Sometimes it is relatively easy to make simple improvements and achieve results. Once these improvement gains are realized, it is critical that the organization invest these gains in further improvements. However, it is imperative that we continue to improve upon the more complex issues if CQI is to be attained. Even if the final improvement is never made, it is important to continue to try to improve each time a process takes place.

Management's overall role in this process is to drive CQI while realizing the complex nature of doing so. They must support associates with training and coaching, and provide the necessary tools and resources to make improvement plans a reality. Perhaps where management assists most is helping others understand the process rather than choosing the hassles to minimize or eliminate.

The CQI Journey

The continuous quality improvement process is applied to each and every intervention that is put in place. There could be as many as 100 interventions being measured at any given time. As actions take place in the PDCA Cycle, other new interventions are being added to the process. At HDS Services, we are now in our twelfth year since implementation of the quality effort. While we can claim to be a company that continuously strives to improve quality after all this time, we have barely scratched the surface in making improvements through the CQI process. This is why it is considered a journey. Fifty years from now, the CQI process will still be used as a primary tool.

Decisions resulting from current interventions will change over the years as the company, the processes, the internal and external customers, and the market forces change. Therefore, the CQI process is dynamic and fluid rather than static. Many companies have failed in the implementation of the quality management philosophies because management was impatient and expected to get immediate transformation. Instilling the quality culture in any organization is a long-term task.

Summary

In the continuous quality improvement process, progress is made in small consistent increments. Managers who expect to make major improvements through intervention will be disappointed to learn that it does not work that way, even though a major breakthrough takes place once in awhile. Use of the decision-making process steps outlined in this chapter is the key to bringing about positive change. The primary ingredient for success is getting everyone involved in the process; this assures that the most appropriate action is being taken.

Key Terms

Indicators—Used to measure the quality of products and services.

Interventions—The action taken after the root causes of the problem are identified and prioritized, and solutions are developed.

Key Functions—Have the greatest impact on the quality of products, services, and experiences ultimately created for and delivered to the customers.

Service Guarantees—Promises made to customers.

Stretch Goals—Frequently the way that improvements get started.

Threshold—Specifically related to an indicator and may be thought of as a "yard stick" of what is an acceptable level of performance.

Review Questions

1. What are the steps in the decision-making process?
2. Why is CQI referred to as a journey?
3. What are the steps in the CQI process?
4. What happens in the four-step PDCA Cycle? Why is it essential to CQI?
5. What is management's role relative to CQI in the high performance service organization?

Activities in Your Organization

Listed below are some activities designed to reinforce the key chapter concepts in your organization. If you are a student and not currently working in the industry, interview an industry leader about one of these topics.

1. Using Exhibit 7.1 in this chapter, select one of the following categories: external customer feedback or innovative ideas/suggestions, internal customer feedback, or supplier feedback. Use this as the one top-priority category on which you will begin to focus in your organization. Meet with a group of associates to determine an idea or issue facing those in the category that you have selected. Who will be assigned to the team to address this issue, implement this idea, or drive the improvements?

2. The 10-step CQI process is detailed in the chapter. For the issue, idea, or improvement that you selected in the first activity, evaluate the process for quality improvement using the 10-step process. What important aspects of the products/services will you monitor? How will you measure the CQI? What standard(s) or threshold(s) will you use to determine the acceptable level of performance? Answer the questions in step 6 of the process. What action(s) might you take to improve the product/service? How will you assess the effectiveness of the action(s)? What results will you communicate and to whom?

3. Management plays pivotal roles in the CQI process. As a leader in your organization, what role will you play in short-term and long-term planning? Which organizational practices and policies require evaluation if the CQI process is to begin or to continue in your organization? What results will you measure? How will those who contribute to CQI and the improvement of

these results be recognized? What will you communicate and how will you go about doing so? What assessment will take place as a part of CQI?

Relevant Web Sites

Continuous Improvement and TQM:
http://academic.emporia.edu/smithwil/s99mg423/eja/hill.html#Continuous
Dictionary of TQM Terms:
http://www.mazur.net/tqm/tqmterms.htm
Merging Six Sigma and The Balanced Scorecard (by Bradley Schultz):
http://healthcare.sixsigma.com/library/content/c031028a.asp

Chapter

8 Tools of the Trade

Quality isn't a noun, but a verb, an action, a process. Quality requires measuring, monitoring, and retooling, over and over again.

Richard D. Farrar
Vice President, Owner and Franchise Services
Marriott International, Inc.
Washington, D.C.

Learning Objectives

1. Explain how a structured style of management improves the organization on an overall basis.
2. Define ISO 9000.
3. Understand how and when to use the 11 "tools of the trade."
4. Describe how the tools are used in completing the Strategic Quality Plan Development Guide.

Customer requirements, both external and internal, drive the efforts of an organization that is committed to managing for quality. For example, a banquet chef in a restaurant or hotel food service organization creates and delivers the memorable experiences for guests (Exhibit 8.1). Achieving management's objectives and being a successful manager cannot be accomplished entirely through common sense and good people skills, however. Our objective in this chapter is to introduce proven metrics, or tools of the trade, that are combined into systems and used along with solid management principles to improve quality. Not only does this improve the odds for success, it also adds to and assures **structure** within the management process. Structural styles of managing give the organization more direction and continuity. And while management should not be totally predictable, consistency is very important to front line associates.

Exhibit 8.1 A banquet chef in a restaurant or hotel foodservice organization creates and delivers memorable experiences for guests. *(Source: HDS Services. Used with permission.)*

As managers we must recognize the importance of using structure in leading people and managing resources and recognize that managing is a process by which achievements are gained through the use of the tools and the proper steps in the decision-making process. A large part of the structure takes place at cross-functional action group team (AGT) meetings. An example of the agenda for an AGT meeting at the Detroit Athletic Club is presented in Exhibit 8.2. While not strictly 1 of the 14 tools, meeting agendas help everyone keep focus and stay on track while working through the process for implementing interventions and measuring the effectiveness of the changes. **Consensus** is defined as a decision or position reflecting the collective thinking of the team that all members participate in developing, understand fully, believe is workable, can live with, and will actively support. The real issue in building consensus are the questions: 1) Can we live with it? and 2) Will we actively support it? The reason for the consensus must be valid and not personal; we must never implement a process to accommodate an individual.

ISO 9000

ISO 9000 is an abbreviation for International Organization for Standardization. This organization develops quality standards. These standards are objective measurements against which an organization can be measured and certified. As of this writing, the three most important quality standards are:

1. ISO 9001—the requirements and standards for an organization with processes ranging from design and development to installation and servicing.

Agenda Item	Why Critical
I. Ground Rules	[agreements on how we will behave while together]
A. Speak up (if wondering, disagree, do not understand, confused).	
B. Share your opinion.	
C. Resolve it here or determine how to resolve it. (Do not leave the meeting with a problem or a concern.)	
D. Remain open and non-defensive (Do not take this personally; do not reject ideas.).	
E. Use consensus to make decisions.	
II. Mission of the AGT	[consensus and mutual understanding]
A. Each person writes what he or she believes the mission to be.	
B. Each person reads his or her statement and it is recorded.	
C. The AGT decides on one representative statement.	
III. Roadmap—list on a flipchart	[comprehensive list of steps to achieve the mission]
A. Identify all areas of focus.	[comprehensive brainstorming]
B. Prioritize all areas of focus.	[consensus on which to begin first]
C. Work through the prioritized list.	[identify ways to reduce/eliminate the hassles]
1. Identify success criteria.	
2. Identify current successes.	
3. Identify hassles (problems/obstacles to improve).	
4. Identify possible solutions.	
5. Choose a solution (i.e., intervention).	
6. Assess solution against current service guarantees and alter as needed.	
7. Develop a plan to implement the solution.	
8. Implement the plan.	
9. Monitor the plan using metrics and revise the plan as needed.	

Exhibit 8.2   AGT meeting agenda. *(Source: Detroit Athletic Club. Used with permission.)*

2. ISO 9002—the requirements and standards for an organization that does not offer design and development services.
3. ISO 9003—the requirements and standards for an organization whose processes do not include design control, process control, purchasing, or servicing. This is the standard for those involved with the testing and inspection of final products and services compared to the specified requirements.

The ISO standards include eight principles of quality management in the evaluation: 1) continual improvement, 2) customer focus, 3) factual approach to decision making, 4) involvement of people, 5) leadership, 6) mutually beneficial supplier relationships, 7) process approach, and 8) a systems approach to management. In the spirit of CQI, the standards are updated regularly.

Measuring Standards

The primary reason that tools and systems are absolutely essential in a high performance service organization is that they help answer the question:

> Are our customers (external and internal) receiving what they need, want, and expect in the products, services, and experiences that we are creating and delivering?

The answer to this question resides in the standards that have been created based on an understanding of those customers. These standards are communicated and reinforced through orientation and ongoing training programs. In addition to awareness of the standards, associates and management need some set of measurements or metrics (we call them **tools of the trade**) linked to ongoing procedures for testing whether we are meeting, exceeding, or falling below the standards. Various tools also encourage associates and managers to intervene with a needed change and measure the effect of the change on the standard, and a number of these tools permit several cycles of interventions.

Some standards only can be measured by direct feedback from customers. Two sources of information from the customer that we have already explored are: 1) observations of reactions to the products and services that are created and delivered, and 2) conversations asking probing questions about quality of the experience. The server in Exhibit 8.3 has been trained to use both observation and conversation with external customers of this casual theme restaurant. Other tools we will explore in this chapter include the Cause and Effect Diagram, Pareto Chart, Check Sheet, Run/Control Chart, and Force Field Analysis. These tools could be used to collect more data from the customer to identify the root cause of a problem or hassle.

Exhibit 8.3 A restaurant server uses both observation and conversation to gather data about external customers. *(Source: Index Stock Imagery, Inc. Used with permission.)*

Once the data are collected from all sources using one or more of the tools, it will be analyzed. Then, the team of associates can choose an action to intervene and change part of the process, if necessary. Once the intervention is implemented, the PDCA Cycle (see Chapter 7) may be used to determine whether the acceptable quality improvement occurred. Afterward an additional intervention (or two or three) could be tried and assessed using the PDCA Cycle. This procedure would take place until the acceptable level of the standard is achieved.

The tools of the trade are very much tied to the process of Continuous Quality Improvement (CQI). CQI requires analysis (through measurement) of standards continually, and it dictates innovation and change based on decisions that improve quality. Once the change is tried, the action to improve is begun. Remember that it is also important to review the progress in this process and make additional changes if necessary.

All skilled trade professionals use tools in accomplishing tasks related to their jobs; professional hospitality managers and associates do so as well. It is unusual for us to associate managers with the use of tools, but the more successful managers use them every day in the workplace. The best managers seldom "fly by the seat of their pants" when managing the organization; they use a systematic approach to improve and grow the organization.

These tools are used in varying degrees. Some offer critical information while others are "nice to know," but are not necessarily essential to monitor with the frequency of the "need to know" indicators. **Brainstorming,** for example, is categorized by some as the most essential quality tool because it helps generate multiple ideas and it encourages the participation of all on the team. By contrast, a Force Field Analysis or a Run Chart may not be used with the same regularity in the same organization. It is essential then to try each of the tools and determine how applicable they are to the organization's unique quality improvement efforts. Do not be afraid to alter or modify the tools to fit the organization's needs, as well as the skill level of your organization's managers and associates. Perhaps a simple combination of four tools—brainstorming, nominal group technique, a cause and effect diagram, and PDCA Cycle—is all that is needed to start. More complex metrics may be added later if there is a pressing need for additional information. The determining factor will be the overall CQI process in the organization. The continuous quality improvement process is supported by five basic steps which effective managers follow in making decisions to achieve their objectives. The various management tools are used to support these five steps.

Step 1

This step involves *identifying the issues, problems, and areas requiring action.* Where does this information come from? Managers and executives must ask a lot of questions, talk to the people directly involved with the hassles and problems and use the appropriate tools to determine the burning issues within the organization. Hassles may be doing things wrong (e.g., waste in a vending company), having to do things a second time to get them right (e.g., redoing an overcooked steak entrée in a restaurant), and/or frustrations (e.g., comments among staff of a private club that begin with "it seems stupid to me when [fill in the blank] happens").

The feedback process is vital for achieving success with this process. Feedback should be flowing constantly from associates, management, and outside partners, such as key suppliers. The most effective tools to use in getting feedback are brainstorming and surveys. Brainstorming sessions provide a format which can include everyone in the organizational structure, thus no one has to be concerned about going outside the reporting structure to make the point that an issue, hassle, or barrier exists. However, in order to get adequate feedback, management must schedule these brainstorming sessions as frequently as necessary. Another factor supporting the use of brainstorming is the "free-for-all" nature of the session. Information is more comprehensive and complete when it is garnered in these open sessions.

Step 2

Once the issues, problems, or hassles have been identified, they must be *prioritized* as soon as possible. They should be prioritized by the individuals who brought them to management's attention. In most cases, prioritizing is a fairly simple procedure; however, in the early stages of this process, when the organization as a whole is being "dehassled" by its associates, the list is bound to be quite lengthy and not as easily prioritized. Resolving the biggest issues in the organization will generate the most profound results, thus the rationale for prioritization.

In order to avoid prioritization being based on "whoever speaks the loudest gets the highest priority," a tool referred to as **Nominal Group Technique (NGT)** is used to give everyone the opportunity to equally voice their opinions. In this case there are no winners and losers; everyone in the group must acknowledge that their idea or concern received its fair amount of consideration.

Step 3

This step relates to *determining the root causes* of the problems, hassles, and issues. The team assigned the task of identifying the root causes should be comprised of those individuals closest to the issue. This likely will be a cross-functional team (individuals from more than one work group or department in the organization). The normal request for information on causes of issues will result in a myriad of ideas concerning the subject. Once the information is gathered, the team will prioritize them.

Step 4

This step involves the *development of a workable solution* and constructing an effective action plan. Through idea generation among the group, interventions are discussed and plans are made for implementation. Using more than one intervention for the hassle or barrier is quite common, but the results of each intervention might be measured separately.

Step 5

Once in practice, the results of the process are thoroughly *monitored for effectiveness.* If the intervention is found to be effective and productive, it must become part of the organization's strategic business plan and adopted as an effective procedure for improving quality.

Asking the Right Questions

Rather than focusing on blaming who did not perform or who screwed up, the "better way" organizations ask and answer the right questions. With the overall goal of improving the process, the answers to the right questions lead to ways to continuously make the better way organization even better. Consider questions such as the following:

- Who are our customers? How do we create and deliver products, services, and experiences that they truly love, not just like?
- What quality opportunity are we targeting? What do we want to accomplish?
- What information is necessary to understand the present process, hassles, barriers, obstacles, problems, and the gap between what our customers need, want and expect and what we deliver?
- Why is an improvement to the process necessary? Are we off target? Have we drifted? If so, by how much? What are the expected outcomes and goals?
- Are we managing the process with facts vs. simply making tampering decisions or managing based on assumptions?

- How is the improvement to the process to be organized? What specific actions are necessary to achieve the desired improvements? Are we going to begin with just one change and then test the results?
- What resources are required to improve the process at each step of the way? Where will the resources come from?
- What metrics will be used and how will feedback be provided to those affected by the changes?
- What is the financial impact and benefit of the process improvement?
- How can we get those directly involved in the changes to analyze the situation, develop the plan for improvement and measure the outcome?

The process of using the right questions to lead improvements is ongoing. This is part of the CQI process. Since needs and wants change and expectations are progressively increased or heightened over time, yesterday's information will simply lead to achieving yesterday's results. Rather, one must try to identify today what will be tomorrow's needs and expectations. Anticipation of these needs and expectations leads to customer loyalty, both for internal and external customers.

Management "Tools of the Trade"

There are approximately 11 tools managers can use in achieving continuous improvement:

1. Brainstorming
2. Nominal Group Technique
3. Cause and Effect Analysis
4. PDCA Cycle
5. Flow Chart
6. Check Sheet
7. Pareto Chart
8. Run Chart
9. Run/Control Chart
10. Force Field Analysis
11. Strategic Quality Planning

To merely learn the tools is only part of the process. We also must know when and what tools apply to each process because each task has applicable tools. The guide in Exhibit 8.4 will assist in determining the application.

Not all of the suggested tools need to be used for the application or task at hand. Oftentimes, one or two will be sufficient in producing the appropriate outcome. Continued use of the tools will give management the experience required to make the right selection of tools.

Brainstorming

The first and most commonly used tool is brainstorming. In its simplest form, brainstorming is a technique designed to generate a large number of ideas, causes, and solutions through a process of total interaction. The outcome that management seeks from a brainstorming exercise is quantity rather than quality of ideas. The session is coordinated by a facilitator. Team members attending the session should not voice their ideas until being recognized by the facilitator after the previous idea has been documented. Typically, an associate will signify that he or she wishes to be called upon for an idea by raising a hand. *The facilitator must encourage creativity* (Exhibit 8.5) *in a brainstorming session to maximize the ideas*

Application	Tool
• Identify the burning issues.	Brainstorming
• Prioritize the issues.	Nominal Group Technique
	Flow Chart
	Pareto Chart
• Describe the issue in statement form in terms of what it is, where it occurs, and when it happens.	Pareto Chart
	Run Chart
• List all possible root causes of the issue.	Brainstorming
	Cause and Effect Diagram
• Prioritize root causes.	Nominal Group Technique
	Brainstorming
	Pareto Chart
• Develop solutions and action plan.	PDCA Cycle
	Brainstorming
	Force Field Analysis
• Implement the plan and monitor.	Pareto Chart
	Control Chart

Exhibit 8.4 Quality management tools and applications. *(Source: HDS Services. Used with permission.)*

generated. Sometimes the ideas thought to be the "furthest out of the box" end up being the best and most effective. The documentation process is very important. The objective is to document as fast as possible so that the documentation process does not slow the flow of ideas or change someone's thought process.

There are nine basic rules that apply to effective brainstorming. When these rules are followed, the results will be optimal.

1. *Everyone involved must fully understand the objective.* For example, the objective may be to brainstorm possible reasons a resort lacks interdepartmental communication. The facilitator must give a comprehensive explanation of the subject, including why the subject was chosen and what the expected outcome is. The facilitator will keep the group mov-

Exhibit 8.5 The facilitator of a brainstorming session must encourage creativity. *(Source: HDS Services. Used with permission.)*

ing forward on the subject matter throughout the process. He or she should write the objective on a flip chart or board in clear view of all the participants in order to keep everyone focused on the objective. Brainstorming could be used to generate:

a. Ideas to dehassle the department or organization (this is a general session which encourages staff to identify their perceptions and opinions of the hassles in the workplace). Perhaps the reason for a lack of interdepartmental communication in the resort mentioned earlier is poor communication between management and associates, management tuning out internal customer feedback, and a lack of feedback from external customers.

b. The root causes of issues or problems (identification of the causes is critical to the success of resolving the issues). Let us assume that the root cause at the resort is poor communication between management and associates.

c. Solutions (ways and means of correcting the root causes through intervention). Perhaps in this case the solution is to have regular meetings with members from the management staff and the associates.

2. *Everyone's participation must be encouraged.* To quote Dr. Deming, "Everyone must be involved." The atmosphere at the meeting must be open in order to obtain the maximum number of ideas. Usually, the higher the level of trust, the higher the amount of input. Most brainstorming sessions have the environment of a free-for-all, which is encouraged and productive for the most part. However, sometimes this creates a situation where most of the input is coming from just a few individuals in the group. One method of assuring input from all members is to solicit ideas from each individual in the order they are seated. This sequential pattern of idea gathering should be followed until there are more "passes" than inputs. This method of brainstorming forces more participation and increases the amount of input.

3. *All ideas must be documented* regardless of their content, and all documented ideas must be posted in the meeting room. Often, the posted ideas create other ideas because someone relates the documented idea to another thought. Documentation is necessary because the next step in the process involves prioritizing. If the ideas are written and posted, the group will be able to prioritize them. One effective method of documentation is to use flip charts and post the lists on the walls of the room in clear view of all participants.

4. During the brainstorming session *everyone must refrain from criticizing and passing judgment.* Each individual presenting an idea has the floor until the idea is documented and the facilitator indicates it is time to proceed. Often, the facilitator will ask for clarification of the idea, but he or she must never be judgmental in doing so. Other members of the group must maintain their composure regardless of the content of the ideas. In cases where groups are judgmental or critical, participants are reluctant to present their ideas.

5. The facilitator and each participant in the group must *work for quantity;* they must generate as many ideas as possible. As previously stated, the session should resemble a free-for-all in terms of how many ideas are recorded. Some individuals may think that a large number of ideas will make the prioritizing task more difficult. Prioritizing is not as complex as it would seem, however, because many ideas are immediately combined with each other. Others are easily placed on the back burner and only a few will stand out as priorities.

6. Throughout the process the facilitator must *encourage creativity.* Make certain the participants are involved with the initial objectives. The more

involved someone is, the more creative that person will be with his or her ideas and suggestions.

7. During the brainstorming process, the facilitator should allow individuals to present **piggyback input**—to build on the ideas of others. Some ideas can be augmented by another participant in the group.
8. The size of the group is critical to the success of the brainstorming effort. The *preferred number of participants is between 8 and 12 people.* The only exception to this would be a department or organization-wide de-hassling exercise.
9. The preferred length of time for the introductory phase of brainstorming sessions is about *10 minutes.* This does not mean you must stop at that point if input is still being received, however.

The typical brainstorming session contains three phases:

1. The *Generation Phase.* During this time the facilitator reviews the rules of brainstorming with all participants, and states the topic and overall objectives of the session. It is the facilitator's responsibility to make the subject clear and "visible." One participant is selected to document all ideas on flip charts at this point. For example, the issues facing the food and beverage department in a resort generated during this phase include difficulty catering to children, boring menus, poor food quality, understaffing, theft, customers not paying for desserts, poor working conditions, and equipment not working. The generation phase ends when all ideas have been exhausted.
2. The *Clarification Phase.* This phase includes a thorough review of the idea list so that all participants understand each and every item. It is important to not discuss the items at this time.
3. The *Evaluation Phase.* This last phase involves the review of all items to eliminate duplication, irrelevancies, and issues that are off limits. An irrelevant idea would be one that has absolutely nothing to do with the original subject. Duplicate items in the resort are theft and customers not paying for dessert. These could be combined. Ideas that are off limits are those that only executive level staff can address.

Ideas that are not relevant to the current topic but have value for consideration at another time should be "parked" on a pending ideas list to avoid being lost. These ideas can be evaluated at a later time when the proper, related topic is discussed.

A sample list of brainstormed ideas for the question "What are the pros and cons of managing for quality in a service organization?" is presented in Exhibit 8.6.

This completes the brainstorming session, and at this point the ideas must be prioritized. This is generally accomplished by using nominal group technique.

Nominal Group Technique

Nominal group technique is often referred to as NGT. The objective of this technique is to prioritize ideas, issues, problem statements, hassles, and interventions in order to create a set of priorities that represent the input from all members of the team or group. An example of the NGT in action in a health care organization is presented in Exhibit 8.7. There are several methods of using nominal group technique; the method is determined by the number of items to prioritize.

The first method is used for a small number of items. It is somewhat more formal than others. Assume we are attempting to prioritize issues related to poor

PROS	CONS
Constant improvement	More costly
Less subjective	Wouldn't work with high turnover
New ideas	Too much paperwork
Associates' voices heard	Expensive
Long-term commitment	Cut in profitability
Improved communications	Too many meetings
Process improvement based on facts	Time consuming
Customer satisfaction	Slow process
Empowering	Confused associates
Builds loyalty	Too many steps
Creates value	Can't find quality suppliers
Higher morale	Associates will not "buy in"
Teamwork	Associates unwilling to change
Competitive advantage	Customers just want best price

Exhibit 8.6   A brainstormed list of pros and cons of managing for quality in a service organization.

Exhibit 8.7   NGT in action in a healthcare organization. *(Source: HDS Services. Used with permission.)*

customer satisfaction in our restaurant. The brainstorming session yielded seven root causes for the problem. These issues are:

1. Poor sanitation
2. Tight seating arrangement in the dining room
3. Attitude of the maitre d'hotel
4. Weak drinks
5. Old boring menu
6. Insufficient parking
7. Server turnover

These items are listed on a flip chart, then the facilitator asks each member of the group to rate the problem statements according to severity. Ratings are listed on a scale of 1 through 7, with 7 being the most severe. Members of the group write this information on a piece of paper. The facilitator asks for ratings by taking each problem in the order they were documented. Members identify their ratings verbally and the total of the ratings for each problem is written on the flip chart adjacent to the listed problem. Once the totals are posted, the problem with the highest number becomes the number one priority. The problems are arranged in the order of priority as determined by the nominal group technique. This is the order in which the problems will be addressed in the future.

If a very small number of items need to be prioritized, the facilitator can use an informal, raised-hand method. This tends to save time and is just as effective. Be careful not to merely select the number one priority, however. In some cases, if the problems are somewhat sensitive, such as those that infer the involvement or connection with the boss, the numbers will be presented in writing to the facilitator who will tally and post the results. With this method, members of the group do not know how others have prioritized the problems; they only know the aggregate rankings.

In the case where there are more items to prioritize, the **one half plus one method** can be applied. Let's say we have 30 items on our list. One half of 30 is 15, and 15 plus 1 is 16. Members of the group will be asked to write down the top 16 problems in order of severity or effect, with the number 16 representing the highest priority item and 1 representing the lowest priority item. The facilitator then will ask each member to give their score for the items one by one. The facilitator records the total numbers and determines the priorities by highest total number.

Cause and Effect Analysis

So far, we have listed all the problems and issues and prioritized them. Now we must take the number one priority item and identify the root causes of the problem. The **Cause and Effect Analysis** can be used to identify the root causes. The effect is the problem statement which was brainstormed and prioritized through nominal group technique. The goal is to select the root cause that has the largest effect and solve/address that cause. A **Cause and Effect Diagram** helps analyze the cause(s) of the variation. This diagram is sometimes called the "fishbone diagram" because it looks somewhat like the skeleton of a fish.

There are two methods to generate the root causes from the group. One is to request each member to write down what they believe the root causes are and to track the processes involved with the root causes before the next group meeting. The other method involves a very structured brainstorming session, to be conducted without preparation, to determine the various root causes. The causes then are documented on a cause and effect diagram. The diagram sorts out and organizes the causes as the brainstorming session progresses. The environment includes things that are out of the control of those trying to manage for quality in the organization. The organization's location, the political situation in the organization's community, poor weather, and the economy would be examples of environmental issues. The major causes are either organized using the categories Methods, Manpower, Machinery, and Materials (Exhibit 8.8) or factors in administrative areas—People, Products, Procedures, or Equipment (Exhibit 8.9). Keep in mind that these categories are only suggestions. The facilitator can use whatever categories best apply to the problem statement.

When discussing each root cause, search for changes from the norm or patterns that have developed slowly over time. Reach a group consensus of the most important root causes, and always focus on curing the problem or cause. Do not evaluate the symptoms of the problem.

Once constructed, the diagram is used in the following way:

1. Place the effect or problem statement in the right-hand box at the "head" of the diagram. (Remember to restate it before brainstorming.)

2. Write in the major categories, including the environment, at the "tail" of the diagram.

3. Begin the brainstorming session to determine various causes and place the causes in the appropriate categories. For each brainstormed cause, ask the question: Why does it happen? Record the answers on the branches off the horizontal lines under "Causes." (Note the use of *"why"* rather than *"who."*) *Include a brainstormed listing of relevant environmental issues.* When the brainstorming is completed, it is time for interpretation and prioritization to determine the predominant causes.

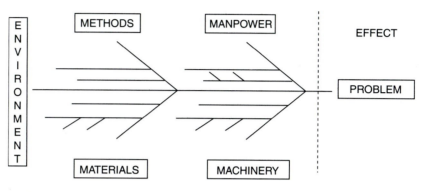

Exhibit 8.8 Cause and effect diagram.

A classic example of the application of these tools to a hospitality business would be "poor customer service" as the problem statement. This application is shown in Exhibit 8.9.

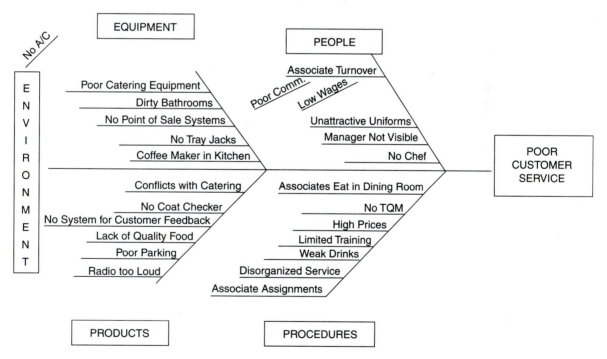

Exhibit 8.9 Application of a cause and effect diagram to a poor customer service problem.

Again, in some cases the group can add a category as the "tail" of the fish and identify it as the environment (in this case, no air conditioning).

Now the group must prioritize the root causes of the problem by first identifying duplicate causes or related causes. In using the previous example, our group identified the following as the top five root causes:

Rank	Cause
1.	Associate turnover
2.	Poor food quality
3.	Limited training
4.	Disorganized associate assignments
5.	No customer feedback system

Remember, prioritization is based on the level of impact that resolution of the root cause will have on the overall operation. Assuming there is no need for additional information (such as identifying the processes, charting the history of the problem, or the relationship between the variables), it is time to use the PDCA Cycle.

The PDCA Cycle

The PDCA Cycle is a four-step process of intervention for eliminating the root causes of key issues in the organization (see Chapter 7). The PDCA Cycle is pictured in Exhibit 8.10. The steps include Planning, Doing, Checking, and Acting.

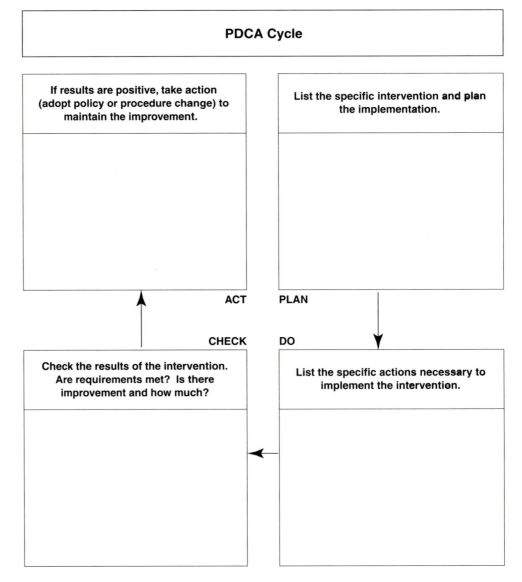

Exhibit 8.10 The PDCA Cycle.

- Planning is developing the actions and steps necessary to eliminate the root cause.
- Doing is putting the actions and plans into motion.
- Checking is monitoring progress in each step of the intervention process.
- Acting is adopting the steps in either policy, accepted procedure, or permanent core value.

We want to develop actions that will assist in the elimination of the hassle and help us understand the problem and the effect the root cause is having on the poor outcome. We will need to get beneath the surface to discover the best long-term solutions. In some cases we want to select the action with the most provocative effect; however, it may also be wise to select an action on a smaller scale to test the waters and to get a more immediate positive change. The planning stage involves getting a complete understanding of the customers, their perceptions, their requirements, their background, and their socioeconomic status. Other tools are available for use in acquiring this information. These tools, which are listed below, will be discussed in more detail later in the chapter:

- **Flow Chart.** This is used to get a more complete understanding of the processes involved in providing our present services. We cannot make educated or informed decisions on plans of action unless we thoroughly understand every step in the process of providing customer service. Many of the steps were listed in the cause and effect diagram, but the flow chart also describes how the various steps relate to one another and follow in a sequence.
- **Check Sheet.** This sheet is used to gather data on the problem or root cause.
- **Pareto Chart.** The Pareto Chart is used to determine which problems to resolve in what order. This directs our attention to the most important issues.
- **Run/Control Chart.** This is used to measure the long-term effects of the root causes and presents them graphically over a period of time that is meaningful to the possible resolution. It identifies shifts or changes in the average result. Obviously, random variation plays a role in changes, but this tool resolves this issue because of the length of time over which the results are reported.

Through in-depth analysis and knowledge of the process, we can arrive at five effective interventions for the first root cause in our example in Exhibit 8.9, "associate turnover."

1. Conduct an associate attitude survey or dehassle the organization. Subject to the results of the dehassling process, recommend additional actions from the planning process.
2. Build the level of empowerment.
3. Improve the associate orientation/training program.
4. Conduct a wage/benchmarking study.
5. Use self-directed work teams to resolve the issues.

The results of the Planning Stage tell us what action we need to take in the *Do Step:* conduct the survey or dehassling session and begin to improve the orientation/training program (Exhibit 8.11).

So, at this stage, we have just completed the staff dehassling session and have initiated changes in the associate orientation/training program.

The *Check Step* involves gathering the information and data to determine if there are changes, improvements, or positive results. In this case, we find the information received through dehassling confirmed our belief that associate training was an issue, and the associates wanted a voice in determining the future direction of the organization (self-directed work teams). Initial findings from improvements

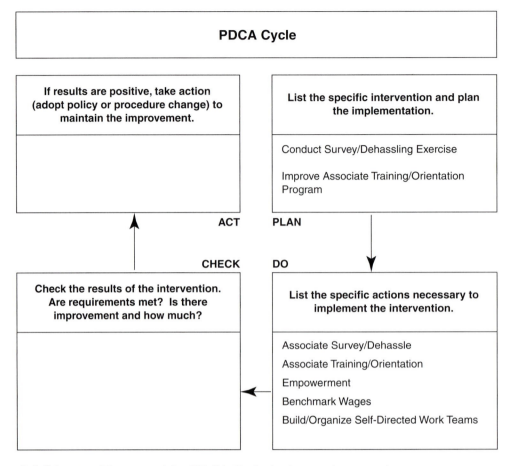

Exhibit 8.11 The start of the PDCA Cycle for improving associate turnover.

in the orientation/training program have been positive. This is seen in improvements of associate attitudes, positive customer feedback, and an immediate slow down in turnover of internal customers. This leads us to the *Action Step* of the process. At this stage we adopt a policy on conducting semi-annual associate attitude surveys and adopt the changes made to the training program (Exhibit 8.12).

The PDCA Cycle does not end here. We will continue to add to the Do list and Check the results for implementation of changes in procedure, policy, and core values. Each work group, including those in management, should have several Dos in process at the same time. If the results of the **Check** step are negative, the intervention must be discarded and another Do implemented. However, before discarding an intervention, be certain that the analysis was complete and that sufficient time was given to the Check step.

To quote Ken Blanchard from *The Heart of a Leader,* "Managers should recognize that good performance, both their own and others', is a journey, not a destination. Everyone learns from doing. It takes time and practice to achieve specific goals. Anything worth doing does not have to be done perfectly—at first."

Flow Chart

Flow Charts are used to identify the detailed steps in a process and how these steps relate to one another. The symbols used in charting a process are easy to use and recognize. They are pictured in Exhibit 8.13.

In order to identify flaws in a process, a flow chart must be developed based on actual experience and compared to the flow chart that represents how the process would work if everything went according to plan. The comparison will

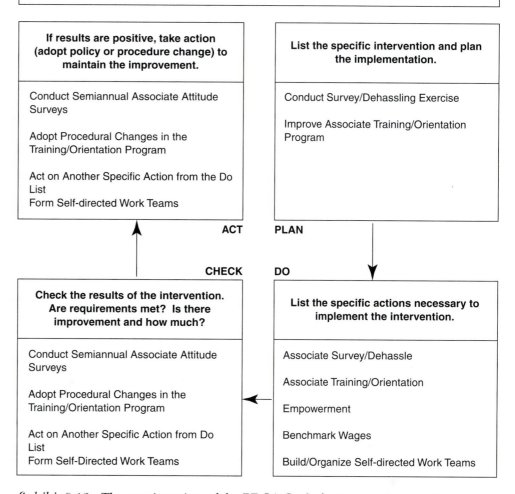

Exhibit 8.12 The continuation of the PDCA Cycle for improving associate turnover.

⬭ = Start or Stop

▭ = A Process Step/Action

◇ = A Question/Decision

Exhibit 8.13 Flow chart symbols.

identify problem areas in the process so that corrective action can follow. Always include the associates who are directly involved and closest to the process for development of the flow charts. Also, use a facilitator and recorder when developing flow charts with a group of people.

It is not unusual that processes in the organization are very difficult to identify. Essentially, the term "process" refers to a set of related activities required to bring about a result. The result is a product or service. Processes start with the supplier, go through the organization, and wind up with the external customer. So, it is safe to say that the resources and results of the process lie outside the organization.

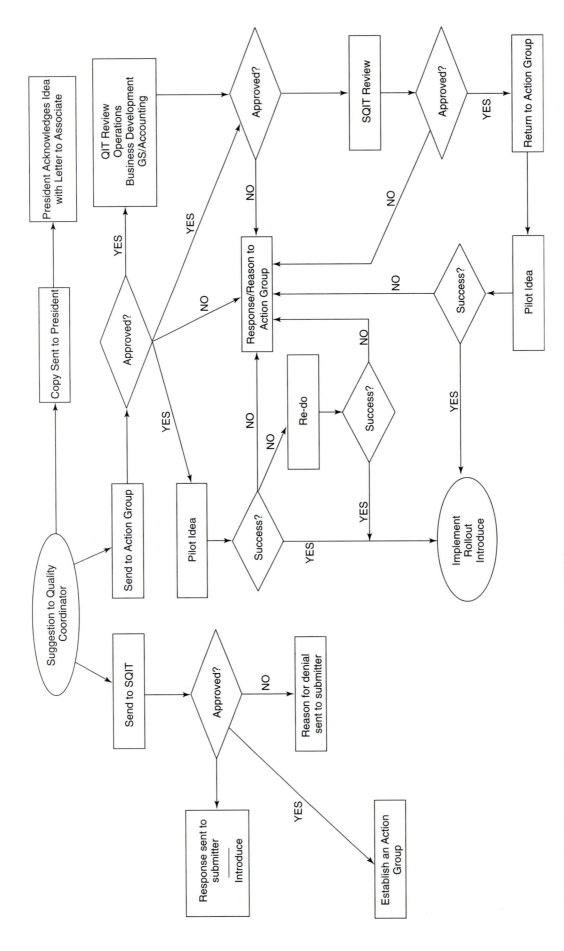

Exhibit 8.14 A flow chart for processing a suggestion at HDS.

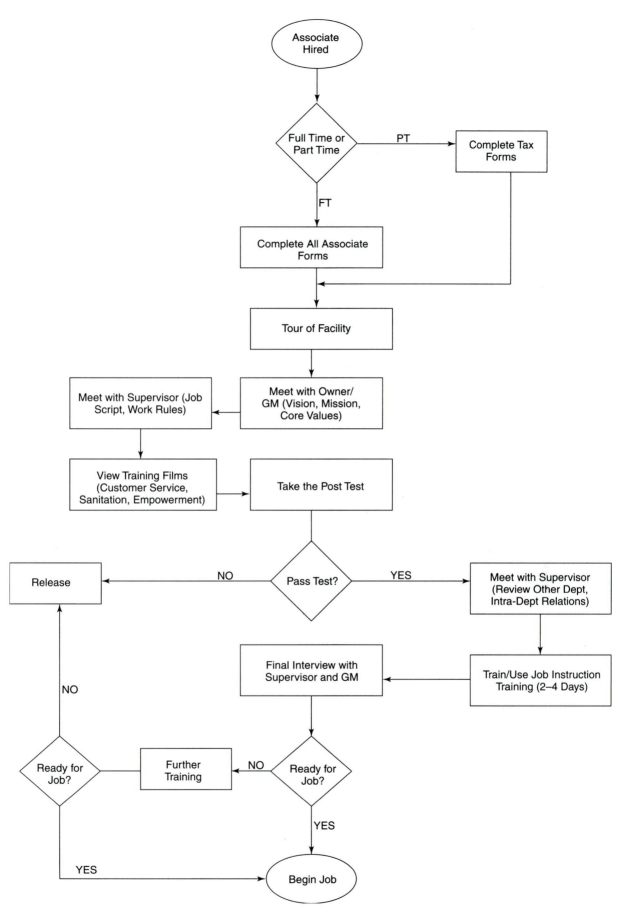

Exhibit 8.15   A flow chart for improving the associates' orientation/training process.

Exhibit 8.14 is an example flow chart for processing a suggestion at HDS Services. It begins at the top left with a suggestion being submitted to the quality coordinator. Exhibit 8.15 shows a flow chart for improving associates' orientation and training process.

Before charting the process, you must clearly define its boundaries. Never bring parts of other processes into the flow chart, other than to list the results of a decision. Also, try to use the simplest symbols possible and make sure all feedback loops have somewhere to go for decision and finality.

Check Sheet

The **Check Sheet** is used to record the number of occurrences during a given time frame. In other words, "How often are certain things happening?"

Exhibit 8.16 presents an example of the check sheet used to track reasons for customer complaints about service levels. If this were a very large restaurant with multiple dining service areas, the areas should be checked independently.

COMMENT	Week 1	Week 2	Week 3	Week 4
Service slow	II	III	I	II
Poor associate attitude	I	II	II	I
Associate unaware of standard (no training)	⊬⊬ I	⊬⊬	⊬⊬ II	⊬⊬ I
Associate not empowered	II	I	II	I
Process flow	———	II	I	II
Totals	11	13	13	12

Exhibit 8.16 Check sheet to track reasons for customer complaints about service.

Pareto Chart

Following the development of the information on the check sheet, the information can be transferred onto a Pareto Chart which tells us what problems we must focus on. A **Pareto Chart** is a columnar graph that depicts causes of issues and their frequency of recurrence over a specified, standard time frame.

The cause categories are listed on the horizontal axis according to frequency from left to right. The number of occurrences is enumerated vertically. The Pareto Chart tries to focus the analysis on the "vital few" while ignoring the "trivial many." The goal is to do what will have the greatest impact. Exhibit 8.17 presents a Pareto Chart.

Run Chart

A **Run Chart** (Exhibit 8.18) is used to monitor a process to determine how the results are changing over a long period of time. Because we are looking for continuous improvement, the chart should indicate steady positive change. In the following example we are tracking customer complaints on poor service over a period of six months.

This chart tells us that the average number of poor service complaints has been reduced in the last month or so. In addition to trying to continuously improve, management needs to know what is acceptable and what is not acceptable

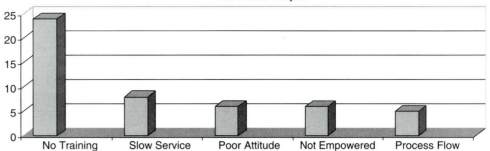

Exhibit 8.17 A Pareto chart showing the causes of poor customer service.

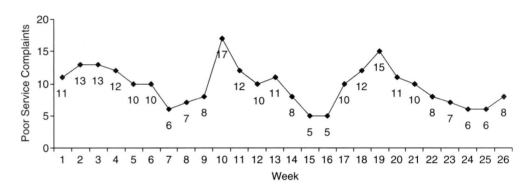

Exhibit 8.18 A run chart showing customer complaints on poor service over a six-month period.

by placing control limits on the graph. There are upper control limits (over the average), and lower control limits (under the average). When the number of complaints falls within the lower and upper control limits, this is acceptable because normal variation is built into the process. However, when the number of complaints falls outside the limits, the process is said to be out of control. Those "out of control" results normally arise from special causes such as people error, unplanned events, or unusual occurrences. These special causes must be eliminated before the chart can be used as a monitoring tool.

Control does not necessarily mean that the service will meet our needs. It only means that the level of service is consistent (this could mean consistently poor as well). As the monitoring and CQI processes proceed, we either have to improve the process or change the specifications or standards. Specifications or standards refer to what we think we need, and control limits are what the process can do.

Run/Control Chart

The Run Chart for poor customer service complaints is now converted into a **Run/Control Chart** (Exhibit 8.19). In this chart, the average number of weekly complaints is 9.7 and our target is a minimum of 40% fluctuation for forming our control limits.

So, the process can be said to be out of control when the number of complaints exceeds 14 or is less than 6. These numbers call for possible process adjustment or change. How do we make adjustments in the process or our systems? First, we need to understand Force Field Analysis.

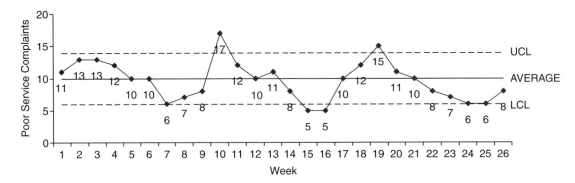

Exhibit 8.19 A run/control chart showing customer complaints on poor service over a six-month period.

Force Field Analysis

Force Field Analysis is a technique developed by Kurt Lewin. It simply presents the **driving forces** that move a situation toward change, and **restraining forces** that block that movement and prevent change. Therefore, when there is no change, the restraining forces are equal to or greater than the driving forces for adjustment.

Exhibit 8.20 shows the driving forces and restraining forces in deciding to make a change. If the restraining forces are stronger than the combination of all the driving forces, the objective for a shift in process will not occur.

Exhibit 8.20 A force field analysis showing driving and restraining forces in deciding to make a change.

How can Force Field Analysis assist management or an Action Group Team or a Work Team in bringing about change?

- It compels individuals to think in depth about all the positive factors and negative forces related to the desirable change, and it encourages creativity.
- It promotes the use of in-depth analysis and consideration of all the factors involved, and it brings personal agendas and paradigms to the surface. This is true for items on both sides of the ledger. There is a place here for the use of Nominal Group Technique at this stage in the process.
- It provides a clear view of where the forces are as a starting point.

To accomplish change or movement in the process we need to strengthen the driving forces or reduce the restraining forces. Be careful, however. Strengthening the positive often has the unexpected outcome of strengthening the negative. Therefore, it is best to concentrate on the restraining forces to either diminish or eliminate them.

If change is to come about, everyone in the group must be honest with themselves and other members of the group in the expression of their feelings. Furthermore, remember that the work environment is changing fast these days and the leaders who once "knew everything" about their organization and the industry find themselves very vulnerable. It is important that management openly admit when they are out of the loop. This opens the door for associates to share knowledge. Finally, if the organization's values include customer focus, change is more easily achieved because everyone will relate the benefits of the change to the customer. Remember that working on issues using the tools and other graphic techniques discussed in this chapter produces better and stronger solutions than any unstructured process. Quality is best achieved by removing the causes of the hassles; those closest to the problems know most about the causes and issues. So, everyone must work together.

Transition from Tools to the SQPD Guide

Another tool managers have available is a **Strategic Quality Plan Development Guide (SQPD).** (See Chapter 9 for a more complete discussion of this tool.) The SQPD Guide allows us to list our objective (the P in the PDCA Cycle), our plans for action (the D and A in the PDCA Cycle), and the impact of these actions on quality and the organization's proforma financial statements.

The dehassling process gave us our overall objective and the cause and effect analysis gave us the root causes of the issue and, ultimately, the interventions. From there, the financial and quality impacts are identified before placing the information in the Strategic Quality Plan. The SQPD Guide is presented in Exhibit 8.21.

Each objective listed in the Planning section of the PDCA Cycle is repeated in complete detail in the SQPD Guide. The bulk of the organization's strategic quality business plan is built around these objectives. As previously indicated, there could be as many as one hundred objectives that are active at any given time. Each Do item from the PDCA Cycle is listed adjacent to the objective, but only one Do item is listed in each box of the SQPD Guide. Therefore, the same objective could be listed a number of times if there is more than one Do item for that objective. The Do item becomes the Action plan. Adjacent to each Action plan is listed the impact of that action on Cost, Revenue, and Quality.

Summary

The tools presented in this chapter are simply yardsticks used to measure the effectiveness of our efforts. They could be thought of in much the same way that a chef and a manager evaluate the quality of products (Exhibit 8.22) when they are received at the restaurant's back door prior to storage. There are hundreds of other tools and metrics that are used in service organizations. For example, some of the key operating metrics often include service interruptions per 1,000 customers, customer complaints per associate, number of units produced per staff member, customers per associate, and many others. Some additional quality measures may include number of mistakes or errors, delivery time, total quality costs, and various customer satisfaction indexes. Customer feedback could be measured in the form of comments about product quality, comments about service quality, comments about the quality of the experience, rating on quality relative

STRATEGIC QUALITY PLAN DEVELOPMENT GUIDE

DEPARTMENT: _____   TEAM MEMBERS: _____
                                                      _____

OBJECTIVE	ACTION PLAN	COST/REVENUE/QUALITY IMPACT
		C = R = Q =
		C = R = Q =
		C = R = Q =
		C = R = Q =
		C = R = Q =

Exhibit 8.21   Strategic quality plan development guide.

162

Exhibit 8.22   A chef and a manager evaluate the quality of products received at the restaurant's back door, prior to storage. *(Source: HDS Services. Used with permission.)*

to the competition, and other metrics. The costs of quality could be reported and analyzed from the perceptions of the customers (internal and external) or financial or management. In all cases, it is important to measure what is meaningful, and what is defined as meaningful is based on our customers' views of quality and the world. Given the experiences with managing for quality, and the resultant improvements in quality, at HDS Services we feel that the most important metrics are presented in this chapter. (We have also presented additional copies in a tear-out appendix section in this book.)

It is important to share the findings and discoveries made from the use of the tools with the team members and others in the organization. Findings can be shared by posting them on a board in a central location, using them as discussion points in meetings, and printing them in associate newsletters. Sharing keeps the team focused on the results and the progress toward the agreed upon, shared goal.

Key Terms

Brainstorming—Technique designed to generate a large number of ideas, causes, and solutions through a process of total interaction.

Cause and Effect Analysis—The effect is the problem statement which was brainstormed and prioritized through nominal group technique. The goal is to select the root cause that has the largest effect and solve/address that cause.

Cause and Effect Diagram—A tool used to analyze causes of a variation; sometimes called fishbone diagram.

Check Sheet—Used to gather data on the problem or root cause.

Consensus—A decision or position reflecting the collective thinking of the team that all members participate in developing, understand fully, believe is workable, can live with, and will actively support.

Driving Forces—Move a situation toward change.

Flow Charts—Used to get a more complete understanding of the processes involved in providing present services; also describes how the various steps relate to one another and follow in a sequence.

Force Field Analysis—It simply presents the driving forces that move a situation toward change, and restraining forces that block that movement and prevent change.

ISO 9000—International Organization for Standardization. This organization develops quality standards. These standards are objective measurements against which an organization can be measured and certified.

Nominal Group Technique (NGT)—Used to give everyone the opportunity to equally voice their opinions and prioritize.

One Half Plus One Method—Used in the case where there are many items to prioritize.

Pareto Chart—Used to determine which problems to resolve in what order.

Piggyback Input—Build on the ideas of others during brainstorming.

Restraining Forces—Block movement and prevent change.

Run Chart—Used to monitor a process to determine how the results are changing over a long period of time.

Run/Control Chart—Used to measure the long-term effects of the root causes and present them graphically over a period of time that is meaningful to the possible resolution. It identifies shifts or changes in the average result.

Strategic Quality Plan Development (SQPD) Guide—The SQPD Guide permits the listing of objectives, the plans for action, and the impact of these actions on quality and the organization's proforma financial statements.

Structure—Gives the organization more direction and continuity.

Tools of the Trade—Combined into systems and used along with solid management principles to improve quality; set of measurements or metrics linked to ongoing procedures for testing whether the organization is meeting, exceeding, or falling below the standards.

Review Questions

1. Internally, why is it better to be a predictable manager?
2. What are the guidelines for identifying hassles?
3. What are the nine rules of brainstorming?
4. What is ISO 9000?
5. Identify two methods of Nominal Group Technique (NGT).
6. What are the features of the cause and effect analysis and what is it used for?
7. What are the three symbols used in flow charting and what do they mean?
8. What is the importance of the SQPD guide?

Activities in Your Organization

Listed below are some activities designed to reinforce the key chapter concepts in your organization. If you are a student and not currently working in the industry, interview an industry leader about one of these topics.

1. Assemble a cross-functional group of associates and use brainstorming to develop a list of possible causes of a lack of training in your organization. If possible, focus the brainstorming on a lack of *service* training, particularly in those positions that have direct contact with the organization's external customers.

Now use one of the forms of nominal group technique to prioritize the list. Select the top priority reason and discuss next steps. What could now be done to intervene and improve the process of training in your organization? Be specific in your causes and possible improvements.

2. Using Exhibit 8.8, the Cause and Effect Diagram, (recall that there are additional tear-out sheets of this and the other tools in the Appendix) generate the root cause for the lack of service training discovered in Activity #1. As an alternative, identify a different problem related to customer satisfaction either internal customers or external customers in your organization. Using the Cause and Effect Diagram, generate the possible causes. Then use the NGT to prioritize the causes so you reach consensus on the top priority cause for the problem.

3. Using the top priority cause that you have identified in Activity #2, discuss the Planning, Doing, Checking, and Acting steps of the PDCA Cycle. What are the possible interventions? What intervention will your team select to try first? Now fill in the PDCA Cycle using the top intervention that your team has selected (P) and follow it through to the D, C, and A steps. Was it successful? Are you going to alter the procedures or policies based on your experience with trying the intervention using the PDCA? Will you try an additional intervention to further address the problem? If so, which intervention will you select and why? What is the result of trying that intervention? What has happened to the original problem? Has quality been improved?

References

Harnish, Verne and Kathleen Harnish. *Implementing Total Quality Management.* Boulder, Colorado: Career Track, 1994.

Blanchard, Ken. *The Heart of a Leader.* Colorado Springs, Colorado: Honor Books, 1998.

Brossard, Michael. *The Memory Jogger.* Metheun, Massachusetts: Goal/QPC, 1988.

Relevant Web Sites

Balanced Score Card (A Method of Grouping Performance Measures):
   http://www.jit-software.com/documents/vsj2.pdf
Conducting a Cost-Effective Root Cause Analysis:
   http://www.rootcauseanalyst.com/costeffective.htm
Force Field Analysis:
   http://erc.msh.org/quality/example/example5.cfm
Implementing ISO 9001:
   http://www.iso.ch/iso/en/iso9000-14000/iso9000/selection_use/implementing.html
ISO 9000 in plain English:
   http://www.praxiom.com/iso-9000-1.htm
ISO 9000 Resource Center:
   http://www.iso-9000-2000.com/
Nominal Group Techniques:
   http://www.institute.virginia.edu/services/csa/nominal.htm

Chapter

Strategic Quality Plan

Managing quality is often a topic we only assume is being addressed until reality tells us otherwise.

Allegra Johnson, CCM
Club Manager
Dunwoody Country Club
Dunwoody, GA

Everyone in the organization must believe in the Strategic Quality Plan and integrate the plan's directives into all actions and decisions. When the plan is used, the associates and the customers know it, and teamwork and partnerships are created.

Bob Wills
Executive Vice President Operations
HDS Services
Farmington Hills, MI

Learning Objectives

1. Define what is meant by the word "vision" and the desired link between a personal vision and an organization's vision.
2. Describe the characteristics of a shared vision.
3. Detail the question that core values answer and how the vision, mission, and core values fit together in an organization.
4. Describe strategic goals and the areas of the organization that they typically address.
5. Define how to generate the strategic quality plan and make it operational.
6. Understand how to build commitment for a strategic quality plan.
7. How are the Balanced Score Card and the Strategic Action Plans linked?

Quality is an integral part of the **strategic planning process** in an organization. Both concepts are interdependent and interrelated; quality is achieved through a set of defined processes that are continuously improved while strategic planning provides a comprehensive approach that helps position the organization for the long term and addresses key strategic issues in the near term. Internally developed strategies take the organization along the pathway to its vision. When internal customers are asked for their input in the creation of the vision, they see the vision as their own and are committed to making the vision reality, as is the case with this chef in a steakhouse restaurant (Exhibit 9.1).

Exhibit 9.1   When internal customers are asked for their input in the creation of the vision, they see the vision as their own and are committed to making the vision reality. *(Source: Getty Images Inc.—Image Bank. Used with permission.)*

The vision and mission in a strategic plan describe what the organization will become and how it will get there. An organization cannot get to where it wants to go without a firm understanding of quality and all that quality encompasses. Quality helps us identify the needs and expectations of customers so we can build capabilities that customers will value and the competition cannot replicate or provide. If we can achieve that set of outcomes, the organization's strength will be built for the long term. The organization will not only survive; it will thrive and prosper.

In order to survive and thrive in the long term, an organization must evolve and grow every day. One example of this is an organization that raises its level of quality service delivery just slightly every day. Over time, revenues will be expanded leading to the growth of the organization. Together, a quality commitment blended with concepts of strategic planning will help create an organization that satisfies customers, both internal and external, and delivers results on financial objectives for the owners and investors.

The most effective strategic plans are those that align the organization's vision, mission, core values, strategies, and metrics. The strategies are developed by the various Action Group Teams to enable the organization to reach or surpass specific **targets**. For example, as of February 2004, RARE Hospitality had 239 restaurants, including 194 LongHorn Steakhouses, 26 Bugaboo Creek Steak Houses, and 17 Capital Grilles. (The other two properties are specialty restaurants and franchise concepts.) These RARE restaurant concepts are growing because the organization's mission and core values are used to help ensure that team members and guests are treated well. RARE's strategies include food that is carefully selected and prepared by dedicated people who love to serve great food. These targets are measurable, but the metrics are never the goal. The goal is the improvement of quality, and the metrics simply report the progress toward the goal.

It has been suggested that high performance service organizations have a "soul." When vision, mission, and values capture the purpose, uniqueness, and methods, the organization's soul is apparent. The soul provides a distinctive source of value for internal customers connected to the organization because their individual and personal values and visions are leading in the same direction as the organization's values and vision. The soul also provides a distinctive source of value for external customers because the organization is connected with the customers' needs, expectations, and other defining characteristics.

Vision, mission, and values translate concepts and ideas into reality and performance. Leaders provide an optimistic outlook on the future and its possibilities; customers inside and external to the organization must be asked to help define the mission, vision, and values so that they will reflect the customers' needs and expectations. While the mission, vision, and values of the organization may remain consistent throughout the years, the commitment of the personal visions of those who make up the organization will modify the organization's implementation of these aspects. The vision, mission, and values provide compelling reasons to commit to and energize change. These three items connect the organization, the internal customers, and the external customers to the future.

During the process selecting of internal customers, it is important to assess the alignment between the individual's core values and mission and the core values and mission of the organization. RARE Hospitality uses its eight core values as primary interview guidelines during selection. The series of questions that are used to interview prospective team members assesses the compatibility of the two value systems. If it is discovered subsequently that a team member is not living the core values of RARE Hospitality, the root cause is determined and categorized into either a lack of knowledge or a lack of commitment. A lack of knowledge can be rectified through training in most cases. A lack of commitment has the potential to invalidate the core values of the RARE organization. Successful team members cannot simply mimic the core values; the values must be present in their hearts and reflected in their behaviors to be genuine.

Shared Vision

A **vision** is simply a picture of the future. It is the ideal view of where we want to be or the answer to the question: What do we want to create? Vision is the expected impact or result of our performance today and in the future.

In his book *The Fifth Discipline*, Peter Senge writes about the power of a shared vision utilizing the movie *Spartacus,* an adaptation of the Roman gladiator/slave-led conflicts in 71 B.C. as an example. After defeating the Roman legions twice, (and subsequent to a long battle,) the slave-led army was conquered by the Roman legions (led by Marcus Crassus.) In the movie, the scene shows Crassus on a hill telling thousands of survivors that they have been slaves before and will be slaves again. To be spared the punishment of crucifixion, Crassus tells them to turn over the leader of the slave army, Spartacus, because they didn't know what he looked like. In the movie there is a long pause, and the camera moves in on Kirk Douglas who plays Spartacus, the slave leader.

Spartacus stands and says: "I am Spartacus!" In turn, each slave stands and announces, "I am Spartacus!" Within moments, all are standing and loudly declaring, "I am Spartacus!" Each man made a clear choice to stand for what he believed in. The loyalty of the individuals in the slave army was *not* to Spartacus the man, but to the vision that Spartacus inspired. The vision was both a reflection of each person's individual vision and the collective **shared vision** of the group.

Personal Vision

Personal vision provides the purpose for which a person exists. When an individual is in touch with a personal vision, it makes the person alive and vital. Every thought you think, every emotion you feel, every action you take, are all related to your personal vision. A personal vision has the power to focus your energies to create what is not yet created and fulfill a purpose that is not yet complete. It makes people passionate about doing what will make the vision become real.

Like organizational visions, personal visions evolve over time. It is important for people to separate themselves from the intensity of daily demands and periodically revisit their personal vision.

Shared Visions in High Performance Organizations

Shared visions in high performance service organizations use personal visions as their seeds—they grow from personal visions. In an organization, a shared vision is a reflection of the personal visions of the people in that organization. As such, it utilizes the synergy of the combination of many to make itself stronger than each personal vision individually. Shared visions grow as a result of the connection and interaction of personal visions in an organization.

Shared visions stimulate the **enrollment** of individuals. Enrollment is dramatically different than the typical concept of "buy in" practiced in most traditional organizations. Buy in works like this: management comes up with the management program (sometimes referred to as the "flavor" of the month). The program grows from an idea that management has (without consulting either internal or external customers) about a way to either control costs or boost revenues. In order for management in a traditional organization to put this program into play, they have to "sell" it to the employees. Usually the sales process inflates the benefits, minimizes the problems, and focuses on the needs of the seller (i.e., the manager), not the needs of the buyer (i.e., the employee). If the sales effort doesn't work, management has no other choice but to resort to autocratic methods to try to force compliance. If the effort is not met with compliance, it is met with defiance and resentment.

This set of strategies is not found in a high performance service organization. Rather than using a buy-in strategy, leaders focus on enrolling others in the organization's vision. Enrollment results when people are free to choose and individual choice stems from the individual's personal vision. If an associate's personal vision (with its purpose, goals, actions, and beliefs) is heading in the same direction as the organization's vision, it is easy for that person to enroll in the shared vision.

A leader encourages enrollment of others by enrolling first. Others detect the leader's genuine enthusiasm and willingness to let others freely choose the course of their lives. These individuals then feel fully responsible for their own personal visions. They are the architects of their own visions, creating their own purpose.

Because the enrollment in a shared vision is a free choice, the resulting commitment is very personal. It comes from the individual choosing to contribute to making the organization's vision a reality. Both the personal vision and the organization's vision are aligned in synchronous harmony. A shared vision is based on trust and placing the needs, wants, and expectations of others first. Shared visions focus attention and help associates and leaders set and achieve goals. When personal and organizational visions are in harmony, individuals are likely to have a high degree of commitment to the organization.

Some sample **vision statements** are presented in Exhibit 9.2.

Visions are crafted by discussing the completion of this statement:

The vision of the [*organization*] is to be [*state what we want to create to complete this sentence*]._____

_____

_____

Vision Statement for HDS Services
We will be the <u>PREFERRED PARTNER</u> in Providing Management and Consulting in the Dining Service and Hospitality Industries.

Vision Statement for the Detroit Athletic Club
The vision of the Detroit Athletic Club is to be recognized as the premier private gathering place in Southeast Michigan.

Vision Statement for The University Club of Michigan State University
The vision of The University Club of MSU is to be the preferred source for social, recreational, and professional experiences.

Vision Statement for Elk Creek Resort
We will be the Pinnacle in Hospitality, Unmatched Among Destinations.

Vision Statement for The Escape
The vision of The Escape is to be the world's foremost destination for creating a pleasurable experience for business or leisure.

Vision Statement for Nordic Lights Resort & Conference Center
The vision of Nordic Lights Resort & Conference Center is to be the premier destination for world-renowned experiences.

Vision of On the Rocks
The vision of On the Rocks is to be the premier destination for the ultimate resort experience.

Exhibit 9.2 Sample Vision Statements for High Performance Service Organizations (*Sources: HDS Services, Detroit Athletic Club, The University Club of MSU. Used with permission.*)

Mission

A **mission statement** answers the questions: Why do we exist? What is our purpose? In what interest do we function/operate? The **mission** seeks to clarify how the organization adds value by contributing to the world in a unique way. A mission is often expressed in terms of what we are in business to do or the line of work we are in. While the vision for the organization usually remains consistent over time, the mission may evolve and change as the purpose of the organization changes. Missions tend to be more dynamic than visions for both organizations and individuals.

Sample mission statements for high performance service organizations are presented in Exhibit 9.3.

Mission Statement for HDS Services

HDS Services is dedicated to providing hospitality based
dining services management at a level which exceeds
our customers' expectations.

Mission Statement for RARE Hospitality

The mission of RARE Hospitality is to be financially successful
through GREAT PEOPLE consistently delivering
GREAT FOOD, GREAT SERVICE and making every guest a loyal guest.

Mission Statement for the Detroit Athletic Club

The mission of the Detroit Athletic Club is to provide a distinguished private club that promotes
friendship, athletics, and opportunities for social and professional interactions.

Mission Statement for The University Club of Michigan State University

The mission of The University Club of MSU is to consistently exceed the
expectations of our members, guests, and staff. We will deliver exceptional
experiences through the efforts of a professional, empowered team,
generating pride and success in all our relationships.

Mission Statement for Elk Creek Resort

The mission of Elk Creek Resort is to provide exceptional service, quality,
and comfort for our guests. We will commit to the growth and development
of our internal customers and empower them to service perfection. We will effectively
manage our resources to assure long-term financial success.
Elk Creek is dedicated to consistency of quality, high standards, and thrilling our guests.

Mission Statement for The Escape

The mission of The Escape is to empower our associates to exceed the expectations of guests
100% of the time and enhance the quality of living when traveling, create long-lasting
partnerships with suppliers, create jobs and community pride,
and be profitable and financially healthy.

Mission Statement for Nordic Lights Resort & Conference Center

The mission of Nordic Lights Resort & Conference Center is to empower our associates
to make decisions that benefit themselves and the organization; to provide our associates with
opportunities to succeed and grow with the organization; to provide our guests with exceptional
service and unparalleled facilities; to instill the principles of Continuous Quality Improvement
throughout the organization and our partners; to commit resources to enrich the community that
we represent; and to prosper as a business and create a sound financial foundation.

Exhibit 9.3 Sample Mission Statements for High Performance Service Organizations *(Sources: HDS Services, RARE Hospitality International, Inc., Detroit Athletic Club, and The University Club of MSU. Used with permission.)*

Mission of On the Rocks

The mission of On the Rocks is to offer quality of life, education, and training opportunities for internal customers; to provide lasting impressions through unique experiences and service, and by exceeding expectations for external customers; to have lasting, loyal, and secure relationships, and maintain consistent communication, with supplier partners; to promote a commitment to the environment, education, and economic stability in the community; and to be a progressive business focusing on financial goals and quality to improve the bottom line.

Exhibit 9.3   continued

A mission is crafted by discussing the completion of this statement:

The mission of the [*organization*] is to be [*state the purpose for internal customers/associates*]

_____

_____;

[*state the purpose for external customers*]

_____

_____;

[*state the purpose for partners/suppliers*]

_____

_____;

[*state the purpose for the community*]

_____

_____;

and [*state the purpose about financial expectations*]

_____

_____.

Core Values

In our experience, it is best to start the "vision, mission, and values" discussion with values since values are the foundations for a vision and a mission, both personally and in organizations. These **core values** guide the planning process, decision making regarding which plans are the highest priorities, and the resulting action to make the plans become reality. Values help us define the direction that we take, while the vision defines our ideal destination. Values live in the present, whereas visions apply to the future. Values help sustain the effort of all in the organization when they are faced with trying times and values provide the tenacity to persevere. The core values of an organization are more than words on paper; they become real when they are acted upon and surface in the behaviors of all involved.

Core values answer the question: How do we want to act? They describe intended behaviors that the organization deems important. Personally, our values help us develop our responses to others, determine our morals, and decide which personal and professional commitments we are willing to make. Values help guide individuals and their interactions with others, such as internal and external customers. Core values of an organization may include customer satisfaction, merit, credibility, efficiency, honesty, quality, integrity, service, loyalty, personal development, mutual respect, and continuous improvement.

Sample **statements of core values** are presented in Exhibit 9.4.

The core values of the organization are determined by discussing the completion of this statement:

The core values of the [*organization*] are [*state the ways that we will act/how we will behave*] _____, _____, _____, _____, _____, _____, _____, _____, _____, _____, _____, _____, _____, and _____.

Sometimes when trying to pinpoint core values, it is easiest to think about the historic and modern day leaders we admire most and the values they exhibit that we admire. Other times, if we identify the values that we are most drawn to in our mentors and role models, it will help us articulate our values. If we use others at the start of the process of discovering our own values, we are **benchmarking** others' values. The same process may be used in an organization by studying past and current leading industry organizations and those organizations that serve as role models in the industry. However, at some point we must articulate our own values; we cannot simply mimic those of others. This holds true for organizational values as well as personal values.

Gaining this self-knowledge requires honesty with oneself and the ability to accept feedback from others regarding behavior. Asking and answering the following questions will help begin to clarify personal values:

- What values are attractive to me in others (historic and modern day leaders, role models) and why?
- Who do I admire and why?
- Who do I try to emulate because I respect the other person?
- What do I believe in and why?
- What do I stand for and why?
- What do I hold as precious above all else and why?
- How do I act repeatedly and why?
- What behaviors characterize me?
- What behaviors have I committed to practicing?

Following this self-discovery, ask and answer the following questions to clarify the organization's values:

- What values are attractive to our organization in other organizations (e.g., leaders in our industry) and why?
- Who do we admire most in our industry segment and why?
- Which organization(s) does our organization try to emulate because we respect the other organization(s)?
- What do the leaders in our organization believe in and why?
- What do the leaders in our organization stand for and why?
- What do the leaders in our organization hold as precious above all else and why?
- How do the leaders and associates in our organization act repeatedly and why?
- What behaviors characterize the leaders and associates in our organization?
- What behaviors has our organization committed to practicing?

Core Values of HDS Services

Core Values of RARE Hospitality

At RARE . . .
1. We treat each other with dignity, respect, honesty, and integrity.
2. We hire great people, we set clear expectations, we provide regular feedback, and we celebrate great performance.
3. We function as a team . . . "we all look good together, we all look bad together."
4. We are committed to continuous training and development.
5. We act first . . . we do it right or fix it fast. The guest wins "moments of truth."
6. We believe in continuous improvement . . . in getting better day-by-day and shift-by-shift.
7. We maximize long-term shareholder value through profitable sales growth.
8. We are a good business citizen . . . we follow the law and we positively contribute to our community.

Guests at RARE's restaurants are affected by a number of the Core Values. For example, Core Value #1 says that guests are treated with dignity, respect, honesty, and integrity. This is true if a guest books a party at Capital Grille, visits LongHorn with a friend for a salad at lunch, or dines at Bugaboo in the evening with their family. RARE operates with integrity and honesty. If an error is made, it is fixed fast (see Core Value #5).

Core Values of the Detroit Athletic Club

At the Detroit Athletic Club, the most important item we sell is The Spirit of Service. Our very personal relationship with the guest is what sets us apart from other businesses.
SERVICE is:

Smile—to motivate yourself and those around you
Enthusiasm—for the hospitality industry
Respect—for the co-workers who make up your team
Vision—to know yourself and what you want from your job
Initiative—your honest commitment to your employer
Customer Care—understanding who you serve and how to do it well
Energy—what it takes to pull it all together

Exhibit 9.4 Sample Core Values Statements of High Performance Service Organizations *(Sources: HDS Services, RARE Hospitality International, Inc., Detroit Athletic Club, and The University Club of MSU. Used with permission.)*

Remember the Golden Rule of our industry: Do Unto Others as Though You Were the Others. Basically, we all want the same things: to be treated fairly; to be recognized for what we do; to have the chance to be good at our jobs. And all it takes is a little SPIRIT!

<u>Core Values of The University Club of Michigan State University</u>
The core values of The University Club of MSU are personal and professional growth, communication, integrity, teamwork, balance, leadership, and excellence.

<u>Core Values of Elk Creek Resort</u>
The people at Elk Creek value honesty, trust, loyalty, equality, fairness, professionalism, sincerity, pride, having an open mind, and customer focus. We hear those who don't say much, respect others' ideas, and work towards the team goals.

<u>Core Values of The Escape</u>
The core values of The Escape are teamwork, empowerment, integrity, honesty, diversity, hospitality, professionalism, passion, communication, and respect.

<u>Core Values of Nordic Lights Resort & Conference Center</u>
The core values of Nordic Lights Resort & Conference Center are loyalty, integrity and ethics, mentoring, honesty and trust, diversity, positive attitude, respect, empowerment, fun, teamwork, continuous quality improvement, and a passion for excellence.

<u>Core Values of On the Rocks</u>
The core values of On the Rocks are mutual respect; hospitable friendliness; positive and consistent attitudes; knowledge; profitability; empowerment; reliability; ethics and integrity; trustworthiness; commitment to the company; giving back to the community; continuous quality improvement; and exceeding customers' expectations through consistency of products and services.

Exhibit 9.4   continued

What We Are All About

Some of the visions, missions, and values statements presented in the previous sections of this chapter came from actual organizations. Others were hypothetical organizations developed by our students in our senior-level Managing for Quality in Hospitality Businesses course at Michigan State University. Obviously, the HDS Services vision, mission, and values statements are "real." Study the others to determine which are the actual operations and which are hypothetical organizations created by our students as part of their class project.

The "real" organizations are the Detroit Athletic Club, RARE Hospitality, and The University Club of MSU. The vision, mission, and values statements were developed by the members of the club's executive team, reviewed with supervisors and associates for their input, modified, and then presented to the club's board of directors for approval. Even though the Elk Creek Resort, The Escape, the Nordic Lights Resort & Conference Center, and On the Rocks are organizations that exist only in the minds and hearts of our students, the vision, mission, and values statements should be studied to find applicable concepts that may be applied to your organization (Exhibit 9.5). While these statements may seem too idealistic, they reflect knowledge of quality principles, an understanding of what makes an organization effective, and a maturity beyond what might be expected in college seniors. These students will be able to apply these tools to whatever organization or career they choose and they have a keen understanding of what managing for quality is all about.

Vision: The Vision of The Escape is to be the world's foremost destination for creating a pleasurable experience for business or leisure.

Mission: The Mission of The Escape is to empower our associates to exceed the expectations of guests 100% of the time and enhance the quality of living when traveling, create long-lasting partnerships with suppliers, create jobs and community pride, and be profitable and financially healthy.

Core Values: The Core Values of The Escape are Teamwork, Empowerment, Integrity, Honesty, Diversity, Hospitable, Professionalism, Passion, Communication, and Respect.

Exhibit 9.5a The Escape's core values, vision, and mission.

Strategic Quality Plan
2000

Vision: The vision of Valhalla is to be recognized world wide as the premier resort destination. Valhalla strives to provide unparalleled quality, safety and service in an adventurous, yet relaxing, environment.

Mission: The mission of Valhalla is to strive to achieve the highest quality in destination resorts through continuous improvement of our products and services. We will foster growth for our team members and our investors in order to provide unparalleled satisfaction and comfort. Valhalla provides quality experiences for the benefit of our guests, team members, investors and community.

The Senior Quality Improvement Team

Andre, Mangier Alexandrei Night Club Manager	Russell Abdul Allen Purchasing Manager Non Food and Beverage
Andris Namejs Antons Transportation Manager (AM)	Tori Lynn Arnott Banquet and Catering Manager
Elizabeth Ann Barlage Manager of the Stables	Shadi Yacoub Bayouk Front Office Manager (PM)
Lissandra Bertagnoli Human Resources Manager	Michael W. Bird Deli Manager

Exhibit 9.5b Valhalla's core values, vision, and mission.

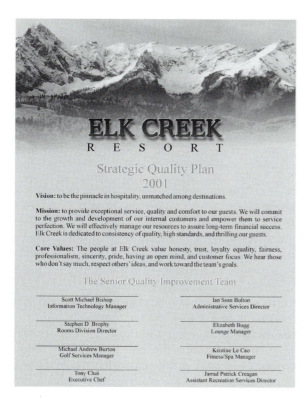

ELK CREEK
R E S O R T
Strategic Quality Plan
2001

Vision: to be the pinnacle in hospitality, unmatched among destinations.

Mission: to provide exceptional service, quality and comfort to our guests. We will commit to the growth and development of our internal customers and empower them to service perfection. We will effectively manage our resources to assure long-term financial success. Elk Creek is dedicated to consistency of quality, high standards, and thrilling our guests.

Core Values: The people at Elk Creek value honesty, trust, loyalty equality, fairness, professionalism, sincerity, pride, having an open mind, and customer focus. We hear those who don't say much, respect others' ideas, and work toward the team's goals.

The Senior Quality Improvement Team

Scott Michael Bishop Information Technology Manager	Ian Sean Bolton Administrative Services Director
Stephen D. Brophy Rooms Division Director	Elizabeth Bugg Lounge Manager
Michael Andrew Burton Golf Services Manager	Kristine Le Cao Fitness/Spa Manager
Tony Choi Executive Chef	Jarrad Patrick Creagan Assistant Recreation Services Director

Exhibit 9.5c Elk Creek Resort's core values, vision, and mission.

NORDIC LIGHTS
RESORT & CONFERENCE CENTER

Strategic Quality Plan
2002

The vision of Nordic Lights Resort & Conference Center is to be the premier destination for world-renowned experiences.

The mission of Nordic Lights Resort & Conference Center is to empower our associates to make decisions that benefit themselves and the company; to provide our associates with opportunities to succeed and grow with the company; to provide our guests with exceptional service and unparalleled facilities; to instill the principles of Continuous Quality Improvement throughout the organization and our partners; to commit resources to enrich the community that we represent; and to prosper as a business and create a sound financial foundation.

The core values of Nordic Lights Resort & Conference Center are loyalty, integrity and ethics, mentoring, honesty and trust, diversity, positive attitude respect, empowerment, fun, teamwork, Continuous Quality Improvement, and a passion for excellence.

Exhibit 9.5d Nordic Lights Resort's core values, vision, and mission.

2004 Strategic Quality Business Plan

The Core Values of On the Rocks are mutual respect; hospitability friendliness; positive and consistent attitudes; knowledge; profitability; empowerment; reliability; ethics and integrity; trustworthiness; commitment to the company; giving back to the community; continuous quality improvement; and exceeding customers' expectations through consistency of products and services.

The Vision of On the Rocks is to be the premier destination for the ultimate resort experience.

The mission of On the Rocks is to offer quality of life, education, and training opportunities for internal customers; to provide lasting impressions through unique experiences and service, and by exceeding expections for external customers; to have lasting, loyal, and secure relationships, maintain consistent communication, with supplier partners; to promote a commitment to the environment, education, and economic stability in the community; and to be a progressive business focusing on financial goals and quality to improve the bottom line.

Exhibit 9.5e   On the Rocks' core values, vision, mission.

Together, the vision, mission, and core values tell others why we exist, how we think, and how we act. They spell out the governing ideas for the organization that answer the questions:

- What? (the vision)
- Why? (the mission)
- How? (the core values)

Strategic Goals

Once the vision and mission are defined and the aligned core values are selected to get us there, **strategic goals** must be articulated. The vision, mission, and values are the "what"; strategic goals are the "how." At the Detroit Athletic Club (DAC), strategic goals are developed after benchmarking the best in the hospitality business—elite clubs and leading hotel companies—that the senior DAC leaders believe are in line with the DAC's vision. The results of the analysis are used as the benchmark. At the Detroit Athletic Club an example of a strategic goal is to provide an extraordinary club experience that retains current members, attracts new members, and encourages all members to use the DAC frequently.

Strategic goals are action plans and each should be identified with a prime mover (associate, manager, supervisor, or team) that will drive the goal. Strategic goals for RARE Hospitality are identified in a rolling five-year plan that contains the strategic plan as well as the business plan. RARE continually assesses the macro elements (e.g., state of the economy, competitive benchmarking) of the environment as well as internal elements when formulating these plans. Internal elements can include capital structure, strength of leadership, relevance of the concepts, and current state of the organization's culture. In addition, many indicators of health (e.g., management retention, team member retention, guest satisfaction scores) are constantly reviewed and verified. Each strategic goal also should have a time frame indicating a start and end date. Strategic goals are broad definitions of how the organization intends to assign resources to move toward the mission and vision. They also describe how people intend to focus.

Those strategic goals that can be measured are placed on a **Balanced Score Card (BSC)**. This tool identifies the performance levels of the previous year and the targets for the new year and provides a means to measure actual current performance against the targets. Because the strategic plan drives change, the Balanced Score Card is a change process rather than a metrics project. There are strategies that "run" the business, and there are those that "change" the business. Only the "change" strategies are used in the measurement process.

There are five categories of strategies on the Balanced Score Card: 1) Financial 2) Marketing/Growth, 3) Organizational Effectiveness, 4) Human Resources, and 5) Customer Satisfaction. Some examples of considerations in strategizing are presented in Exhibit 9.6.

FINANCIAL
- Increase in overall dollar volume
- Increase in profit
- Productivity

MARKETING/GROWTH
- What to sell
- Who is the customer
- Pricing
- Advertising
- Promotions and sales
- Marketing
- New products
- Maintaining the competitive edge

ORGANIZATIONAL EFFECTIVENESS
- Process identification
- Organizational functions
- Staffing requirements
- Control procedures
- Technology
- Materials, equipment, and facilities
- Scheduling
- Hassle identification

Exhibit 9.6 Sampling of Strategic Goals

HUMAN RESOURCES
- External growth rate vs. internal talent
- Associate expectations
- Idea generation
- Associate training
- Associate selection
- Benefits
- Wage/salary administration
- Associate turnover rates

CUSTOMER SATISFACTION
- Feedback
- Areas for improvement
- Expectations

Exhibit 9.6   continued

Critical Processes

The **critical processes** are those that are necessary to meet the present and future needs of the organization's customers. Some examples of critical processes that we have already explored are the human resources process and the continuous quality improvement process. Critical processes help institutionalize our strategic goals and core values and indicate how we will execute the goals while staying consistent with the organization's values.

At the Detroit Athletic Club (DAC), the Five Points of Hospitality are part of the critical processes. In dealing with members and their guests all at the DAC are urged to always remember the following:

- Greet all members and guests with a friendly and sincere smile and strive to use member and guest names at all times.
- Anticipate needs and exceed expectations.
- Instill a positive impression of our club.
- Suggest – Discuss – Take Action – Follow Up
- Continuously improve

These processes describe the steps that we will use to interact with members and their guests to satisfy their needs and serve their expectations. Many of the critical processes describe what happens in the organization on a day-to-day basis, and they define how people should spend their time and focus their efforts. The processes also translate the vision, mission, core values, and strategic goals into action through behaviors and activities.

RARE Hospitality believes that quality can be a consistent competitive advantage. The ultimate measure of quality is guest satisfaction, which leads to guest loyalty. Several critical processes relate to guest satisfaction. Among the most important of these is the delivery of high quality food. Guests want team members to help them escape from the pressures of their world and make them happy. Guest loyalty is defined as the guest's intent to return to that restaurant. It is measured in terms of behaviors that may include: 1) guests who like to return frequently, 2) zealots who are frequent guests and talk about it to others, and 3) apostles who educate others to become loyalists. Apostles insist "this is my favorite restaurant and you must try it" to others.

Critical processes at RARE Hospitality are designed to affirm guests, lift their spirits, nurture the guests, and "show them love." Many of RARE's guests develop an abiding affection for a specific RARE restaurant location. There is a direct correlation between how the guest is treated, how their personal needs are answered, and their commitment to frequent a restaurant. Guests will abandon their loyalty to the competition if you use their names, create a bond with them, and consistently exceed their expectations.

Strategic Results

The outcomes produced in the organization are the **strategic** results. Each of RARE's restaurant concepts continues to grow same store sales (sales in an individual restaurant this year compared to sales in that restaurant last year) year after year. The market value of RARE has grown in six years from $100 million to $800 million. RARE Hospitality serves over 30 million people as guests in its restaurants each year. These guests could choose to take their food home in a box and eat at home, relaxing in familiar surroundings. Instead, they pay the RARE team members a "commission" (i.e., gratuity) to sit and enjoy the experience in the restaurant, on the restaurant's timetable. The guests are willing to do this because they want to feel the human touch, be served, and feel compassion. These are examples of strategic results.

Beginning with the vision and moving through the process described in Exhibit 9.7, the common goal of all is to achieve the desired results. Results are measured in financial, numerical, or binary terms (dollars, number progression, or a yes/no answer, respectively).

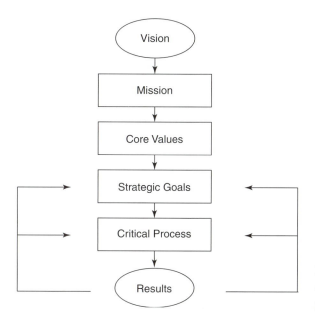

Exhibit 9.7 Strategic Quality Planning Process Model *(Source: HDS Services. Used with permission.)*

Note the alignment and the feedback loop in the **strategic quality planning process model.** Strategic goals may be altered based on what is learned in the critical processes. There is also a set of feedback loops between the results and the strategic goals and the results and the critical processes. The feedback continuously provides information for the alteration of strategic goals, if necessary. The primary end result is customer satisfaction.

HDS SERVICES
BALANCED SCORE CARD
Fiscal Year 2004

OUTCOME AREA	TARGET PERFORMANCE	CURRENT PERFORMANCE	BASELINE PERFORMANCE	MEASUREMENT TOOL	REPORTING FREQUENCY
1. Financial/Cost					
1.1 Increase gross profit dollars					
1.1a Increase new sales revenue					
1.1b Increase sales of P&Ls					
1.2 Increase pre-tax contribution					
2. Marketing/Growth					
2.1 Improve new business GPD growth (management and consulting)					
2.1a Increase sales closure rate					
2.1b Increase system/alliance relationships					
2.2 Improve client retention rate					
2.3 Strengthen HDS/HHA alliance by increasing the number of accounts sold and managed jointly					
2.4 Establish a tour-ready Center of Excellence in all regions/markets (*aggregate measure*)					

Exhibit 9.8 Balanced Score Card *(Source: HDS Services. Used with permission.)*

HDS SERVICES
BALANCED SCORE CARD
Fiscal Year 2004

OUTCOME AREA	TARGET PERFORMANCE	CURRENT PERFORMANCE	BASELINE PERFORMANCE	MEASUREMENT TOOL	REPORTING FREQUENCY
3. Customer Satisfaction 3.1 Overall client satisfaction 3.1a Sanitation of department 3.1b See value in HDS 3.1c Would recommend HDS 3.1d # of Red Flagged accounts 3.2 Improve internal customer satisfaction 3.2a Operations Staff Survey 3.2b Accounting 3.2c General Services					
4. Organizational Effectiveness 4.1 Enhance our primary vendors' satisfaction with our systems and processes 4.1a Satisfaction with primary vendors 4.2 Compliance with basic programs in all accounts over six months tenure 4.3 Balanced Score Card in place in all current units of operation by July '03, new units within 90 days					
5. Human Resources 5.1 Improve EEOC compliance 5.2 Fill open management positions 5.2a Unit Director 5.2b Assistant Director 5.2c Chef 5.2d Registered Dietitian 5.3 Improve associate satisfaction					

Exhibit 9.8   ccontinued

183

Balanced Score Card

The Balanced Score Card included as Exhibit 9.8 lists and compares current performance level (where we are now) with the targeted performance level (where we want to be based on the activation of all strategies). As the year progresses, we measure and record where we actually are in relation to the targeted levels. The strategies that support and drive performance improvement are listed as Initiatives/Action Plans to "change" the business. The BSC aligns performance measures with the activation of strategies that affect any particular metric. Performance measurement items are listed separately on the action plan and refer to the strategies that ultimately and directly affect that area of performance. Therefore, strategies are transformed into measurable results. All measures on the BSC must be quantifiable and consistent. The total number of measures per category should be held to approximately the top six.

The Strategic Quality Improvement Team (SQIT) is aware of the major items to measure each year, such as external and internal customer satisfaction, bottom line financial contribution, new business contribution, associate turnover, and new product development. These items form the preliminary framework for the BSC. The various Action Groups comprised of associates from all levels of the organization develop the initiatives and strategies that drive improvement.

The BSC will strengthen the customer relationships and create more organization advocates. It also improves communications and reinforces goals at all levels of the organization. The BSC identifies the customers' value needs and how the organization can support them and creates a higher level of accountability, more meaningful time frames, and strengthens team focus. There will be mileposts that are clearly identified along the way toward improvement. The BSC keeps everyone focused on the future, rather than the past.

Generating and Operationalizing the Strategic Quality Plan

Jerry McVety, president of McVety & Associates (a division of HDS Services), frequently consults with organizations (Exhibit 9.9) to generate **strategic quality plans** and *then* make *them* operational. His process begins with the organization's vision, mission, and core values. If these are already developed, the team of participants reviews them and determines if they are still relevant or need modification. If they are nonexistent, the team, facilitated by McVety, develops the vision, mission, and core values.

Following the review and agreement that the vision, mission, and core values accurately reflect what we want to create, why we exist, and how we act, the attention is focused on the organization's internal and/or external strengths, weaknesses, opportunities, and threats. This is often referred to as **S.W.O.T. analysis.**

Then participants are asked to help develop a "wish list" of the direction they hope the organization can move in the next one, three, and five years. Input from everyone is again critical at this point. After brainstorming the wish list, the group is divided into smaller groups and the wish list items are arranged by importance. (The Nominal Group Technique tool or some other method of prioritizing can be used to sort and rank the items.) These are recorded on a Strategic Directional Worksheet (Exhibit 9.10).

Here are some suggestions for using the worksheet:

- Identify items by both numbers *AND* key words to facilitate discussion.
- When working as a team to rank items (Column 3), try to achieve the ranking everyone can live with rather than a perfect score.

Exhibit 9.9 Strategic quality plan consulting.
(HDS Services. Used with permission.)

| | | | Year_____ |
| **Individual Section** | | **Group Section** | **Final Rankings** |
Column 1 (Least Important to You)	**Column 2** (Most Important to You)	**Column 3** (Group's Ideas of Important Issues)	**Column 4** (Rank Ordering of Items)
1)	1)	1)	1)
2)	2)	2)	2)
3)	3)	3)	3)
4)	4)	4)	4)
5)	5)	5)	5)
6)	6)	6)	6)
7)	7)	7)	7)
8)	8)	8)	8)
9)	9)	9)	9)

Exhibit 9.10 Strategic Directional Worksheet *(Source: HDS Services. Used with permission.)*

- Talk through each item. See how the other team members perceive this strategic direction. Be persuasive, not stubborn.

Once the small groups achieve consensus, the large team is reconvened and the mission is reviewed to determine whether it is still accurate and applicable. Then the team agrees on priority listings by year, beginning with the first year. The next step is to set target implementation dates for each issue, as well as tentative completion dates for each. A project manager is selected for each project and quantitative goals are established along with the frequency of measuring the progress.

Once all the information is gathered and assembled, there is a ceremonial signing of the approved vision, mission, core values, and the goals. The commitment for a strategic quality plan must be built by giving everyone the opportunity to freely enroll in the plan's direction. The best strategic quality plans are open-ended—they do not have finite goals but are based on the process of continuous quality improvement.

The strategic quality plan provides a framework or platform for how the direction takes place and there must be mileposts that we can clearly identify along the way. It may imply a change in the level of resources needed, either an increase or a decrease. A part of planning is to make some choices about what the organization will do, given the finite nature of the resources.

Strategic quality planning has, at its heart, the laying out of high priority directions for the future. A strategic quality plan is not a business plan, but its principles are translated into a business plan and various other plans (e.g., marketing plan).

Building Commitment

The process of planning is relatively easy compared to the process of **building commitment** for the strategic quality plan. As previously stated, if people are involved and asked to participate in planning the things that affect them, they commit to the plan. One way to understand each person's point of reference in this process is to ask the individual to complete the following statement:

This strategic quality planning process will be worth the effort if we
_____.

Some additional questions to ask at the onset of the planning process include the following:

- What is my personal definition of quality?
- What is our internal customers' definition of quality?
- What is our external customers' definition of quality?
- How does our organization's definition of quality fit with these definitions?
- How does our organization survive?
- How do we build customer loyalty and business?
- What does it mean to be a high performance organization?
- How can I contribute to providing memorable customer service?

Following a discussion of some or all of these questions, a commitment can be strengthened by giving team members the time to reflect on the shared vision, including how the individual fits into making the vision a reality. Each person has to be clear about where he or she wants to go. Only then can the individual help the organization, as well as herself or himself, get there. The vision must be compelling and the way to get there must be clear. Once the vision is clear, commitment is strengthened and we can determine how to move toward our goals together.

Plans, whether they are strategic quality plans, marketing plans, or training plans, are implemented by individuals (Exhibit 9.11), not organizations. The individual associate or manager must first decide to make the plan a reality, to take it from ideas on flip charts and from words in a document to actual practice in the daily workings of the organization. Each individual should identify just a few parts of the plan that he or she wants to make real in the next year. Then, take that project on by committing to personally doing what it takes to make it a reality in service of the organization's customers. The choices need to be specific, measurable, and appropriate to the goals of improving quality, and the assistance of others must be solicited in the process of transforming the ideas into realities.

Exhibit 9.11   Commit personally to doing what it takes to make the strategic quality plan a reality in service of the organization's customers. *(Source: HDS Services. Used with permission.)*

Implementation of a system for managing quality is a team effort at most organizations. So, too, at RARE Hospitality the implementation begins by constantly identifying the best practices within the organization's restaurant concepts as the baseline. The goal is to consistently present the attributes of each concept to their guests, executed perfectly and synchronous with the goals, by integrating the core values and individual behaviors. The RARE team strives to continue this course, adjusting as it progresses, and is relentless about continuous quality improvement.

Throughout the implementation of a strategic quality plan, the lines of communication must be open and used frequently. There is no such thing as communicating too frequently. Communicating stories of successful quality improvements demonstrates evidence of achieving results and stimulates others to strive even harder to improve quality. Often the process of strategic planning is more important for building commitment than the actual implementation of every detail of the plan. Communication and interaction throughout the process help build commitment that fuels improvements in quality.

Summary

The process of strategic quality planning is, in many ways, the core process in any high performance service organization. The other processes should be established and continuously improved in service of the organization's strategic quality plan. In that regard, the strategic quality planning process is embedded in all of the other processes. The strategic quality planning process is the heart and soul of the organization; everything we do each day should be consistent with the elements of this plan. This is the only way that we can achieve the desired results on the road to becoming a high performance service organization.

Key Terms

Balanced Score Card (BSC)—Identifies the performance levels of the previous year and the targets for the new year and provides a means to measure actual current performance against the targets.

Benchmarking—Helps an organization study a process at another organization and adapt, modify, and apply the process at their own organization.

Building Commitment—Inviting people to be involved and participate in things that affect them.

Core Values—Guide the planning process, decision making regarding which plans are the highest priorities, and the resulting action to make the plans become reality.

Critical Processes—Necessary to meet present and future needs of the organization's customers.

Enrollment—Results when people are free to choose and individual choice stems from the individual's personal vision.

Mission—Seeks to clarify how the organization adds value by contributing to the world in a unique way.

Mission Statement—A mission statement answers the questions: Why do we exist? What is our purpose? In what interest do we function/operate?

Personal Vision—Provides the view of the future for which a person exists.

Shared Vision—A vision that all embrace in the organization.

Statements of Core Values—(same as core values)

Strategic Goals—The action plans; each should be identified with a prime mover (associate, manager, supervisor, and team) that will drive the goal.

Strategic Planning Process—Provides a comprehensive approach that helps position the organization for the long-term and addresses key strategic issues in the near term.

Strategic Quality Plan—Result of Strategic Quality Planning Process Model.

Strategic Quality Planning Process Model—Ties together vision, mission, core values, strategic goals, critical processes, and results.

Strategic Results—Outcomes produced in an organization.

S.W.O.T. Analysis—Organization's internal and/or external strengths, weaknesses, opportunities, and threats.

Targets—Action Group Teams (AGT) develop strategies to reach or surpass these; must be measurable.

Vision—A picture of the ideal future; answers question "what do we want to create?"

Vision Statements—(same as vision)

Review Questions

1. What is the definition of vision, mission, and core values?
2. What is the link between a personal vision and an organizational vision called? How is it created and strengthened?
3. What are core values and how do they fit together with vision and mission?
4. What are strategic goals of an organization? What do they typically address in the strategic quality plan?
5. How is a strategic quality plan generated and made operational?
6. How can you build commitment for a strategic quality plan?

Activities in Your Organization

Listed below are some activities designed to reinforce the key chapter concepts in your organization. If you are a student and not currently working in the industry, interview an industry leader about one of these topics.

1. Your personal vision is the purpose for which you exist. Separate yourself from the intensity of daily demands and revisit your personal vision. Begin by

asking two questions: Why do I exist? What do I want to create? Based on the answer to these questions, where will you focus your energies to create what is not yet created and fulfill a purpose not yet complete? How will you devote your energy, talents, and time to continue to make the vision a reality? When you have contemplated these questions and written a note or two for each, ask yourself why it is important to answer the questions. Repeat the "why" question a couple more times to really get to the heart of the personal vision. Reflect on what makes you uniquely you. Ponder what it is you care about. Meditate about for whom and for what you are important. How does your personal vision tie to the organization's vision? What are the similarities? What are the differences? Is there alignment?

2. Your core values can be identified by thinking about the historic and modern-day leaders that you admire most and the values that they exhibit. If you identify the values of the mentors and role models you are most drawn to, it will help you articulate your values. Use these at the start of the process of discovering your own values (i.e., benchmark others' values). Begin to record a list of your personal core values. Ask and answer the following questions:
   - What values are attractive to me in others (historic and modern-day leaders, role models) and why?
   - Who do I admire and why?
   - Who do I try to emulate because I respect the other person?
   - What do I believe in and why?
   - What do I stand for and why?
   - What do I hold as precious above all else and why?
   - How do I act repeatedly and why?
   - What behaviors characterize me?
   - What behaviors have I committed to practicing?

   Now compare these values to those in your organization. How do your personal values tie to the organization's values? What are the similarities? What are the differences? Is there alignment?

3. Review the Balanced Score Card (BSC) included in Exhibit 9.8. What metrics would be included on a BSC for your organization? Create a BSC for your organization using the blank BSC tear-out sheet in the appendix. For your organization, list and compare current performance levels (where you are now) with targeted performance levels (where you want to be based on the activation of all strategies). What strategies that support and drive performance improvement would be listed as Initiatives/Action Plans to "change" the business? Who generates all of the strategies, and who provides the framework for the general items in the BSC in your organization? What items form the preliminary framework for the BSC in your organization? Are the measures on the BSC for your organization quantifiable and consistent? What does the BSC do to strengthen customer relationships and create more organization advocates? What does the BSC do to improve communications and reinforce goals at all levels of the organization? How does the BSC identify the customers' value needs and how the organization can support them? How does the BSC create a higher level of accountability, more meaningful time frames, and strengthen team focus in your organization? How does the BSC keep everyone in the organization focused on the future rather than the past?

Reference

Senge, Peter. *The Fifth Discipline: The Art and Practice of the Learning Organization.* New York: Doubleday/Currency, 1990.

Relevant Web Sites

Best Practices in Resolving Customer Complaints:
http://govinfo.library.unt.edu/npr/library/papers/benchmrk/bstprac.html
Detroit Athletic Club Web Site:
http://www.thedac.com/
HDS Services Web Site:
www.hdsservices.com
RARE Hospitality International, Inc. Web Site:
http://www.rarehospitality.com
Strategic Quality Plan:
http://www.co.mecklenburg.nc.us/cobudget/pdf/Introduction/StrategicQualPlan01.pdf
Strategic Quality Planning Through Quality's Five Dimensions (by Richard Winder):
http://www.ldri.com/articles/93stratqualplan.html
University Club of MSU Web Site:
http://www.universityclubofmsu.org
What Is Strategic Planning?:
http://www.allianceonline.org/FAQ/strategic_planning

Chapter
10 *Assessing Quality*

Connecting to the guests and associates and delivering to them what they need are the foundation of a solid, growing, profitable organization.
Kevin Brown
Chief Executive Officer
Lettuce Entertain You Enterprises, Inc.
Chicago, IL

Learning Objectives

1. Understand why assessment is so important in the CQI process, how assessment reduces the need for inspections, and why it is critical to conduct baseline surveys.
2. Be able to identify who the customers are and what their needs are and understand the differences between quality in fact and perceived quality.
3. Describe quality indicators and what the information reveals.
4. Detail some of the questions that might be asked on external customer satisfaction surveys and internal customer satisfaction surveys.
5. Explain the role of benchmarking in assessment.
6. Describe some of the recognition awards, including the criteria for selection, associated with the results of the assessment process.

Feedback is an extremely important piece of the Continuous Quality Improvement process. We get feedback from many sources by conducting assessments of our products and services. For example, feedback comes in the form of verbal comments from vending machine customers, completed guest satisfaction surveys from hotel guests, completed associate satisfaction surveys from internal customers of an office coffee service company, written suggestions placed into a suggestion box by those who are customers in a hospital cafeteria, and listening to customers in a restaurant. If we do not know what our internal and external customers think, there will be little improvement.

Assessment Defined

Walter A. Shewhart, Ph.D., a pioneer of the quality movement, worked with the management team at Western Electric in the early part of the twentieth century. Western Electric had 45,000 associates, which was a huge organization in those days. Over 25% (over 10,000) of these associates were quality inspectors. What we have learned since that time, especially from the teachings of Dr. Deming, is that "inspecting quality in" is ridiculously expensive and a waste of associate talent. Today we define quality as doing the right things right the first time. Therefore, most inspectors were removed from the workplace, and the burden of quality production fell on the shoulders of each and every associate involved in the process.

So, if there are no quality inspectors, how does management know that quality targets are being achieved and customers are satisfied? Now inspecting is accomplished on a random basis; the initial step is to manage by walking around (MBWA). Many Malcolm Baldrige Award winners, including The Ritz-Carlton Hotel Company, use this management practice in every area of each hotel. At HDS Services, MBWA is part of the company's culture. We stay as close to the internal and external customers as we can on a continual basis. If management is present at the sites of production and point of customer service, the targeted levels of customer satisfaction are more readily met.

Assessing Customer Wants

Basically, almost everyone is a customer, including *associates*. Remember the Model for Doing the Right Things presented how associates, customers, and financial expectations interact and how all three must be considered before implementing change. Change cannot be successful unless the requirements of all three are met. Never improve customer service at the expense or detriment of your associates; highly motivated and happy associates make a company very successful.

Current external customers should never be taken for granted or forgotten. At HDS every client customer is engaged in a business meeting with one of three company executives on an annual basis. This special attention separates HDS from other firms in the industry and sends the message that we are customer focused. Some of these meetings are conducted president to president. Remember, current clients are the company's best sales representatives.

Prospective customers are an excellent source of information regarding how the company stacks up against the competition and how the company's products and services can be modified to better meet the needs of future clients.

It is crucial to remain in contact with **former customers** as well. We can learn a great deal from them because they had the opportunity to compare our products and services with those of other organizations. Who knows, it also might be possible to bring them back to the current client base. At HDS Services, we pay special attention to former customers. Rather than send the normal sales materials to them, we contact them regularly to inform them about the new programs and events at HDS, and how we might assist them in reaching their operational and strategic objectives.

There are two other groups of customers that are important for success. Most organizations come in contact with government groups and associations that support industries. These customers have an effect on the company's processes and the way we operate. The other customer group is the company's vendors. These suppliers are your business partners. Dr. Deming, in one of his 14 points (see Chapter 2), indicated that management must not base purchasing on price alone; management should partner with as few suppliers as possible and treat them as customers. If we bring the vendors into our work processes, quality delivery will be greatly enhanced. When the vendors are involved in the operating processes of HDS Services and the delivery of quality services to the client facilities, client satisfaction will be at a higher level.

Now that we have defined the various types of customers, we must look at what the customer wants before we can assess whether or not we are delivering it. For starters, we know the customer wants us to meet the specifications and the technical aspects of the product and service. This is referred to as **Quality in Fact.** Today, quality goes well beyond meeting these technical requirements, however. At HDS Services, when a client does not compliment us about the on-site associate and the regional support staff, we know there is an underlying issue. Our quality objectives include making the association with HDS a memorable one. In other words, we want our customers to *love* the services. This is referred to as **Quality in Perception.** The best-known classic example of this is the love affair people have with their Harley-Davidson motorcycles. The company successfully sells the romance of the machine. A customer is not considered to be loyal until they *rave* about the service or product. (The totally loyal Harley Davidson customers even tattoo the Harley Davidson logo on themselves!)

There are several methods of determining what the customer wants. One involves bringing a customer into the product development process, which involves the highest level of contact and loyalty. At HDS we meet with the client [our customer] in a business setting at least once each month. This meeting is led by the operations-based regional director and the regional vice president. We also get feedback from customers via comment cards. In many of the HDS operations, there are customer focus groups that meet regularly and give management continuous feedback and formal surveys are conducted on a quarterly basis. (The written comments on survey forms are also very important because they often provide the specifics behind the score. As much specific information as possible is desired.) These five types of communication provide management with a tremendous amount of information about client requirements.

Keep in mind, however, that client requirements change on an ongoing basis, especially in the health care arena. Continued assessments must be conducted on a regular basis using criteria common to previous assessments so that comparisons can be made. This will ensure consistency. The goal of assessments is to measure the results. The tools used to do this can be any or all of the following:

- Formal, periodic surveys
- Focus groups
- Customer comments submitted via associates or obtained when MBWA
- Complaint analysis
- One-on-one discussions
- Customer involvement in research and development—product tastings, asking for ideas

The data gathering has to be based on sampling or other statistically sound methodology and all associates should be involved as much as possible in data gathering to keep them close to the external customer. We must determine how to accurately measure and interpret the data so the information gathered will be specific to the quality improvements sought.

What happens to the results of the customer surveys? At HDS these survey results are used as the foundation of our business plan for the upcoming period. Teams are assigned to the issues, and the tools are put into action for resolution. At HDS we also share the results with our customers, including internal customers. In addition, the survey information is used to identify the critical processes in the company. The results of these processes must be measured for continuous improvement. A company should be tracking and measuring at least 10 critical processes at any given time. How do we identify the critical processes? The customer survey results will be a good source for several of the processes. Then, it is important that management and teams ask this question: What is it that we do that is essential? When the processes are measured, be certain that they are measured based upon the customer's perspective.

Once measured, we also put assessment information on the Quality Board at HDS Services (please see Chapter 7, Exhibit 5.7) so it will be read by all. The board contains information such as:

- Sanitation score graphs
- Customer comment cards
- All survey results
- Notes from customers
- Safety graphs
- Food cost graphs
- Revenue graphs
- Signs with messages about quality
- Newsletters

Quality Indicators

The implementation schedule for quality management has six steps (see Chapter 11). The second step, assessing internal and external customer satisfaction levels and the financial ramifications of meeting customer requirements, is done early in the implementation schedule because we need a base assessment on which to form positive change. (Some organizations elect to use an outside consultant to conduct the initial surveys or baseline assessment.) When we examine the financial ramifications early in the implementation phase, we are more compelled to accurately budget for the costs of quality.

All teams and individual members have the same goal: to improve quality. Members realize that the first step is to define the **valid quality requirements,** based on the needs and expectations of customers. **Quality indicators** then are used to measure the degree and/or frequency of conformance to the valid requirements. In other words, how do we objectively know that the level of quality created and delivered is in line with what the customer wants and expects? Think of these indicators in the same way you would think of daily specials offered on a restaurant menu (Exhibit 10.1). The frequency in which each special menu item is ordered determines the popularity of the menu item. Both (frequency and popularity) are assessments.

Exhibit 10.1 Quality indicators may be thought of in the same way that you would think about the frequency of guests ordering daily specials from a restaurant menu. Both are assessments. *(Source: Dorling Kindersley Media Library. Used with permission.)*

Some examples of quality indicators follow:

- the number of telephone calls answered after 30 seconds in an auto dealership service center
- the number of unsatisfactory items on a foodservice sanitation checklist
- the number of customers that return freshly laundered, unused shirts with broken buttons
- the number of times a banquet set-up has to be changed on the banquet event order in a hotel
- the number of times customers complain because the windshield washing container at a gas station doesn't have any washing fluid
- the number of reports past due in the corporate office of a management company
- the number of late deliveries by an overnight express delivery service company
- the amount of time customers at a theme park have to wait in line to enjoy the most popular roller coaster ride

Quality indicators are used to establish the current level of quality; this provides a **baseline** which consists of the results of the initial quality assessments and surveys. The baseline helps an organization know where it is beginning. Use baseline data for both internal and external customers.

So, how do we know what questions to ask in the base survey? In the case of HDS Services, we had been conducting informal surveys for many years, so we had a good idea of what areas to cover. If you are not confident about what to ask in the initial survey, you can get the information directly from your customers by way of asking a key question and completing an **Affinity Diagram.**

Assemble about 8 to 12 customers in one room, and ask them to respond to this question: Exactly five years from today, you are talking to a peer or friend about HDS Services. What points would you use to express your belief that HDS is the leader in the industry and what suggestions for improvement would you make?

They can make as many responses as they want, (the more the better). Have them write their responses on small Post-it™ notes and arrange the responses in groups of similar ideas. This will form an Affinity Diagram similar to the one in Exhibit 10.2.

Networking	Training	Financial	Marketing
• Hire a visionary at HDS • All HDS regional directors of operations and regional vice presidents are on the same page • Strategic Planning Process is excellent, involves the client • HDS e-mail system efficient • Networked recruiting works • HDS is a synergistic company	• Training tools—Good • TQM training • Managers Development Program-Plus effective • Manuals/videos are comprehensive • Need more hourly associate training at start up	• Always hit budget • Look for economies each year • Financial reporting system • Industry stats report helps us	• Proposals informative • Sales associates talented • Selected markets make sense

Communications	Products	Corporate
• Very responsive • Visits by corporate executives are excellent • Compliance is strong • Client assessments a good tool • HDS associate visits monthly • Regional office very close	• State of the art programs • Food quality is excellent • We now have all the tools in our department • Many value added services	• Excellent reputation as a company • Strong leadership • Privately held • Many tenured executives

Exhibit 10.2 Affinity diagram. *(Source: HDS Services. Used with permission.)*

In this case, the suggestions for questioning came directly from the customer group. This information is used both as an assessment tool and for the short- and long-term strategic planning process.

Quality indicators also are used to track the number (and/or percentage) of hassles, errors, changes, or improvements over time. Some quality indicators used at HDS Services include the following:

- the number of unsatisfactory items on a sanitation checklist
- the number of errors in filling a menu request
- the number of reports past due
- compliance with acceptable hot food temperature
- the number of calls answered after 45 seconds
- the number of late deliveries

The quality indicators help track the process and the effect of changes to the process. They are selected after choosing the problem/opportunity, but before analyzing root causes of hassles, problems, obstacles, or barriers, since they are an integral part of fact-based decision making. Quality indicators are a way of involving everyone in identifying, tracking, analyzing, and improving the quality of the work that we are all doing. They also assist the high performance service organization by involving associates, giving them many opportunities to participate, and letting them see first-hand the trends in the levels of quality created and delivered.

External Customer Assessment at HDS Services

At HDS, external customer satisfaction is assessed using **surveys.** Initial surveys are conducted by the Assessment Team and include client (e.g., hospitals) surveys, associate surveys, client's customer (e.g., hospital employees) surveys, and vendor surveys. All future survey results are compared to this base measurement, and all process changes that have taken place since the time of the base surveys (1992) have produced higher levels of satisfaction in most cases. Subsequent survey results indicate this to be factual. For example, Exhibit 10.3 represents the results of a client-based survey (for the years 1994 through 2003) and compares it to future expectations.

CLIENT SATISFACTION SURVEY
1994 - 2003

TOGETHER
TQ
FOR QUALITY®

Issue	Grade	1994	1995	1996	1997	1998	1999	2000	2001	2002	2003
Sanitation	A	18.5%	20.4%	22.5%	31.2%	28.0%	28.4%	34.4%	32.0%	25.0%	35%
	B	69.1%	69.6%	56.5%	46.7%	51.0%	54.1%	41.7%	48.8%	49.0%	55%
	C			14.5%	16.8%	17.0%	13.5%	19.8%	14.4%	24.0%	9%
	D	12.4%	10.0%	6.5%	3.8%	4.0%	4.0%	4.1%	3.2%	2.0%	1%
	F				1.5%	0.0%	0.0%	0.0%	0.0%	0.0%	0%
	TBD								1.6%	0.0%	0%
Food Service Quality	A	25.7%	34.6%	18.6%	23.7%	28.0%	35.1%	35.4%	35.2%	28.0%	36%
	B	68.3%	63.4%	70.5%	64.5%	61.0%	52.7%	54.2%	53.6%	60.0%	52%
	C			9.4%	11.8%	11.0%	10.8%	8.3%	10.4%	11.0%	10%
	D	6.0%	2.0%	1.5%	0.0%	0.0%	1.4%	2.1%	0.0%	1.0%	1%
	F								0.0%	0.0%	1%
	TBD								0.8%	0.0%	0%
Customer Satisfaction	A	9.0%	26.9%	16.0%	25.9%	23.0%	27.4%	30.2%	34.4%	31.0%	33%
	B	85.0%	67.4%	67.0%	57.2%	57.0%	61.6%	56.3%	52.8%	53.0%	56%
	C			16.0%	15.6%	19.0%	9.6%	13.5%	11.2%	14.0%	9%
	D	6.0%	5.7%	1.0%	1.3%	1.0%	1.4%	0.0%	0.0%	1.0%	2%
	F								0.0%	1.0%	0%
	TBD								1.6%	0.0%	0%
Creativity / Innovation	A	13.3%	32.7%	40.5%	35.0%	37.0%	37.4%	37.5%	40.8%	45.0%	45%
	B	76.8%	55.8%	41.0%	48.0%	45.0%	44.4%	38.5%	42.4%	37.0%	39%
	C			13.5%	15.7%	17.0%	15.9%	21.9%	12.8%	16.0%	14%
	D	9.9%	11.5%	5.0%	1.3%	1.0%	2.3%	2.1%	1.6%	2.0%	1%
	F								0.0%	0.0%	1%
	TBD								2.4%	0.0%	0%
Cost Effectiveness	A	20.8%	23.5%	43.0%	47.4%	36.0%	56.2%	45.8%	44.8%	38.0%	38%
	B	73.3%	68.7%	33.0%	40.5%	45.0%	34.2%	38.5%	40.0%	42.0%	47%
	C			21.0%	9.5%	13.0%	5.5%	10.4%	12.0%	16.0%	12%
	D	5.9%	7.8%	3.0%	1.3%	6.0%	4.1%	4.2%	1.6%	3.0%	3%
	F				1.3%	0.0%	0.0%	0.0%	0.0%	1.0%	0%
	TBD							1.1%	1.6%	0.0%	0%
Regulatory Requirement Compliance	A			54.5%	49.5%	43.0%	59.7%	52.1%	55.2%	49.0%	59%
	B	New	New	33.5%	38.4%	47.0%	34.7%	31.3%	34.4%	39.0%	35%
	C			7.0%	10.7%	7.0%	4.2%	9.4%	6.4%	10.0%	5%
	D			5.0%	1.4%	3.0%	1.4%	4.2%	0.0%	2.0%	1%
	F								0.0%	0.0%	0%
	TBD							3.0%	4.0%	0.0%	0%
On-Site Team	A	13.7%	35.8%	41.0%	43.4%	26.0%	44.4%	44.8%	46.4%	44.0%	53%
	B	82.9%	58.6%	51.5%	43.5%	58.0%	44.4%	40.6%	40.0%	45.0%	38%
	C			6.0%	13.1%	12.0%	11.2%	11.5%	7.2%	9.0%	8%
	D	3.4%	5.6%	1.5%	0.0%	4.0%	0.0%	1.0%	0.0%	2.0%	0%
	F								0.0%	0.0%	1%
	TBD							2.1%	6.4%	0.0%	0%

Exhibit 10.3 Sample Client Survey Results *(Source: HDS Services. Used with permission.)*

Issue	Grade	1994	1995	1996	1997	1998	1999	2000	2001	2002	2003
Unit Support	A	33.2%	41.0%	50.5%	68.0%	55.0%	48.6%	46.9%	59.2%	52.0%	58%
	B	62.3%	55.1%	41.5%	23.7%	35.0%	44.6%	39.6%	34.4%	41.0%	36%
	C			8.0%	6.9%	9.0%	4.1%	10.4%	3.2%	6.0%	5%
	D	4.5%	3.9%	0.0%	1.4%	1.0%	2.7%	3.1%	1.6%	1.0%	1%
	F								0.0%	0.0%	0%
	TBD								1.6%	0.0%	0%
Value HDS	Yes	93.4%	94.0%	98.0%	98.6%	99.0%	98.6%	90.6%	96.0%	96.0%	97%
	No	6.6%	6.0%	2.0%	1.4%	1.0%	1.4%	3.1%	2.4%	4.0%	3%
	TBD							6.3%	1.6%	0.0%	0%
Recommend HDS	Yes	89.0%	94.0%	98.0%	98.6%	100.0%	98.6%	88.5%	92.8%	94.0%	97%
	No	11.0%	6.0%	2.0%	1.4%	0.0%	1.4%	2.1%	4.0%	6.0%	3%
	TBD							9.4%	3.2%	0.0%	0%

Issue		1994	1995	1996	1997	1998	1999	2000	2001	2002	2003
Return Rates	Sent			120	135	124	159	170	172	205	196
	Returned			64	77	78	78	96	125	171	181
	%		35.0%	53%	57%	63%	49%	56%	73%	83%	92%

NOTE: 1994 and 1995 was a 1–10 scoring system. To compare 1996 "grade" score, 9 and 10 were considered A, 1–4 was a D/F grade. These were the only breakdowns available from 1994–1995. Starting in 2000 the range was 5 for an A to 2 for an F. Starting this year the following was utilized.

A	=	4	C+	=	2.3
A–	=	3.7	C	=	2
B+	=	3.3	C–	=	1.7
B	=	3	D+	=	1.3
B–	=	2.7	D	=	1
			F	=	0

CLIENT ISSUES IMPORTANCE RANKING (Asked to pick top 3)	1995	1996	1997	1998	1999	2000	2001	2002	2003
Keep costs low	1	1 (32)	2 (38)	2 (31)	3 (35)	1 (48)	2 (62)	2 (77)	1 (85)
Enhance quality/appearance of meals	2	2 (28)	1 (48)	1 (37)	1 (39)	2 (44)	1 (71)	1 (85)	2 (80)
Interdisciplinary teams work	3	3 (22)	3 (28)	3 (30)	2 (38)	3 (40)	4 (43)	3 (65)	3 (55)
Hire/train better staff	4	4 (21)	3 (28)	6 (21)	5 (25)	5 (31)	5 (35)	6 (36)	6 (35)
Innovative methods of service	5	5 (16)	4 (26)	5 (26)	4 (28)	4 (35)	3 (45)	4 (55)	4 (52)
Provide more specials/theme meals	6	6 (9)	7 (6)	7 (19)	7 (10)	7 (17)	6 (21)	8 (22)	7 (26)
Improve kitchen/dining environment	7	7 (6)	6 (8)	8 (8)	8 (8)	8 (15)	7 (16)	7 (29)	8 (23)
Improve meal delivery system	8	8 (5)	5 (22)	4 (28)	6 (23)	6 (25)	*	5 (42)	5 (51)
Other						9 (2)	8 (4)		

* Improved kitchen/dining equipment omitted from 2001 survey.

Exhibit 10.3 continued

Internal Customer Assessment at HDS Services

As with external customers, internal customer satisfaction should be assessed regularly. The survey in Exhibit 10.4 is distributed to all HDS Services internal customers at least on an annual basis. The internal customers complete the survey and return it to the unit director in the organization. The unit director is responsible for tallying the results.

The survey data from client's customers (Exhibit 10.3) and associates (Exhibit 10.4) are summarized and compared with the targets for customer satis-

Associate Satisfaction Survey

In order to create an atmosphere of open communication and good working conditions for each associate, we hope you feel free to share your opinions with us on any subject that you believe has an effect on this facility, our customers, and associates. Open communications are of extreme importance if we are to successfully work together as a team in achieving common goals.

By answering the following questions as honestly as you can, we can identify concerns that you are dealing with while performing your daily duties.

To keep this survey confidential, please do not put your name on it unless you wish to do so or would like individual feedback. Your cooperation in completing and returning this survey is appreciated.

Please Circle the Number That Best Describes Your Opinion for Each Statement:

5–Strongly Agree   4–Agree   3–Neither Agree or Disagree   2–Disagree   1–Strongly Disagree

A.	5 4 3 2 1	I like working at _____.
B.	5 4 3 2 1	The people that I work with are a team.
C.	5 4 3 2 1	I enjoy serving the customers here.
D.	5 4 3 2 1	I feel that my job has importance in satisfying our customers.
E.	5 4 3 2 1	I take a great deal of pride in my work.
F.	5 4 3 2 1	I do my work very well.
G.	5 4 3 2 1	I have the tools I need to do my job.
H.	5 4 3 2 1	My supervisors here help me to do my job better.
I.	5 4 3 2 1	I believe I have received adequate training to do a good job.
J.	5 4 3 2 1	I know what is expected of me by my supervisors and what my responsibilities are.

Exhibit 10.4   Associate satisfaction survey. (*Source: HDS Services. Used with permission.*)

K.   5 4 3 2 1   My supervisors are really interested in my work performance, and let me know how I am doing on a regular basis.

L.   5 4 3 2 1   If I bring a concern to my supervisor, I will get a response.

M.   5 4 3 2 1   I feel that the working conditions are good and/or improving.

N.   5 4 3 2 1   I have a voice in decisions affecting my work area and/or job functions and department.

O.   5 4 3 2 1   All employees are treated equally by supervisors.

P.   5 4 3 2 1   I feel that I am treated fairly by supervisors.

Q.   5 4 3 2 1   I have the opportunity to learn new skills if I choose and advance to another position.

R.   5 4 3 2 1   Communication between employees and supervisors is good.

S.   5 4 3 2 1   I understand how the job I do impacts or affects people working in other areas.

For existing HDS accounts:

T.   5 4 3 2 1   The programs/tools that came from HDS Services have helped improve quality.

U.   5 4 3 2 1   HDS employees are working to improve quality.

V.   5 4 3 2 1   HDS employees and unit employees work together as a team.

W.   YES/NO   I understand the role of HDS Services.

X.   YES/NO   I am aware that HDS Services is interested in management development candidates from units they manage.

Please Answer the Following:

1. What suggestions do you have that you believe would enable you to do your job better?
_____
_____
_____

2. What one suggestion do you have that you believe would improve our service to our customers? (i.e., residents/patients, associates, and community)
_____
_____

3. What do you like most about your job?
_____
_____

4. What do you like least about your job?
_____
_____

5. List two or more ideas of how you suggest changing the item listed in #4.
_____
_____
_____

6. List any suggestions for reducing costs or increasing revenue in the food service department.
_____
_____
_____

ANY ADDITIONAL COMMENTS:
_____
_____

Return to _____ By _____

Exhibit 10.4   continued

faction in the Balanced Score Card (see Chapter 9). Then, issues, hassles, obstacles, problems, new ideas, and negative trends are assigned to an Action Group for root cause analysis, PDCA development, and application of the CQI process. Further measurement is conducted for results and success.

Of the 24 opinions asked in the Associate Survey on pages 199–200, 6 are tracked over time. These opinions have to do with critical processes such as togetherness, training, expectations, performance feedback, communications, and the adequacy of HDS tools/programs. These 6 opinions are:

1. The people that I work with are a team.
2. I believe I have received adequate training to do a good job.
3. I know what is expected of me by my supervisors and what my responsibilities are.
4. My supervisors are really interested in my work performance, and let me know how I am doing on a regular basis.
5. Communication between employees and supervisors is good.
6. The programs/tools that came from HDS Services have helped improve quality.

Another way to get feedback from internal customers is to use the survey presented in Exhibit 10.5. This information not only includes the hassle, prob-

---

List the top 10 "hassles, problems, obstacles, or barriers" you encounter in our company that cause rework, waste, and frustration. Another way to think about this is to list things that get in the way of doing your best in your day-to-day activity. We would also like you to estimate the time that is consumed each week by these "hassles."

Describe the hassle, problem, obstacle, or barrier   **Wasted time per week**

1. _____   1. _____
2. _____   2. _____
3. _____   3. _____
4. _____   4. _____
5. _____   5. _____
6. _____   6. _____
7. _____   7. _____
8. _____   8. _____
9. _____   9. _____
10. _____   10. _____

Now, list below the top 10 things that help you get your work done effectively and efficiently.

1. _____
2. _____
3. _____
4. _____
5. _____
6. _____
7. _____
8. _____
9. _____
10. _____

Exhibit 10.5   Internal customer assessment. *(Source: Verne Harnish, Gazelles, Inc.)*

lem, obstacle, or barrier, it also addresses the time wasted per week and ideas for getting the job done effectively. As an alternative, the statement, "It seems stupid to me when . . ." could be completed by each internal customer to try to pinpoint hassles.

ASSOCIATE SATISFACTION SURVEY
1994 - 2003

Issue	Grade	1994*	1995**	1996** 187 Responses	1997** 222 Responses	1998** 121 Responses	1999** 123 Responses	2000** 189 Responses	2001** 155 Responses	2002** 193 Responses	2003** 281 Responses
RDO Support	A	47.9%	48.6%	54.8%	45.4%	50.0%	47.6%	50.8%	55.8%	60.9%	63.9%
	B	42.3%	48.0%	30.6%	30.0%	33.3%	38.1%	33.0%	27.9%	26.1%	28.5%
	C			11.8%	17.5%	16.7%	14.3%	12.4%	8.8%	10.3%	4.7%
	D	9.8%	3.4%	1.0%	3.1%			3.2%	5.4%	2.2%	2.2%
	F			1.8%	4.0%	0.0%	0.0%	0.6%	2.1%	0.5%	0.7%
Communication with Corporate is Good?	Yes	94.0%	83.3%	87.4%	87.4%	92.6%	79.5%	82.8%	86.3%	90.1%	95.4%
	No	6.0%	16.7%	12.6%	12.6%	7.4%	20.5%	17.2%	13.7%	9.9%	4.6%
Clinical Support	A	30.6%	38.0%	59.8%	48.9%	59.8%	43.8%	53.7%	50.5%	57.8%	54.9%
	B	52.5%	57.8%	25.2%	33.0%	26.8%	38.4%	29.6%	25.2%	29.7%	31.2%
	C			10.3%	11.3%	11.0%	10.9%	12.0%	16.5%	10.7%	11.6%
	D	16.9%	4.2%	2.8%	6.0%	2.4%	1.4%	1.9%	5.8%	1.1%	2.3%
	F			1.9%	0.8%	0.0%	5.5%	2.8%	2.0%	0.7%	0.0%
Clinical Programs/ Tools	A						41.2%	47.3%	43.3%	44.4%	48.8%
	B						39.2%	37.8%	42.5%	43.1%	42.0%
	C						15.5%	12.8%	10.0%	11.7%	6.8%
	D						3.1%	1.4%	3.3%	0.1%	2.4%
	F						1.0%	0.7%	0.9%	0.7%	0.0%
Purchasing Program	A	21.9%	17.5%	22.6%	19.3%	33.3%	28.2%	26.4%	35.1%	33.9%	38.3%
	B	65.5%	68.9%	54.0%	48.9%	48.6%	41.9%	49.1%	41.4%	51.3%	50.0%
	C			18.2%	24.4%	17.1%	23.9%	15.7%	20.3%	11.5%	9.5%
	D	12.6%	13.6%	4.4%	6.3%	0.0%	6.0%	6.9%	3.2%	3.2%	1.3%
	F			0.8%	1.1%	1.0%	0.0%	1.9%	0.0%	0.1%	0.9%
Signature Programs	A	17.9%	7.2%	24.6%	32.8%	27.3%	28.0%	24.0%	31.0%	40.8%	34.1%
	B	79.5%	79.2%	46.0%	42.4%	53.6%	52.0%	46.8%	51.4%	41.4%	50.9%
	C			22.1%	21.5%	16.4%	16.0%	25.3%	15.5%	15.9%	14.6%
	D	2.6%	13.6%	7.3%	2.8%	0.9%	3.0%	3.3%	0.7%	1.9%	0.4%
	F				0.5%	1.8%	1.0%	0.6%	1.4%	0.0%	0.0%
MDP Effectiveness	A	7.9%	24.0%	24.3%	25.7%	29.1%	32.5%	25.8%	25.5%	31.0%	32.2%
	B	85.7%	71.8%	49.3%	48.0%	42.7%	45.6%	44.5%	46.8%	47.5%	48.2%
	C			22.9%	21.8%	26.4%	17.5%	24.5%	19.7%	16.0%	15.0%
	D	6.4%	4.2%	3.5%	4.5%	1.8%	2.6%	4.5%	4.0%	4.9%	3.2%
	F						1.8%	0.7%	4.0%	0.6%	1.4%
Other Support & Tools from HDS	A	34.2%	30.4%	48.8%	41.4%	47.5%	39.4%	41.8%	41.7%	51.4%	49.4%
	B	58.4%	68.3%	42.6%	45.8%	40.7%	47.2%	45.7%	45.3%	40.8%	44.5%
	C			7.5%	10.0%	9.3%	11.8%	10.9%	10.9%	6.1%	5.3%
	D	7.4%	1.3%	1.1%	2.3%	2.5%	1.6%	1.1%	1.4%	1.7%	0.8%
	F				0.5%	0.0%	0.0%	0.5%	0.7%	0.0%	0.0%
Career Opportunities	Yes	91.0%	87.0%	96.5%	94.1%	91.7%	94.0%	91.4%	94.5%	94.8%	95.3%
	No	4.0%	11.0%	3.5%	5.9%	8.3%	2.0%	8.6%	5.5%	5.2%	4.7%
	Undecided	5.0%	2.0%	0.0%	0.0%	0.0%	4.0%	0.0%	0.0%	0.0%	0.0%
Fair Promotion	Yes	92.0%	78.0%	90.0%	87.8%	91.7%	85.0%	93.0%	87.3%	85.9%	92.8%
	No	6.0%	20.0%	10.0%	12.2%	8.3%	6.0%	7.0%	12.7%	14.1%	7.2%
	Undecided	2.0%	2.0%	0.0%	0.0%	0.0%	9.0%	0.0%	0.0%	0.0%	0.0%
Replacement HDS personnel efficient	Yes	69.0%	69.0%	80.0%	86.3%	92.2%	68.0%	84.0%	82.9%	90.6%	87.7%
	No	26.0%	1.0%	20.0%	13.7%	7.8%	12.0%	16.0%	17.1%	9.4%	12.3%
	Undecided	5.0%	30.0%	0.0%	0.0%	0.0%	20.0%	0.0%	0.0%	0.0%	0.0%

Exhibit 10.6 Sample associate satisfaction survey results. *(Source: HDS Services. Used with permission.)*

Issue	Grade	1994*	1995**	1996** 187 Responses	1997** 222 Responses	1998** 121 Responses	1999** 123 Responses	2000** 189 Responses	2001** 155 Responses	2002** 193 Responses	2003** 281 Responses
Agree personal gain	Yes	92.0%	93.0%	95.5%	95.2%	95.7%	90.0%	91.0%	92.0%	94.2%	97.5%
with trained	No	5.0%	7.0%	4.5%	4.8%	4.3%	3.0%	9.0%	8.0%	5.8%	2.5%
promotables	Undecided	3.0%	0.0%	0.0%	0.0%	0.0%	7.0%	0.0%	0.0%	0.0%	0.0%
	Yes	82.0%	84.0%	81.0%	83.3%	77.6%	73.0%	76.0%	85.6%	86.5%	91.0%
Fair Salary/Benefits	No	1.0%	0.0%	0.0%	0.0%	22.4%	17.0%	24.0%	14.4%	13.5%	9.0%
	Undecided	17.0%	16.0%	19.0%	16.7%	0.0%	10.0%	0.0%	0.0%	0.0%	0.0%
Value of HDS seen	Yes	86.0%	87.0%	97.0%	95.7%	94.8%	90.0%	93.8%	93.6%	93.8%	95.3%
by Client	No	12.0%	13.0%	3.0%	4.3%	5.2%	2.0%	6.2%	6.4%	6.2%	4.7%
	Undecided	2.0%	0.0%	0.0%	0.0%	0.0%	8.0%	0.0%	0.0%	0.0%	0.0%
Vision Supported	Yes	94.5%	99.0%	96.0%	97.2%	96.5%	97.5%	93.8%	95.8%	98.9%	96.4%
by Actions	No	5.5%	1.0%	4.0%	2.8%	3.5%	2.5%	6.2%	4.2%	1.1%	3.6%
	Undecided	0.0%	0.0%	0.0%	0.0%	0.0%	0.0%	0.0%	0.0%	0.0%	0.0%
	Yes	91.5%	90.0%	94.4%	95.7%	92.2%	91.7%	93.6%	94.4%	97.3%	95.3%
Empowerment		8.5%	8.5%	10.0%	5.6%	4.3%	7.8%	8.3%	6.4%	5.6%	2.7%	4.7%
		0.0%	0.0%	0.0%	0.0%	0.0%	0.0%	0.0%	0.0%	0.0%	0.0%

*   Unit Directors Only
** All Salaried Unit Employees

Note: In 2000, 468 surveys were sent with 189 responses (40.4%).
In 2001, 473 surveys were sent with 155 responses (32.8%).
In 2002, 487 surveys were sent with 193 responses (39.6%).
In 2003, 470 surveys were sent with 281 responses (60.0%)-33% were anonymous

Exhibit 10.6 continued

Another example of a survey that can be used is presented in Exhibit 10.6. This exhibit shows the results of the HDS Salaried Associate Satisfaction Surveys over a seven-year period. Using such a presentation of these data makes it possible to track trends in associate satisfaction.

The information in the issue column was developed by the Senior Quality Improvement Team (SQIT) prior to the first survey in 1992, and it is visited annually for possible modification. When the data are summarized, the primary issues/ideas are assigned to Action Groups for recommended resolution and further measurement.

These results are indicative of success with the process of Continuous Quality Improvement (CQI). (It is very obvious that we had quality issues at the time we decided to commit to the management of and Continuous Improvement of Quality.)

There are two other indicators that are directly connected to customer and associate satisfaction: associate turnover and client attrition. At HDS, we track both of these key indicators. They are presented in Exhibit 10.7 and Exhibit 10.8. The results of the Salaried Associate Survey in Exhibit 10.7 are directly linked to turnover, which is measured and reported quarterly on the Balanced Score Card.

Many interventions have resulted from the information received from associate surveys at HDS Services. The most notable include the following:

1. Regional director of operations support survey questions have decreased the number of account assignment changes. A general manager position has been added to further support major accounts.
2. Corporate support survey questions have increased account visits by vice presidents and regional vice presidents of operations.
3. Clinical service support survey questions have added consultant and dietitian account visits in the healthcare market segment.

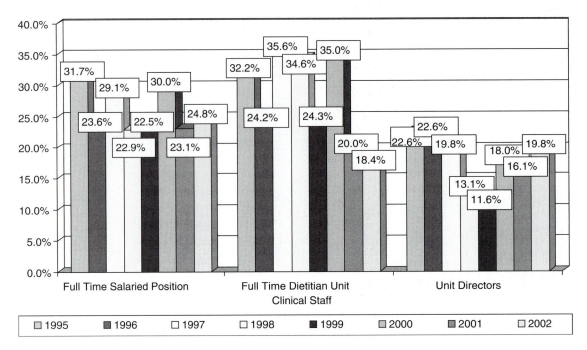

Exhibit 10.7 Unit salaried position turnover rate. *(Source: HDS Services. Used with permission.)*

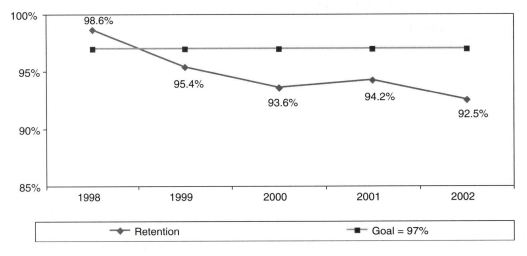

Exhibit 10.8 Account retention. *(Source: HDS Services. Used with permission.)*

4. Fair promotion and transition of management staff survey questions have resulted in posting of all management position openings and added a dietitian recruiter.

The key issues that surfaced in the most recent associate survey included corporate support deficiencies, supplier/purchasing problems, and ineffectiveness of segments of the organization's management development program. All three of these concerns have been addressed in the following year's strategic business plan.

The value of assessing and tracking these two metrics (**account retention** and **associate satisfaction**) in other hospitality organizations and service businesses should be apparent. Associate satisfaction levels are critical to monitor in any organization that depends on its associates to create and deliver quality products and services. For example, the satisfaction of route drivers in a vending company, the satisfaction of servers in a restaurant, the satisfaction of cooks and chefs in a hotel banquet kitchen (Exhibit 10.9) are all related to the levels of satisfaction that the external customers experience at the hands of those creating the products and services. Account retention is an essential metric for hotel management companies who live or die by the number of hotels they sign to management contracts and retain. Account retention is also a critical concern for vending companies that not only want to retain clients but maximize the revenues from each vending machine in service with each client.

Exhibit 10.9 Satisfaction of cooks and chefs in a hotel banquet kitchen is related to the levels of satisfaction that the external customers experience at the hands of those creating the products and services. *(Source: HDS Services. Used with permission.)*

Group Input

Group input is another way to obtain associate input and is accomplished in a group setting, specifically during a meeting of a Work (i.e., departmental) Group Team. The meeting could include a discussion around the following questions:

- What would enable you to do your job better?
- What would enable us to serve our customers better?
- What made you angry today?
- What took too long?
- What was the cause of any complaint?
- What was misunderstood?
- What was wasted?
- What was too complicated?
- What was just silly?
- What job took too many people?
- What job involved too many actions?

These questions help break the ice at the beginning of the meeting, bring a focus to the topics for the meeting, and give each person, no matter how shy or introverted, an opportunity to say something that contributes to the work of the team and the improvement of quality in the organization.

Sanitation Scores

Another assessment tool is **sanitation scores**. Once again, this assessment is essential for any hospitality organization or service business since customers expect cleanliness and safety. This assessment is done system-wide and two awards are given annually: the Mop Bucket Award for most improved sanitation is given to the unit that has the greatest numerical improvements and the highest corporate sanitation score is given to the unit with the highest score for the year. The corporate average sanitation scores are tracked each year and shared with all. (Please see Exhibit 10.10 for the corporate sanitation averages; the goal for all units is 90%.)

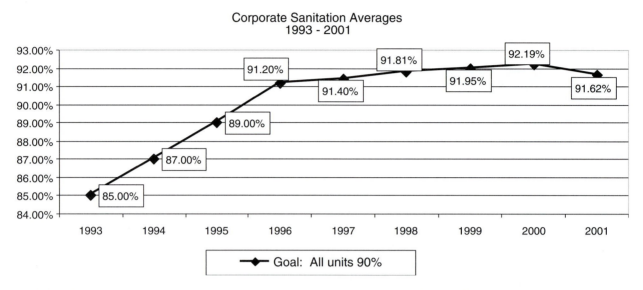

Exhibit 10.10 Corporate sanitation averages. *(Source: HDS Services. Used with permission.)*

Benchmarking

Benchmarking is really another means of assessment since we learn from others. It is a process to compare others within an industry or organizations outside of an industry to help identify, understand, and adapt the best practices and processes. The goal is to use data from others to improve our performance. Benchmarking avoids "reinventing the wheel." When HDS Services was establishing its retail operations, we asked the question: What are the best retail operations in the world to benchmark? After the list was developed, the HDS leaders visited these retailers and learned from them. When HDS rolled out the retail program, it had applications from the best retailers. Benchmarking helps achieve breakthrough improvements and accelerate change and quality improvements. It can help achieve stretch goals and overcome a common problem abbreviated as "NIH"— Not Invented Here. Benchmarking also helps the organization anticipate and head off competitive threats.

Using the Assessment Information at HDS Services

In terms of the client survey results, the notable changes in 2000 included an improvement in sanitation, improvement in customer satisfaction, and, most importantly, the ability to keep the costs low. The key issues from the clients' (external customers') perspectives to include in the 2001 business plan were: cost effectiveness, regulatory compliance, unit support, value of HDS Services, recommending HDS Services, and customer satisfaction.

Through 2002, 684 suggestions were submitted for improvement and 456 were implemented as part of the quality improvement program. Each year, a

Corporate Quality Improvement winner is selected and each year a CQI Checkup is performed, including the customer packet/quality board, associate meeting, work/action groups, patient/resident survey, cafeteria associates survey, associate opinion survey, annual report, and standards assessments (i.e., pre-meal temperatures/taste, refrigerator/freezer logs, dish machine temperature logs, and weekly sanitation checklists.) HDS Services also monitors the inventory timeliness.

In terms of sales and marketing, the number of proposals submitted is tracked. This figure is compared to the number of accounts signed, for both consulting and management services. Each year, the sales activity is tracked in terms of the number of follow-ups on leads, proposals completed, decisions pending, and signed contracts. HDS Services also recognizes/celebrates the award winners each year (Exhibit 10.11). Exhibit 10.12 is a listing of all annual awards presented at HDS Services.

Key Elements of Quality Improvement

Of the four key elements of quality improvement (customer focus, measurement driven, every one being involved, and all management systems aligned), two are covered in this chapter. Associates that are customer focused will succeed. This is precisely why HDS Services has an Associate Code and has developed Associate Commitments (Exhibit 10.13). Organizations that get as much feedback as possible, and continually measure the results, will be successful because they always know exactly where they stand in the eyes of the customer.

At HDS, we literally welcome complaints, because this is the feedback we need to improve our service levels. We make it very simple for customers to complain through monthly face-to-face meetings, monthly surveys, and the formal annual survey process. It is when we do not receive feedback that we immediately get concerned. In this case we contact the client immediately and conduct the survey process telephonically.

Every complaint gets a response, in terms of recognition that it was registered, and what the resolution will be. If a complaint is not recognized, the customer will go elsewhere.

The complaint process helps instill ownership in those associates on the front line. Most associates are proud of the work they do, and complaints tend to "hit home."

Customer concerns are viewed as opportunities to display our ability to respond. Like the hotel industry, the food service business is very sensitive to customer's changing requirements, thus there tends to be more constructive criticism registered.

We share all complaints with the associates, and make them very visible. In fact, the quality boards in each operation contain all feedback, both positive and negative. Again, we do not perceive complaints as negative, but as opportunities for improvement.

Summary

Assessment is essential to the CQI process to establish the baseline and regularly determine the progress toward improvement. Assessment reduces the need for inspections. Quality indicators, based on the requirement of customers, are used to measure the degree and/or frequency of conformance to the requirements and then help track the progress toward CQI. The regular and ongoing assessment of

Exhibit 10.11 A team recognition. *(Source: HDS Services. Used with permission.)*

Award	What is recognized/celebrated
Chairman of the Board	Highest achievement by a member of the corporate/regional staff
Clinical	Best demonstrated clinical program in patient/resident, physician, and community services
Culinary Excellence	Chefs who contribute the most to upgrading and expanding the culinary program
Entrepreneur	Unit with the most creative approach to changes in the income stream
Gold Performer	Most effective hourly associate with respect to customer service, attendance, and loyalty
Outstanding Sanitation	Unit performance in sanitation: "most improved" and "highest score overall"
Quality	Most improved unit of operation; criteria include customer satisfaction, standards implementation, and financial performance
Recruiting	Associate who refers the most individuals to HDS Services overall and contributes the most to the recruiting effort
Rookie of the Year	Best performance by a first-year manager who has been a director for at least nine months
Smart Services	Individual who contributes the most to the joint efforts of HDS Services and HHA Services
Team	Highest performing regional director of operations (RDO) and their units; criteria include client/customer satisfaction survey results, contribution/financial performance, sanitation, basic program standards, and team spirit

Exhibit 10.12 HDS Services annual awards. *(Source: HDS Services. Used with permission.)*

HDS Services Associate Code
To serve all customers with respect, honesty, and sincerity. Customers will be greeted with a
name, a smile, friendliness, and a commitment to quality.

HDS Services Associate Commitments
Honor * Discipline * Service

- Know and pursue the HDS Services vision
- Serve all customers with respect, dignity, and a positive attitude
- Identify a mentor for yourself and be a mentor for someone
- Always be "Inspection Ready"
- Be an HDS ambassador . . . communicate positively and with appropriate people
- Take pride in your appearance
- Be empowered—know your goals
- Keep in mind that it is everyone's job to develop people
- Take part in the quality process by submitting suggestions for improvement
- Demonstrate the right attitude and the appropriate actions
- Manage the financial side as if you personally owned it
- Honor the Associate Code
- Remember that we are a **TEAM**
  - Together
  - Everyone
  - Achieves
  - More

Exhibit 10.13   HDS Services associate code and associate commitments. *(Source: HDS Services. Used with permission.)*

both external customers and internal customers helps establish feedback that can be used to point to areas that need improvement. In other words, they assist in our goal of giving the customer precisely what the customer wants.

Key Terms

Account Retention—Number of clients signed to management contracts that are kept and maintained.

Affinity Diagram—Arranging responses from members of a focus group into groups of similar ideas.

Associate Satisfaction—Assessment of internal customers.

Baseline—The current level of quality; consisting of the results of the initial quality assessments and surveys.

Benchmarking—Process to compare others within an industry, or organizations outside of an industry, to identify, understand, and adapt best practices and processes.

Current External Customers—Should never be taken for granted or forgotten.

Feedback—Extremely important piece of the Continuous Quality Improvement process. We get feedback from many sources by conducting assessments of our products and services.

Former Customers—A great deal to be learned from them because they had the opportunity to compare our products and services with those of other organizations.

Group Input—Another way to obtain associate input is in a group setting, specifically during a meeting of a Work (i.e., departmental) Group Team.

Prospective Customers—Excellent source of information regarding how the organization stacks up against the competition and how the organization's products and services can be modified to better meet the needs of future clients.

Quality in Fact—The customer wants us to meet the specifications and the technical aspects of the product and service.

Quality Indicators—Used to measure the degree and/or frequency of conformance to the valid requirements.

Quality in Perception—Wanting customers to *love* the services.

Sanitation Scores—This assessment is essential for any hospitality organization or service business, since customers expect cleanliness and safety. Also is done system-wide and two awards are given annually: the Mop Bucket Award for most improved sanitation is given to the unit that has the greatest numerical improvement and the highest corporate sanitation score is given to the unit with the highest score for the year.

Surveys—Tools used to assess external customers and internal customers.

Valid Quality Requirements—Based on the needs and expectations of customers.

Review Questions

1. What are the categories of customers?
2. What are quality indicators? Give some examples including the information that they reveal.
3. Why is assessment an ongoing critical step in the management of quality improvements? How do baseline surveys fit into the assessment process?
4. What are some of the questions that might be asked on an external customer survey? An internal customer survey?
5. How does benchmarking fit into the assessment process?
6. How does assessment tie to recognition? What are some examples of possible recognition awards?

Activities in Your Organization

Listed below are some activities you can do in your organization. These are designed to reinforce the key chapter concepts. If you are a student and not currently working in the industry, interview an industry leader about one of these topics.

1. The first step in improving quality is to define the valid requirements, based on the needs and expectations of customers. Quality indicators then are used to measure the degree and/or frequency to which the level of quality created and delivered is in line with what the customer wants and expects. On a sheet of paper list five top requirements that external customers expect from your organization. Now list at least two quality indicators that you will use to establish the baseline and the current level of quality using the results of the initial quality assessments and surveys. Regularly measure the progress toward improving quality of those requirements. Be certain to develop the quality indicators as numbers and/or percentages of changes and improvements. Now repeat the process for internal customers. Share the ideas with a colleague who is also a leader in your organization and ask that colleague for feedback and ways that you could improve the definitions of the requirements and/or the quality indicators. Then, select three of the quality indicators and actually

establish a baseline and measure the change in the indicators for the next three months. What did you discover? What do these data tell you? What are your next steps in improving quality?

2. Review Exhibit 10.4, the Associate Satisfaction Survey. Select questions from the samples provided for a survey of a selected group of associates in your organization. Now survey this group of associates using the questions that you selected. Meet with a different group of associates from your organization and ask them the same questions that you used in the survey. Now compare the responses obtained from the survey and those obtained in the meeting. What are the similarities? What are the differences? If there were differences, why do you think that happened? How will you use this information to improve quality in your organization? What will you do to involve these associates in the process of improving quality?

3. The recognition and celebration of efforts to improve quality are essential to the process of maintaining a commitment to CQI. Review the annual awards presented at HDS Services. Now compare these to the annual recognitions that your organization awards. Are there ideas in the list that you could implement at your organization? If so, which ones? Is it possible to modify or adapt the HDS awards to your organization? If so, how do you plan to do so? What did you learn by benchmarking HDS Services' annual awards?

References

Harnish, Verne and Kathleen Harnish. *Implementing Total Quality Management,* Boulder, CO: Career Track. 1994.

Brossard, Michael. *The Memory Jogger.* Metheun, MA: Goal/QPC, 1988.

Relevant Web Sites

HDS Services' Mission Statement:
http://www.hdsservices.com/our-mission.htm
Measuring Service Quality, Customer Satisfaction, and Customer Value in the Hospitality Industry (by Haemoon Oh):
http://www.extension.iastate.edu/hrim/current/customervalue.htm
Quality and Customer Management:
http://www.sonic.net/~mfreeman/quality.htm

Chapter

11 *Implementing Quality*

Expectation meetings are an essential part of the Clients for Life *program, and have been an effective addition to the HDS CQI process. These annual meetings bring all of our external customers together to tell us what their most important requirements are. We then design the account's Balanced Score Card to achieve these objectives correctly the first time and in the appropriate time frame.*

Mary Westcott
Vice President Operations
HDS Services
Farmington Hills, MI

Learning Objectives

1. Understand how restricting forces create changes in the way we manage the business, how the principles of quality do not change, and how today's high performance managers differ from managers of the twentieth century.

2. Be able to explain the six steps in implementing the principles and philosophies of quality management at your organization and the areas of cost in doing so.

3. Be able to talk about the costs associated with developing a quality management system.

The quality improvement system that is described in this book helps transform managers from enforcers, firefighters, trouble shooters, and police officers into coaches, facilitators, teachers, and leaders for improving change. Consequently, we shift the paradigm from viewing employees as just "workers" to valuing associates as important internal customers and resources who help the organization address the needs, wants, and expectations of external customers. Paradigm shifts resulting from implementing a managing for quality system are presented in Exhibit 11.1.

The paradigm shift from . . .	The paradigm shift to . . .
Making assumptions about customers	Clearly defining customers' requirements
Believing defects/hassles are inevitable	Believing defects/hassles are preventable
Results orientation	Process orientation
Department focus	Customer focus
Resisting change	Leading change

Exhibit 11.1 Paradigm shifts resulting from implementing a managing for quality system.

Once an organization's management team understands the new management philosophy, how do we implement it at all other levels of the organization? Time, patience, and thoroughness are vital requisites to a successful transition. This chapter outlines the basic steps in the implementation process. Our goal is to present the steps as a process. We will also identify the most common types of costs associated with implementation.

Restricting Forces—Spanning the Centuries

How does an organization go about implementing the techniques and systems outlined in this book? And how do the leaders of the organization know that these systems, techniques, and philosophies will work in the twenty-first century? **Restricting forces** vividly point out that many of the techniques that worked in the past will not work in the future. The most commonly presented restricting force is that line associates today are short sighted and are looking for immediate gratification and self-indulgence, as opposed to the mid-twentieth century staff member who was tenured, loyal, appreciative of having a job, and had a strong value system.

Major shifts in this country's culture and the socioeconomic environment continue to change at what seems like warp speed. The availability and flow of information via personal computers is changing the way traditional industries and companies operate. The products, services, and experiences we offer and how we create and deliver them are changing the most. How we manage our resources and develop people and how we improve our service levels has not changed (and more than likely will not change), but these processes may be augmented by more advanced versions of proven techniques.

Diversity will continue to be an issue in the twenty-first century due to the ever changing demographics of our society, especially the tremendous increase in the Hispanic population and other minorities. In fact, more synergism can be achieved in the future because of expected increased diversity, thus tapping into some of the hidden strengths of the organization.

One of the overriding challenges in the early years of the twenty-first century, barring any major catastrophe such as economic depression or major global military conflict, will be minimizing associate turnover and maintaining service quality levels to preserve the competitive edge. One of the prime issues we face today is how associates relate to the organizations that they join. They, like external customers, are searching for an experience and want to be treated with dignity and respect. When associates are treated as peers by management—rather than as peons or the help—the associates, the external customers, and the organization all benefit. Being friendly, helpful, and encouraging works with internal customers as well as external customers. In a high performance service organization that exists to create and deliver products, services, and experiences, both the associates and the external customers must interact to co-create the experiences. This contributes to the sense of pride felt by associates and it builds customer loyalty. It gives associates good reasons to come to work and encourages customers to refer others to the organization.

Twentieth Century Management versus High Performance Management

Twentieth century managers had a management style that was very different than that required in high performance organizations. High performance organizations began with the end of the 1900s. The high performance management style has different requirements than those that led to success in the twentieth century. Twentieth century managers made assumptions; high performance managers clearly define requirements. Twentieth century managers believed that hassles were inevitable; high performance managers know that hassles can be prevented and eliminated. Twentieth century managers were results oriented; high performance managers know that the process must be the focus. Twentieth century managers focused on strengthening departments in their organizations; high performance managers have a laser focus on their customers, both internal and external. Twentieth century managers often resisted change; high performance managers create change.

High performance managers have an open mind regarding the continuous improvement of quality. They realize that they do not have all the answers; therefore, they accept the opinions, comments, and suggestions of those who create and deliver experiences, services, and products in the organization. High performance managers are leaders who facilitate improvements guided by the personal visions of those in the organization and in concert with the organization's shared vision. High performance managers know that the better way to manage helps build associates' pride. These associates then exceed their customers' expectations, and in doing so, deliver higher than expected financial results for the organization.

The Six Steps of Implementation

In all, there are six basic steps for implementing quality improvement on an organization-wide basis:

1. **Education**—an enrollment process
2. **Assessment**—a baseline is critical

3. **Addressing the Burning Issues**—commitment is manifested
4. **Identification of Critical Processes**—also need to decide how the process will be measured
5. **Realigning the Processes**—the most difficult step
6. **Continuous Improvement**—"the journey"

We will talk about these steps using the process that took place at HDS Services as an example.

Education

A part of the educational segment of the plan had already been completed because several of our people were "quality improvement management literate," and many of the organization's executives understood most of the basic principles. The next piece in the educational drive was to teach the principles of managing and improving quality to all senior management, operations executives, marketing associates, and corporate support associates (Exhibit 11.2). Because of our initial perception of quality improvement as a very complex process and technically encumbered, we hired a consultant to take us through the initial steps, or at least to identify the burning issues. In February 1992, two months after the initial approval of the plan, all senior managers went through the first educational process, which was coordinated by the consultants.

Exhibit 11.2 Education, the first step in implementing a system for managing and improving quality, begins with all senior management, operations executives, marketing associates, and corporate support associates. *(Source: HDS Services. Used with permission.)*

The first objective of the session was to get enrollment from everyone. This was accomplished by reviewing the present standards and relating them to the true definition of "quality," our assessment process, and our systems for improvement. While part of this was practical, it was extremely inconsistent, and it was conducted in the absence of a corporate vision. However, most everyone enrolled at that particular meeting.

The agenda for this first session included:

- defining quality
- defining natural variation
- brainstorming
- using the nominal group technique
- using other basic tools (such as cause and effect analysis and the PDCA cycle)

- discussing Dr. Deming's 14 points
- discussing the quality improvement organizational structure
- comparing management styles between those companies that have a plan to manage quality and traditional organizations, and
- organizing and planning the implementation of the management of quality throughout the HDS system

Groups were established to manage the initial transition and to convert HDS Services into an organization that not only professed a commitment to Continuous Quality Improvement, but also "walked the talk." A Steering Team, or Organizational Planning Group, was assigned to oversee management and coordination of the transition. They assigned associates to each of the groups and ensured that the topic of "quality" was on the agenda of each and every meeting. A Management Practices Team was given the responsibility of integrating quality into every position description, every policy, and every procedure within HDS Services. We were given a three-month window of time to complete these tasks because the educational step for our largest associate group, unit management associates, was scheduled for June 1992.

A Measurement Team also was assigned to determine what we were going to monitor and measure as *critical processes* throughout the organization. These processes would include customer (both internal and external) satisfaction, associate turnover, client retention, and other important areas. A Recognition Team was assembled and assigned the task of planning how HDS associates at all levels would be recognized for achievement in the future, both as teams and as individuals, with an emphasis on teams.

A Communications and Education Team was given responsibility for general communication of quality matters throughout the organization, including the establishment of the quality review document called the *QNews*. Their first major challenge was to educate all unit management associates and front line supervisors on the principles of the management of quality. Sometimes this education took place one-on-one (Exhibit 11.3); other times it took place in groups. Finally, an Assessment Team was assembled to determine what and how areas of our business would be assessed and to accomplish baseline assessments in key areas such as customer satisfaction.

Exhibit 11.3 Sometimes quality education takes place one-on-one. *(Source: HDS Services. Used with permission.)*

Between February and May 1992, all corporate and unit-level policies, including the personnel policies, were revised, the *QNews* (an HDS quarterly publication devoted to quality) was established, recognition procedures were established, an education plan was adopted, the baseline assessments were completed, critical processes for measurement were established, a vision and corporate mission were finalized, the core principles or values were published, and the senior management team was 100 percent enrolled. We were ready to take on the next challenge of taking the new principles to our unit managers and supervisors.

Since 1968, it has been normal practice to conduct an Annual Managers Conference for all corporate and regional associates and unit managers. In 1992 this group consisted of 120 food service executives. It was a three-day meeting entirely devoted to quality improvement. In addition to the education process, each attendee signed the Quality Commitment Scroll, which remains permanently displayed in the organization's corporate headquarters in Farmington Hills, Michigan. A celebration was conducted at that meeting and has been duplicated each year thereafter. Everyone left the meeting enrolled in the principles of continuous improvement of quality and committed to implementation on an organization-wide basis. After the meeting our target was to achieve some form of implementation and compliance within a 12-month time frame.

We made all of our external customers aware of our plans to implement the principles and conducted the first customer surveys that summer. These surveys had surprising results: 20 percent of our clients had concerns about the level of service and 7 percent would not recommend HDS if requested. The level of satisfaction among internal customers (associates) was reported at a similar level, with major concerns about the purchasing program, corporate management's concern about its people, and concern about the level of services generated by our support groups in the corporate and regional offices. In other words, it was not difficult to find key processes that required intervention for improvement and monitoring. In addition, we chose one other key process to monitor on an organization-wide basis: sanitation. Our first organization-wide assessment for sanitation yielded a score of about 80 percent, which was well short of our personal goals.

We quickly learned one important thing about the educational process: not every operating unit manager and supervisor needs to learn all the technical aspects of quality improvement before starting its practice at his or her facility. However, we did emphasize that they all understand the basic principles of quality, customer focus, using the basic tools, assessment, measurement, and continuous improvement. Today, this quality education process is applied on a quarterly basis with all new management associates attending the weeklong session.

Leadership in a quality improvement effort initially must be top-down, until others in the organization can become familiar with this six-step process to drive the changes and improvements from the bottom-up. It is the personal involvement of and commitment from the leaders at HDS Services that helped others voluntarily enroll in the quality improvement process. The senior management of the organization led the way by setting the strategic direction of the organization and the strategic long-term goals. At HDS Services our commitment to continuously improving quality continues to challenge all of the senior managers in the organization to accept the responsibilities of leadership.

To summarize, the education process must include a basic summary of the requirements for improving quality. The individuals participating must understand the reasons why the improvement of quality is important and they must understand the principles of quality improvement. To work in any organization, the management of quality improvements must be carefully planned, communicated to all, and coordinated by a group of individuals. The program must be an all-encompassing commitment based on voluntary enrollment by all concerned in the process.

Assessment

This second step in the process of implementation must be done quantitatively. As previously stated, baseline assessments must be conducted with two major groups, external customers (clients) and internal customers (associates). The format for client evaluations at HDS Services was consistent throughout the organization and addressed overall service, associate competency, program effectiveness, response to requirements, and standards compliance. A separate format was developed for external customer groups such as client associates, patients, and catering customers. Baseline assessments were conducted in each operating unit during the initial stages of implementation and have been conducted at each new facility start up since 1992. The baseline survey forms the foundation for continuous improvement and assists HDS in quantifying its value to the customer over time. Again, the assessment information must be factual and we must be able to rate and numerically quantify it. Results of assessments must be posted on the department's quality board and circulated to client management.

Every attempt must be made to standardize the survey formats on an organization-wide basis, because comparisons in the future must be free of exceptions and the degree of improvement must be meaningful. Assessments must be done with the Quality Triangle in mind. There are three basic considerations to make before making any quality-related decisions, as illustrated in Exhibit 11.4. We cannot please the client at the expense of the associates or the financial plan; the needs and expectations of all three in the triangle must be balanced.

Exhibit 11.4 The Quality Triangle *(Source: Verne Harnish, Gazelles, Inc. Used with permission.)*

The goal of assessment is to show the current situation. If a company does not know where it is at the moment (the baseline), it is impossible to accurately chart a course for where it wants to go. The other crucial part of assessment is to define the desired levels of quality in the critical processes. Part of that definition is created by reviewing the organization's vision, mission, and core values. Each or all may need to be redefined and refocused to highlight the continuous improvement of quality. Once these elements have been reviewed, the strategic goals can be assessed and redefined, if necessary, toward the new focus on quality.

Other ways to assess the current situation include the utilization of the Malcolm Baldrige National Quality Award criteria (leadership, customer satisfaction, human resources utilization, information and analysis, quality assurance of products and services, quality results, and strategic quality planning).

Some organizations establish indicators to use for assessment that can be used with the tools of the trade (Chapter 8) or separately. For example, the organization could use a log of customer complaints to identify the 5 or 10 most frequent complaints and then work to define a process to minimize or eliminate each, starting with the most frequent one. The assessment may include focus groups, a review of general trends, a review of some of the costs of quality (described later in this chapter), or a survey of the opinions of associates to identify trends in their needs, wants, and expectations.

One final suggestion for assessment lies in the area of benchmarking. Sometimes the best source of ideas comes from studying, adapting, and modifying the best practices at other companies. If benchmarking is used for assessment, why not benchmark the winners of the Malcolm Baldrige National Quality Award?

Prior to benchmarking, the infrastructure for quality improvement must be in place at the organization. That includes the vision, mission, values, strategic goals, and processes for continuous quality improvement. Once these are in place, the process of benchmarking can help the organization improve the levels of quality created and delivered.

QUALITY IMPROVEMENT SUGGESTION

NAME _____   POSITION _____

UNIT _____   IMMEDIATE SUPERVISOR _____

DESCRIBE YOUR IDEA FOR IMPROVING QUALITY WITHIN HDS SERVICES

_____

_____

_____

_____

CLASSIFICATION OF YOUR QUALITY IMPROVEMENT SUGGESTION

(Check All That Apply)

☐ Saves Time   ☐ Decreases Cycle Time
☐ Saves Money   ☐ Improves Job Satisfaction
☐ Saves Supplies   ☐ Decrease Paperwork
☐ Improve Customer Satisfaction   ☐ Increase Productivity
☐ Improves Work Flow   ☐ Elimination of Repeating a Process
☐ Improves Safety   ☐ Improves Communication
☐ Other _____

DESCRIBE THE BENEFIT OF YOUR SUGGESTION

_____

_____

_____

_____

_____   _____
Employee Signature   **Date**

DO NOT WRITE BELOW THIS LINE

QI REVIEWED BY SQIT – Date: _____   QI REFERRED TO WORK GROUP OR ACTION GROUP

QI Implemented Within Company: ☐ Yes   ☐ No   Date: _____

Date: _____   Coordinator: _____

QI Not Implemented/Reason: _____   Action Taken By Group: _____

_____   _____

_____   _____

Exhibit 11.5 Quality Improvement Suggestion *(Source: HDS Services. Used with permission.)*

Address the Burning Issues

Major dehassling sessions were conducted in all areas of HDS Services, including departments in the corporate offices, regional offices, and in the various client facilities. Most of the "burning issues" were discovered in these sessions, although some came forth in the form of quality improvement suggestions from associates. All units of operation and all offices have access to these suggestion forms (Exhibits 11.5 and 11.6).

IDEA COLLECTOR

DATE	IDEA	SUBMITTED BY	IDEA* CLASSIFICATION

*IDEA CLASSIFICATION MUST BE INCLUDED

WORK GROUP: _____

S1 – Feedback to Supplier	P1 – Increased Revenue	P4 – Reduce Paperwork
C1 – Feedback from Customer	P2 – Reduce Cost	P5 – Reduce Cycle Time
C2 – Improved Customer Service Satisfaction	P3 – Work Flow Improvements	P6 – Increase Productivity
C3 – Marketing for New Customer		P7 – Improve Safety

Exhibit 11.6　Idea Collector　*(Source: HDS Services. Used with permission.)*

The information on these forms receives 100 percent consideration. During the first year, hundreds of these suggestions were reviewed by the Senior Quality Improvement Team. Resolving burning issues early on demonstrated commitment on the part of the organization and literally created a groundswell of incoming suggestions and feedback from brainstorming sessions. Work groups and cross-functional teams immediately went to work to analyze cause and effect information. These were then incorporated into action plans and formal business plans.

Determine Critical Processes and How to Measure Progress

Initially, we wanted to know the five most important critical processes that directly affect external customer (client) requirements. Sanitation and stability/quality of the on-site management team were two of the five selected. The other three were: 1) meeting the financial targets, 2) effectively training groups of associates (Exhibit 11.7), and 3) creatively meeting the requirements of the client's customers. Since that time we have initiated the management of other processes such as attrition and sales success. (Client attrition is the flip side of client retention.) As previously stated, sanitation was the first critical process we tracked because it was easily quantifiable and pertained to all operations. It was also a very high-profile process in the eyes of each client.

Exhibit 11.7 Effective associate training is a critical process. *(Source: Pearson Education/PH College. Used with permission.)*

One of the burning issues that came out during the assessment step was management turnover, or the stability/quality of the onsite management team. This was the cause of many of the client service issues because improvements in unit level services are mostly generated by the direction of the unit management team. With the presence of excessive management turnover, continuous improvement was a challenge since too many HDS managers were in the orientation phase. The initial assessment indicated that overall management/associate turnover was exceeding 22 percent, with clinical services associates in the 30 percent range.

Seven years later the overall management turnover rate had been reduced to 12 percent. This was accomplished through improvements in the recruitment process, including more people in the selection process, and drastically improving our Management Development Program (MDP Plus).

In order to determine what the critical processes are in any organization, one question needs to be asked and answered on a continual basis: What is it that we do that is critically essential? Remember, critical processes often cross functional lines; therefore, the formation of groups to deal with the issues is very challenging. These cross-functional teams are responsible for the next step in the implementation process.

Redesign the Process

Issues identified as flawed processes must be totally redesigned, not simply corrected by making small changes. These major interventions must be put into action and constantly measured for progress and continuous improvement.

At HDS we needed to redesign the entire management process, starting with the vision and corporate mission. We then focused on the new core values and incorporating quality improvement principles in every process in the organization. The process HDS Services followed is outlined in Exhibit 11.8.

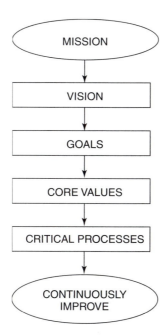

Exhibit 11.8 Corporate Quality Process Model
(Source: HDS Services. Used with permission.)

The *mission* defines the line of work we are in, that is, our purpose and why we exist as an organization. The *vision* is what we want to create, that is, our picture of where we want to be. The mission and vision of HDS Services were presented in Chapter 9. Our *goals* help us live out our mission and move closer to our vision. Our goals take place in the organization when we act or behave according to our *core values.*

The *critical processes* are those processes that are necessary to meet the present and future requirements of our customers. Embedded in all of this is the essential ability to be able to measure the degree of success in meeting the requirements of customers *from their perspectives.* That is why one or more metrics are defined and tracked and analyzed for each critical process. Action Groups work on specific areas for improvement of critical processes.

In keeping with the fact that Continuous Quality Improvement (CQI) is a never-ending journey, 10 years later we continue to discover new issues and improve on others.

Continuous Improvement

Through the use of the PDCA cycle and maintaining many interventions in the process simultaneously, the necessary momentum for continuous improvement is maintained. This CQI process develops associates that listen and are willing to learn. It promotes creativity, enhances customer satisfaction, and challenges traditional thinking. The basic concept of continuous improvement dictates that any form of improvement, quantitatively measured, is acceptable. If the customer satisfaction level was 89.5 percent last year and 90.4 percent this year, that is entirely acceptable because continuous improvement is a journey, not a destination. Quality cannot be forced on an organization and its associates. We must mentor, coach, support, and follow the CQI process.

Remember, improvement takes time and patience. So, at HDS Services the result of the journey is that the organization has evolved into a culture that does not resist change. We do not care who gets the credit for improvements; we simply want the improvements to be continuous. Our associates have been given more responsibility in our empowered culture because we have come to realize that they often know the best ways to improve a process. Our associates have become empowered to make the necessary decisions that affect the quality of products, services, and experiences that HDS Services provides for customers. These associates are given many opportunities to participate in decision making. The HDS Services leaders are individuals who have articulated a clear vision and mission and live by the core values. We use these to guide the implementation of our strategic goals and directions. Along the way our communications of prompt and accurate information has improved, particularly active listening. We have improved our feedback to these associates as they have shared their ideas with us, and we work together for quality in an environment that promotes open and honest solutions to issues that affect our customers and ourselves.

The Costs of Quality

There are costs involved with any long-term, worthwhile evolutionary changes in an organization's culture and method of conducting business. However, if the financial investment and commitment are not made and the quality effort fails, the organization will experience the greatest cost of all, lost customers. The level of costs generally parallel the level of effort put forth in achieving quality-related targets.

The four major categories of expense in achieving quality are:

1. Implementation costs
2. Assessment costs
3. Internal failure costs
4. External failure costs

Implementation costs involve expenses related to getting started. For example, the marketing department must determine the present value of the customers' services to its customers by conducting a baseline assessment of all customers and organization associates. The results of these surveys form the service level foundation on which to build and improve.

Product development, another implementation cost, is accomplished through the monitoring and measurement process. This monitoring system, which involves intervention, is the process which creates improvement in goals and services to the customers

All supplies also must be reviewed and rated from a quality perspective. Preferably the organization will be partnering with vendors that also are focused on quality. (Remember the principles of Dr. Deming as they relate to dealing with as few suppliers as possible and gaining maximum value from each partnership.) This process of vendor review requires a total reassessment of product/service specifications. The vendors can be very helpful in this step due to their vast knowledge of all available products and service benchmarks.

The operations department undertakes the largest and most expensive series of implementation projects. Their initial mandate is to identify the organization's most critical processes (i.e., those processes used in the delivery of products and services to both internal and external customers). In other words, what are the things we do that are critical to our survival? For example, a critical process at a Ritz-Carlton Hotel is having the doorman pleasantly greet guests (Exhibit 11.9).

Exhibit 11.9   A critical activity at a Ritz-Carlton Hotel is a pleasant greeting by the doorman. *(Source: PhotoEdit. Used with permission.)*

Operations must develop a **rollout plan** for all divisions or units within the organization and thoroughly educate all organization associates when changes are being implemented. The process of gathering statistical information must be established, and, undoubtedly, some quality-related equipment will have to be purchased. At HDS Services, for example, over 500 salaried management associates had to be educated on the principles of quality management. We retained a consulting firm for the initial stages and conducted numerous regional and company-wide educational sessions. (This learning process has no end and all 750 current associates are continuing the process of improvement and learning.)

Administrative functions such as program start-up, performance report establishment, and audit must be completed as well.

Assessment costs relate to the processes of monitoring measurement and making assessments beyond the baseline. Assessments will need to be made in purchasing, receiving, and storing procedures, tests, and equipment for quality improvements. A visual inspection of products in storage by a chef in a hotel kitchen is part of the assessment costs (Exhibit 11.10).

As operations tests materials and service processes and adjusts control measurements, planning can be started relative to certification by outside influences such as those criteria found in the Malcolm Baldrige National Quality Award. For those suppliers that did not actively use the principles of quality management, HDS took a proactive approach and included those in the educational process. This was also the case with HHA Services, the support services company that is a partner in the alliance.

Internal failure costs can be described as expenses related to rejects inside the organization's operations. They also involve costs associated with product design and redesign resulting from intervention. It is extremely critical to control how materials are used in order to achieve cost targets. This is particularly critical in the hospitality business where food is a primary product. An example of the control of internal costs is the portioning of food products in a cafeteria (Exhibit 11.11). All internal failures must be evaluated and require intervention to assure improvement. The goal is to reduce and eliminate the internal failures in the long-run.

Exhibit 11.10 A visual inspection of products in storage by a chef in a hotel kitchen is part of the assessment costs *(Source: HDS Services. Used with permission.)*

Exhibit 11.11 An example of the control of internal costs is the portioning of food products in a cafeteria. *(Source: HDS Services. Used with permission.)*

External failure costs involve defects in services and products as perceived by the external customer. An external failure cost is avoided when the resident of a retirement community shown in Exhibit 11.12 is served exactly what she expects. The bulk of the costs of quality are incurred in the external failures category. Immediate and thoughtful feedback, both good and bad, is an essential ingredient in the CQI process. All rejected and returned products require evaluation; therefore, there will be additional costs. In addition, there will always be the costs associated with liability such as insurance and legal expenses. Health insurance for associates and managers is rising at record rates each year. Because of the litigious society in which we live, legal expenses also have risen with the proliferation of lawsuits. The largest cost of all, however, is a lost customer.

Exhibit 11.12 An external failure cost is avoided when this resident in a retirement community is served exactly what she expects. *(Source: HDS Services. Used with permission.)*

Generally, as the number of incoming suggestions and ideas increases so do the costs and opportunities. The impact on quality and the return on investment must be carefully weighed with each evaluation. Remember that management must be committed to quality and must display this in the decision-making process.

Transformation at HDS Services (2003)

The HDS Quality Improvement Installation Plan is presented in Exhibit 11.13. This installation plan was crafted in 1991 and had three phases: Phase 1—Develop Common Understanding and Quality Vision Statement (October 1991–December 1991), Phase 2—Develop the Quality Management Installation Plan (January 1992–May 1992), and Phase 3—Work Groups and Action Groups Make Improvement in Services and Processes (June 1992–present). Phase 1 began with the orientation of the organization's senior leadership to quality management and improvement. It also included the definition of the quality vision for the organization. Phase 2 defined the design of parameters and appointed the Senior Quality Improvement Team (SQIT) and subcommittees (i.e., organizational plan, management practices, measures, recognition, communication/education, and assessment). This second phase also defined the components of the plan and identified/educated internal staff as facilitators. After these initial phases the installation plan document was written. In Phase 3, we began the workgroup education/training and quality improvement team process. We also identified key indicators and formed the Action Group Teams. During Phase 3, which has been active for more than a decade, we have implemented improvements using the process, measured successes, and implemented benchmarking.

On June 13, 1992, as we were beginning Phase 3 of the installation plan, 124 HDS executives, operations staff, and unit directors signed the Together for Quality Declaration of Commitment to the Continuous Quality Improvement Process shown in Exhibit 11.14. This commitment is still proudly displayed in our corporate offices as a reminder of our collective commitment to CQI.

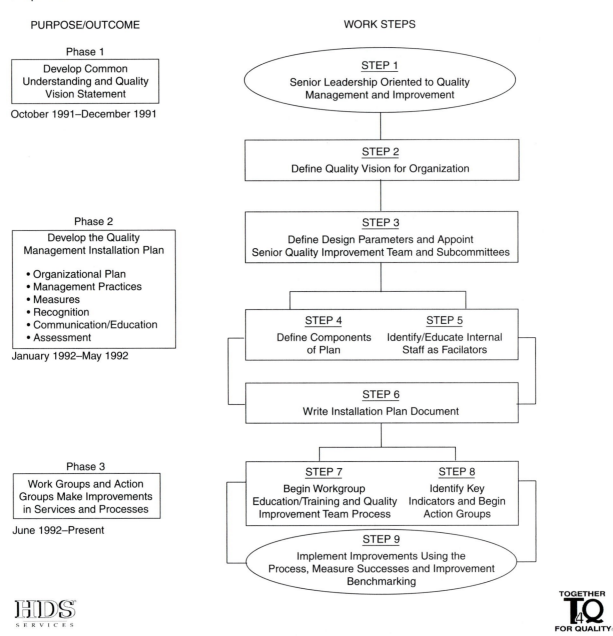

PURPOSE/OUTCOME

Phase 1
Develop Common Understanding and Quality Vision Statement

October 1991–December 1991

Phase 2
Develop the Quality Management Installation Plan

• Organizational Plan
• Management Practices
• Measures
• Recognition
• Communication/Education
• Assessment

January 1992–May 1992

Phase 3
Work Groups and Action Groups Make Improvements in Services and Processes

June 1992–Present

WORK STEPS

STEP 1
Senior Leadership Oriented to Quality Management and Improvement

STEP 2
Define Quality Vision for Organization

STEP 3
Define Design Parameters and Appoint Senior Quality Improvement Team and Subcommittees

STEP 4
Define Components of Plan

STEP 5
Identify/Educate Internal Staff as Facilators

STEP 6
Write Installation Plan Document

STEP 7
Begin Workgroup Education/Training and Quality Improvement Team Process

STEP 8
Identify Key Indicators and Begin Action Groups

STEP 9
Implement Improvements Using the Process, Measure Successes and Improvement Benchmarking

HDS
SERVICES

TOGETHER
T4Q
FOR QUALITY

Exhibit 11.13   HDS Quality Improvement Installation Plan   *(Source: HDS Services. Used with permission.)*

In many ways, the principles and management philosophies practiced by HDS Services associates today are the same as those in place in 1992. We are customer focused, process oriented, intervening, measurement driven, able to change, mentoring, and bottom-up management oriented.

However, in some ways we are totally different because of the many quality improvements resulting from changes that have been implemented in the organization over the years. These changes have been driven by the members of our teams (Exhibit 11.15) and have led to improvements that have transpired one by one through the process of Continuous Quality Improvement. For example, the number of self-directed Action Group Teams has increased dramatically (Exhibit 11.16). This is particularly true with corporate and regional office associates, including the executive team. Exhibit 11.16 includes a monthly quality reminder, which is sent to all salaried HDS associates; these reminders are entitled "STEP-PIN' IT UP."

TOGETHER FOR QUALITY

DECLARATION OF COMMITMENT

TO THE

CONTINUOUS QUALITY IMPROVEMENT PROCESS

We, the employees for HDS Services, are committed to the process of

Continuous Quality Improvement and doing things right the first time.

Together we will provide quality service which meets or exceeds our

customers' expectations.

124 signed

Executives, Operations, Sales Staff, and Unit Directors

June 13, 1992

Exhibit 11.14 HDS Services Declaration of Commitment *(Source: HDS Services. Used with permission.)*

Exhibit 11.15 Improvements resulting from changes that have been implemented in the organization over the years have been driven by the members of our teams. *(Source: HDS Services. Used with permission.)*

STEPPIN' IT UP

- Do you realize that you cannot have a quality program without the support of a **TEAM** or **TEAMS?**
- Have you asked for suggestions from your management **TEAM,** co-workers, and/or hourly staff in the past?
- Do you have work group **TEAMS** within your work environment?
- Do you have cross-functional action group **TEAMS** striving to make your workplace stronger and more customer focused?
- Has a work or action group **TEAM** at your facility made an improvement in the past three months to exceed customer expectations?
- Are hourly associates on **TEAMS** that create and deliver service?

If you can answer "yes" to each of the above questions,
you are on the HDS Services Quality Journey.
If not, you can quickly and easily
implement self-directed **TEAMS.**

ACTION GROUP LIST

Hourly Training	*GOLDEN SERVICE*	Preferred Place to Work
HHA/HDS	Technology	Recruiting
Recognition	Clinical	Safety
GRAND CLASS	Performance Evaluation	Accounting/OPS
Financial	*FOOD IS . . . FASHION & FUN!*	Triplett University
Purchasing	Client Satisfaction Survey	DOE/BSC

Exhibit 11.16   HDS Services Self-Directed Teams *(Source: HDS Services. Used with permission.)*

We continue to have a quality champion who coordinates all quality-related initiatives. Interestingly, there are more suggestions being generated today than ever before. We believe this is a result of increased computerization and improved communication in all areas. Marketing and operations also meet much more frequently now, both regionally and corporately. The one team that has remained intact for the entire nine years is the Senior Quality Improvement Team (SQIT). The team's role has remained intact as well.

The greatest challenge today is the education of newly selected management associates. Those management associates who were introduced to the management of quality at the outset of our journey remain very effective in the use of the various principles and processes. In fact, their **Quality Quotient (QQ)** has improved and matured. We define Quality Quotient as the measure of the management's and associates' knowledge and use of the quality improvement principles. Today's objective is to place the Quality Quotient in the CQI process with various sets of action steps mostly related to education, testing, and measuring.

The two unique root causes of the challenge are growth in accounts and variation in account operating status. Invariably, when a new account is signed, the operational status of the client's facility is in shambles. In spite of the heavy concentration of work we perform during the start-up phase, it requires at least a year to initiate most of the programs and processes. This includes the quality processes as well. So, with an average of 12 percent new account growth, we know the maximum QQ is 90 percent. In addition to this, the account growth and normal associate turnover create at least 125 open positions per year. This is why the education process and QQ are so vital to the organization's success.

Implementation of Service Systems

The steps for implementing a high performance service system are presented in Exhibit 11.17.

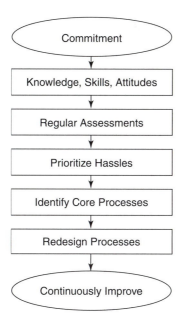

Commitment

↓

Knowledge, Skills, Attitudes

↓

Regular Assessments

↓

Prioritize Hassles

↓

Identify Core Processes

↓

Redesign Processes

↓

Continuously Improve

Exhibit 11.17 Implementation Process Model
(Source: HDS Services. Used with permission)

The implementation process begins with a commitment from top managers and other leaders in the organization. These leaders must paint a compelling picture for all others in the organization, so the others will choose to enroll in the implementation process.

The next step is acquiring the knowledge, skills, and behaviors required to become a high performance service organization. Once these are acquired by top management, it is their responsibility to teach others. All must be included because it takes everyone in the organization to contribute.

The third step is regular assessments. Assessments of internal customers, external customers, and the financial health of the organization encourage all to make decisions based on facts and data, not intuition. This step may include surveys, interviews, ratios, and other tools to categorize the data. Once categorized, it is relatively easy to identify recurring themes and hassles that occur over and over again.

The next step, prioritize hassles, becomes easier when the assessment information is known. The top priorities are those mentioned most frequently in all the assessments. Often it is helpful to select the top priority internal customer hassle and top priority external customer hassle and work in teams simultaneously to solve each. Once the hassle has surfaced, a number of tools can be used to identify the root cause(s) and eliminate these hassles. Then the teams move on to the next high priority hassle and go through a similar process.

Next, the core processes are determined. A core process is one that is essential for meeting the needs and exceeding the expectations of customers in both the short- and long-term. One of the questions to ask is: "What is it that we do that is critical?" Often, these critical processes are cross-functional. This step also includes the identification of ways to measure the effectiveness of each of the core processes.

Redesigning the process is the next step. In a high performance service organization, information flows most frequently from the creators and deliverers of products and services to the top management. This is an example of a process redesign since the traditional process, top-down information flow, did not stimulate the organization to achieve remarkable levels of quality or continuously improve. Cross-functional teams are used for process redesign.

The final step is continuous improvement, a step that is never completed. This helps the organization, as well as the individuals in it, have long-term staying power. When we challenge the status quo, we have a tremendous opportunity to build a better way.

Perhaps the keys to implementing a system for managing for quality are determination and persistence. All must understand, believe in, and coach others in the process. All must be willing to invest the necessary time, effort, and other resources, and all must be convinced that the system of managing for quality is practical for those in operations and that it will yield the desired quality results. It is also essential to establish a common performance language and to link quality improvements to other operational goals. Once the process begins, due dates must be set and regular reporting of progress to all involved is required. This demonstrates how dependent everyone is on others in the organization in the management for quality.

High performance service organizations, by their very nature, improve each day. While the daily improvements may be small, the sum of the improvements is cumulative and helps ensure even higher levels of performance. Performing at a high level requires getting better through the elimination of one hassle at a time, each and every day. The end result is that the organization's products and services are perceived as valuable by customers to the point that they are not available from the organization's competition at the same level of quality. That is a distinct competitive advantage for the high performance service organization.

Summary

There are restricting forces that may affect the way that we do business. However, the principles of quality do not change. What does change is the hassles and things that stand in the way of achieving the quality goals of our customers. The six steps in implementing quality provide a way to organize the efforts of getting underway and continuously improving. The costs of quality result from identifying the processes for improvement, improving the processes, and assessing the improvements.

Key Terms

Addressing the Burning Issues—These are then incorporated into action plans and formal business plans.

Assessment—A baseline is critical; baseline assessments must be conducted with two major groups; external customers (clients) and internal customers (associates).

Assessment Costs—Relate to the processes of monitoring measurement and making assessments beyond the baseline.

Continuous Improvement—Promotes creativity, enhances customer satisfaction, and challenges traditional thinking. The basic concept dictates that any form of improvement, quantitatively measured, is acceptable.

Education—An enrollment process.

External Failure Costs—Involve defects in services and products as received and perceived by the external customers.

Identification of Critical Processes—To include customer (both internal and external) satisfaction, associate turnover, client retention, and other important areas.

Implementation Costs—Expenses related to getting started.

Internal Failure Costs—Related to rejects inside the organization's operations. They also involve costs associated with product design and redesign resulting from intervention.

Quality Quotient (QQ)—The measurement of the management and associates knowledge and use of the quality improvement principles.

Realigning the Processes—Redesigning to continuously improve a process.

Restricting Forces—Point out that many of the techniques that worked in the past will not work in the future.

Rollout Plan—Process of gathering statistical information must be established, and, undoubtedly, some quality-related equipment will have to be purchased; administrative functions such as program start-up, performance report establishment, and audit must be completed as well.

Review Questions

1. How did restricting forces work in paradigm shifts affecting managers at the recent turn of the century?
2. What are the six steps in implementing quality improvements in an organization?
3. What are the five most common teams that are involved in educating associates and implementing the quality process?
4. What is the quality triangle?
5. How would you identify the burning issues in your organization and what would you do to address them?
6. What are the four areas of costs that result from implementing the quality process?
7. What is the most pressing challenge facing HDS Services as quality continues to be transformed?

Activities in Your Organization

Listed below are some activities designed to reinforce the key chapter concepts in your organization. If you are a student and not currently working in the industry, interview an industry leader about one of these topics.

1. The six steps for implementing quality are as follows:
    1. Education
    2. Assessment
    3. Addressing the Burning Issues
    4. Identification of Critical Processes
    5. Realigning the Processes
    6. Continuous Improvement

    Study the *Education* step with regard to the implementation of quality in your organization. How will you teach the principles of managing and improving quality to all senior management, operations executives, marketing associates, and corporate support associates? How will you get enrollment from everyone? What agenda items will be addressed in the first session (e.g., defining quality, defining natural variation, brainstorming, nominal group technique, other basic tools, Dr. Deming's 14 points, the quality improvement organizational structure, a comparison of management styles between those organizations that have a plan to manage quality and traditional organizations, and organizing and planning the implementation of the management of quality)? What groups will you establish to manage the initial transition and to convert the organization to Continuous Quality Improvement? Who will be assigned to the Steering Team, or Organizational Planning Group, to oversee management and coordination of the transition? How will you be sure that the topic of "quality" was on the agenda of each and every meeting? Who will be assigned to the Management Practices Team with the responsibility of integrating quality into every position description, every policy, and every procedure within the organization? Who will be assigned to the Measurement Team to determine what you are going to monitor and measure as "critical processes" throughout the organization? What critical processes will you monitor? Who will be assigned to the Recognition Team to plan for how associates at all levels would be recognized for achievement in the future, both as teams and as individuals, with emphasis on teams? Who will be assigned to the Communications and Education Team with the responsibility for general communication of quality matters throughout the organization? Who will be assigned to the Assessment Team to determine what and how areas of the organization will be assessed?

2. Now turn your attention to the next two steps in implementing quality: *assessment* and *addressing the burning issues.* How will you conduct baseline assessments with external customers and internal customers? What areas will you address for each baseline assessment? How will you ensure that the baseline assessment information is factual, ratable, and quantified numerically? What will you do with the results? How will you balance the needs and expectations of all three in the quality triangle? How will your assessment include both the level of quality that the organization is currently creating and delivering as well as the definition of the desired levels of quality in the critical processes? Will you establish quality indicators using the tools of the trade presented in an earlier chapter? If so, which tools will you use? How will you use the process of benchmarking? With regard to "burning issues," how will you discover what these are in your organization? How will you involve associates in the process? How will you utilize work groups and cross-functional action group teams?

3. Finally, study the last three steps for implementing quality. Consider the fourth step—*determine critical processes and determine how to measure progress.* What are the critical processes in your organization? How will you use the baseline assessment to identify these? How will you use feedback from associates to identify these? What are the five most important critical processes that directly effect customer requirements in your organization? With regard to *redesigning the process,* what interventions must be put into action and constantly measured for progress and continuous improvement? How do the organization's mission, vision, goals, and core values fit together in the organization? What *critical processes* are necessary to meet the present and future requirements of the organization's customers? What metric(s) will be used to track and analyze each critical process? The last step in the process is *continuous improvement.* How will you utilize the PDCA cycle for CQI? How will you involve associates in the CQI process? How will you and other leaders mentor, coach, support, and follow the CQI process? How will you ensure that associates become empowered to make the necessary decisions that affect the quality of products, services, and experiences that the organization provides for customers? How will you promote open and honest solutions to hassles that affect your customers and your organization?

Reference

Harnish, Verne and Kathleen Harnish. *Implementing Total Quality Management,* Boulder, CO: Career Track, 1994.

Relevant Web Sites

Implementing TQM Right the Second Time:
http://twincities.bcentral.com/twincities/stories/1996/10/28/editorial2.html

Linking Covey with Quality—The Five Dimension Denominator (by Richard Winder, Daniel Judd, and Lindon Robison):
http://www.ldri.com/articles/95nqmlinkcoveyqual.html

TQM Has a Place in Your Business:
http://bizjournals.bcentral.com/extraedge/consultants/company_doctor/2000/01/31/column193.html

TQM Process Management: (Article on Improving Quality)
http://www.iqpic.org/pm.htm

When TQM Works:
http://deming.eng.clemson.edu/pub/tqmbbs/tools-techs/whatwrks.txt

Chapter

12 *Leading Quality*

The realization of the improvements inherent in the CQI process requires committed leadership that is visionary, customer focused, empowered, and embraces the value of recognition.

Jerry Fournier
Executive Vice President
HDS Services
Farmington Hills, MI

At RARE Hospitality, the quality delivered to our guests is driven by the quality of the individuals on our teams. All efforts throughout our organization are focused on growing loyalty of both our staff and our guests.

Phil Hickey, Jr.
Chairman and Chief Executive Officer
RARE Hospitality International, Inc.
Atlanta, GA

Learning Objectives

1. Define existentialism as it relates to leadership.
2. Compare an ideal leader you have known with the leadership qualities identified by Peter Drucker.
3. Understand leadership qualities and what they mean to you.
4. Understand leadership keys and what they mean to you.
5. Understand leadership secrets and what they mean to you.

The basics of effective leadership are not new; they have been known throughout the ages. Native Americans taught their young the basics of leadership as part of their time-honored philosophies and used them as a form of instruction for the members of the tribes. Two Native American proverbs in particular address leadership:

"Teaching should come from within instead of without."

—Hopi Native American Proverb

"Our first teacher is our own heart."

—Cheyenne Native American Proverb

These Native American proverbs summarize the idea of getting to know yourself before trying to know others or learning from others. Similar philosophies, including existentialism, may be found as common threads throughout the works of twentieth century authors. The core of **existentialism**, a twentieth century philosophical movement, is an analysis and understanding of individual existence in an unfathomable universe. The philosophy centers on the individual assuming ultimate responsibility for her or his actions. When applied to the concept of leadership, it becomes clear that *leadership is first, foremost, and always, an inner quest.* We must know ourselves before we can lead ourselves or others.

Since 1989 we have explored leadership qualities, keys, and secrets in the United States and Japanese hospitality industries, often with other researchers in *The* School of Hospitality Business at Michigan State University. The studies have ranged from surveying chief executive officers (CEOs) and presidents, chief operating officers (COOs), chief financial officers (CFOs), general managers (GMs), and controllers.

This chapter presents a summary of the top five aggregate leadership qualities, keys, and secrets for United States hospitality industry leaders.

The Leadership Paradigm

It has been said that we do not see the world as it is; we see the world as we are. That is to say, the world, along with the way we lead, is seen through our paradigms, the filters through which we view the world. A classical management paradigm is the following:

1. Do things right (i.e., be efficient)
2. Direct operations
3. Enforce policies and procedures
4. Design procedures and tasks
5. Control results
6. Foster stability

The manager and chef of a restaurant, for example, regularly practice doing things right, in this case monitoring the quality of inventory (Exhibit 12.1).

Contrast the classical management paradigm with the new leadership paradigm:

1. Do the right things (i.e., be effective)
2. Monitor stakeholder expectations
3. Communicate vision and values
4. Manage systems and processes

Exhibit 12.1 The manager and chef of a restaurant practice regularly doing things right, in this case monitoring the quality of inventory. *(Source: HDS Services. Used with permission.)*

5. Support people
6. Engage in continuous quality improvement

The leadership paradigm requires leaders to do the right things by monitoring stakeholder (i.e., external customers and internal customers) expectations (Exhibit 12.2) in this cafeteria foodservice operation. The management paradigm and the leadership paradigm are complimentary in organizations. The management paradigm is essential in the running of an efficient organization; the leadership paradigm is critical in leading an effective organization. The two paradigms work hand-in-hand to present a system of processes that result in meeting

Exhibit 12.2 The leadership paradigm requires leaders to do the right things by monitoring stakeholder (i.e., external customers and internal customers) expectations in this cafeteria foodservice operation. *(Source: HDS Services. Used with permission.)*

customer requirements and exceeding customer expectations while continuously improving quality.

Peter Drucker, having written extensively on the topic of management, states the following about leadership:

- Without followers there can be no leaders.
- An effective leader is someone who achieves results.
- Leaders are highly visible.
- Leadership is a responsibility.

Examining each of these statements provides insight into the topic of effective leadership. The first states that a leader's power comes from his or her followers. Followers empower the leader, rather than the other way around. Achieving results sometimes means that the leader is not loved or admired, but the leader does the right things to be effective. Visibility simply means that the leader sets examples through actions. The responsibility of leadership is in contrast to rank, titles, salary, or privileges that come with a position. Leadership is, most importantly, responsibility.

Think of an ideal leader, whether an historical figure, a mentor, a role model, personal friend, a business associate, a relative, a member of an organization, a volunteer, or someone who is paid for his or her leadership responsibilities. Visualize this leader and ask and answer the following questions:

- What did the followers say/do?
- What results did the leader and followers achieve together?
- In what ways was the leader or the leader's actions visible?
- How did the leader and followers demonstrate responsibility?
- What did you reinforce/discover about leadership?

Individuals who are leaders empower their followers to be effective, and the followers end up becoming living examples of the organization's values, vision, and mission. A leader in such an organization has the responsibility to ask and explain rather than direct and tell because the leader must encourage people to want to follow the shared vision and do the right things.

At RARE Hospitality, as with other service organizations, each individual brings his or her own core values, behaviors, and experiences to the organization. Each person possesses his or her own set of standards for sanitation, food quality, and personal relationship management. RARE presents its own set of standards to its people and expects them to raise their standards accordingly. RARE finds that occasionally, when a long-term veteran of another company is selected as a management trainee at RARE, it is a challenge because RARE wants to honor the veteran's past experiences, yet asks them to set those aside and comply with RARE's standards and culture. This ultimately creates a shared vision in the organization—one that leads to continued success.

Leadership Assessment

Just as the ongoing assessment of levels of quality is important, it is critical to regularly assess individual leadership qualities, keys, and secrets. Sometimes these traits need to be altered to improve the leader's effectiveness. Exhibit 12.3 provides one such simple leadership assessment tool, developed and refined with over a dozen years of research on leadership qualities, keys, and secrets.

Fill out Exhibit 12.3 to assess your personal leadership assets.

LEADERSHIP: WHO ARE YOU?

Self-Assessment Survey

Leadership Qualities

Effective leaders . . .	My Rank (1 = top; 5 = bottom)
have a strong personal value or belief system	_____
listen as well as, if not better than, they speak	_____
make their desired outcomes tangible	_____
provide a compelling message or vision	_____
recognize that the ability to adjust is a necessity	_____

Leadership Keys	My Rank (1 = top; 5 = bottom)
Be an expert	_____
Develop a vision	_____
Keep your cool	_____
Simplify	_____
Trust your subordinates	_____

Leadership Secrets

In our organization or company, leaders must possess:	My Rank (1 = top; 5 = bottom)
accountability	_____
credibility	_____
dependability	_____
responsibility	_____
self-confidence	_____

Exhibit 12.3 A Leadership Self-Assessment Tool

Leadership Qualities

The top five **leadership qualities** are presented in ranked order of importance (based on over a dozen years of research results) in Exhibit 12.4.

Rank	Effective leaders . . .
1	have a strong personal value or belief system
2	provide a compelling message or vision
3	recognize that the ability to adjust is a necessity
4	make their outcomes tangible
5	listen as well as, if not better than, they speak

Exhibit 12.4 The Top Five Leadership Qualities

Strong Personal Value or Belief System

Leaders have told us that they value rallying their associates with a positive attitude, shared vision, and clear direction. They believe that personal values should be aligned with the values of the organization. They also value identifying a mentor and they pick the mentor who exemplifies the person they want to be.

These leaders also have other beliefs or values. They believe in the power of listening to associates. They are open-minded and try to understand others. These leaders value putting themselves second to their people, their organization, or to the issue at hand. They believe in managing as they would like to be led. They always strive to be the best at work and at home and they stay focused.

Leaders are passionate about what they do, believe in themselves so others will also believe, and know that one person can make a difference. They believe that people should not be afraid to test their abilities. They value a balance in life and say that a job is only a job and a career is only a career, but family is non-replaceable. These leaders believe that personal lives need to be put in order first; family should always come before work or any job.

Leaders believe that associates should be clear and focused both in the organization and the family to facilitate what they want to achieve in life and accomplish harmony. They value a vision and setting and achieving goals to move closer toward that vision, and they share the vision and values with others in compelling ways.

Leaders who are part of the quality improvement in an organization believe passionately in those who will help improve the quality through their actions. These leaders do not simply talk about quality. They act on their beliefs and value the improvement of quality and communicate that message to others. Their vision for the organization is one that improves each day, and this vision is at the heart of the message that the leaders regularly share with others in the organization.

Compelling Message or Vision

Vision is one of the four foundations of leadership discovered and reinforced in our research. The other three are **trust, perseverance,** and **communication.** Leaders start with understanding their personal visions, which are clear, strong, compelling, and come alive by sharing these personal visions with others in the form of a series of compelling messages. They identify the vision/desired state of the organization in the future, communicate this to others, develop and facilitate the training that others need to achieve the vision/desired state, and then set out to achieve the vision.

Leaders must be committed to the vision and stick to it in a passionate way. It is this passion that ignites the shared vision in others. Once the vision is developed, the message is centered on helping others see their roles in the organization as the vision describes. To make that message compelling is to articulate it in a way that makes others decide that they simply cannot *not* help achieve the organization's vision through their contributions.

Leaders say that they have to believe in the vision so much that they can be direct, bold, and unwavering. They use these behaviors to stay focused. The vision must be present in all the decisions of the leader. The vision can be used to encourage personal growth in the leader, others, and the organization. Leaders understand the culture of the organization and do not simply have their own personal vision. Rather, the vision represents what is for the good of the organization.

Leaders of quality improvements share the vision with all in their organizations. They know that it is the power of the shared vision that creates the desired outcome. They understand that the shared vision comes from the individual personal visions combined and strengthened through synergy. Quality improvements are a part of each person's responsibility daily in an organization that has a vision of providing its customers with the level of quality that meets their requirements and exceeds their expectations. All of these individuals end up communicating the message of quality and "being" the vision for improving quality.

Recognize the Ability to Adjust Is a Necessity

Leaders adapt to and welcome change. They are flexible and willing to change direction when necessary. This flexibility comes in part from being a good listener and team player and treating others with respect.

Leaders stay with their personal visions as well as the shared visions in their organizations; however, they are willing to alter the visions as needed as conditions change. They adapt the visions to coincide with the customers' expectations of the organization, and they adjust their strategies, actions, and methods to deliver the vision for the organization.

Leaders are not afraid to take risks and do not punish others for doing so or for making mistakes—mistakes are opportunities to learn and grow. Leaders who have quality improvement responsibilities know that change is at the very core of improvement. Improvement requires people to change the way that they look at the world, to be open to input from a variety of sources, and to give up power to those who have the greatest responsibility for leading change. This concept of empowerment results in the leader taking the view that nothing today should simply be done the same way it was done yesterday out of a sense of obligation to simply maintain the routine.

Make Their Desired Outcomes Tangible

Tangible outcomes are those that people can see and touch even before the outcomes exist. They seem real in spite of the fact that they just exist in the minds and hearts of those who dream of achieving the outcomes. Tangible outcomes are those that are compelling. When people in organizations start behaving in the ways that they would like the organization to be, the transformation of the organization is well underway. Outcomes are made more tangible when they are communicated in compelling ways. When a team of individuals in an organization believes that an outcome already exists, half the work to make it happen has been done. This is called bringing the vision to life.

Those participating in improving quality in the organization often rely on tangible metrics to evaluate intangibles (i.e., the level of customer satisfaction or the level of service). In a sense, the metrics help transform the intangible into the tangible or the vague into the understood. However, we must occasionally remind others that the goal of quality improvement is not simply improved metrics (i.e., a higher percentage of customer satisfaction or increased score on the customer service index). The goal is to attract and retain customers who are loyal to the organization.

Listen As Well As, If Not Better Than, They Speak

Communication is one of the four foundations of leadership. The more leaders learn about effective leadership, the better they will be able to communicate and share their vision. Communication experts often remind us that the most important communication skill is listening. Leaders listen to the whole story before making a decision. They are effective listeners for verbal and non-verbal communication, and they know that by "listening" carefully they will often hear and understand what is not being said.

Leaders listen to all sides, evaluate, and learn from the mistakes that are made in the hope of making progress toward the improvement of quality. They are in touch with the feelings of followers and listening is the conduit for this relationship. They know that the associates often see and feel what is not seen or felt by the leader because the associates are more frequently in close contact with the organization's customers.

Leaders listen to external customers as well as associates. The leaders of the quality improvement process must hear the voices of customers so that they can clearly understand the requirements in the forms of needs, wants, and expectations of those customers. Accurate information only can be obtained through listening. Only through listening will leaders know what those in the organization can do to improve quality and be able to assess whether the organization has successfully delivered the level of quality that was promised.

Leadership Keys

The top five **leadership keys** are presented in order of most important to least important in Exhibit 12.5.

Rank	Key
1	Develop a vision
2	Trust your subordinates
3	Simplify
4	Keep your cool
5	Be an expert

Exhibit 12.5 The Top Five Leadership Keys

Develop a Vision

The basics of a leadership vision were already discussed. It is no surprise that this is the top ranked key to leadership. Ponder a number of questions about your leadership vision: What is your vision? What is your vision for you as a person? What is your vision for your family? What is your vision for the relationships that you are nurturing and strengthening? What is your vision for your organization? What is your vision for your life in this decade? Do you know where you are going?

The Hindus have a saying: "If you don't know where you are going, any road will take you there." Yogi Berra said, "You've got to be careful if you don't know where you are going, because you might not get there." Professionally, our shared vision is to seek opportunities to be of service to others. We want to help others and make a positive difference in their lives.

Trust Your Subordinates

Trust is built with frequent formal and informal communication in the organization. It is the responsibility of leaders to create a sense of trust and honesty. Leaders must trust their own abilities and the abilities of their staff. They trust and respect associates and live by a set of exemplary values.

Leaders are open since this builds the trust of others. They develop relationships by following through on what they say they will do, and they practice honest communication by making amends as soon as they recognize that they have made a mistake and caused harm to another. They remain trustworthy and consequently establish the confidence of others in their leadership. Leaders are able to trust others to make the right decisions and trust in the decisions that are made by others.

Leaders are truthful at all times. They realize that trust must be earned and re-earned regularly through being honest with others. When leaders are respectful of and empathetic to others, they earn respect and trust. Leaders treat others with the same respect that they would like in return, and they trust associates and give them direction and respect them as human beings. Leaders understand that people are all different and that they are not to be judged.

Leaders care about people. Leaders develop trust by being themselves first and then being a role model to others. They are not too good or too proud to go into the trenches with associates, particularly in times of overwhelming pressures, rapid change, and trying circumstances.

Simplify

The vision and mission, along with the values and critical processes of an organization, must be simplified so that people can understand them and figure out where they can contribute in ways that are significant. In simplifying the improvement of quality, leaders should be role models. They should communicate the little things that they do to make a difference in the organization and improve quality.

Leadership is first, foremost, and always, an inner quest. A leader must know his or her individual strengths and constantly work to enhance them, and a leader must recognize that sometimes qualities that are strengths are also weaknesses. For example, leaders typically have the ability to achieve and inspire others to be their best. Others sometimes view that same strength as the leader being too intense or driven. Leaders must continuously evaluate inner feelings, motivations, and desired outcomes.

Leaders who are responsible for improving quality must require that they and others keep the process simple so all can contribute. Simplicity leads to understanding and understanding leads to knowledge. Knowledge, in turn, leads to behavior changes and these actions lead to the improvement of quality in the organization.

Keep Your Cool

Leaders stay calm even in the face of adverse pressure. Some do this by maintaining their sense of humor and using common sense. Other leaders make it look like they are having fun and, at the end of the day, laugh at the hard times that they faced that day. Others use trust, confidence, and humility to maintain a level head in the face of controversy.

Above all, leaders at all levels of the organization must view mistakes as learning opportunities, opportunities to fix the process. Mistakes can happen whenever humans are involved in a process; however, mistakes must be viewed as process, not people, problems.

Be an Expert

Over the dozen years that we have been collecting and analyzing leadership research data, in all of our studies of leaders in the United States and Japan, this key was ranked dead last. The mark of a great leader is that he or she surrounds himself or herself with people who are more talented. Leaders bring people with complimentary talents together so that the organization effectively utilizes synergy. A poor leader always hires people who are lesser leaders than he or she. In this way, the poor leader looks better.

As a team, being an expert is important when trying to improve quality because the knowledge and expertise of the collection of individuals is essential to knowing where to fix the critical processes to improve quality. Being an individual expert, on the other hand, is not critical because most of the improvements that affect quality are driven by a number of cross-functional teams known as Action Groups (AGs). These AGs dramatically affect the improvement of quality at the critical point where products and services are created and delivered. Therefore, being an individual expert in the quality improvement system that we have described is not necessary.

Leadership Secrets

The top five **leadership secrets** are listed from most important to least important, in Exhibit 12.6.

Rank	In our organization or company, leaders must possess:
1	dependability
2	credibility
3	responsibility
4	accountability
5	self-confidence

Exhibit 12.6   The Top Five Leadership Secrets

Dependability

Delighting customers by providing them with excellent service makes customers dependent on our organization, creates customer loyalty, and builds repeat business. When we promise superior service, and deliver on that promise, our customers depend on us for more of the same. Leaders say that dependability is synonymous with reliability, since people rely or depend on service organizations to meet their requirements in exchange for the time and money that they spend with the organization. In many ways, dependability is the overarching goal of a quality improvement system.

Dependable products and services are consistent; we know what to expect from them. They also have elements of trustworthiness because they are worthy of our trust and confidence. Dependability is the reason for quality improvement efforts. We undertake the dehassling process to reduce or eliminate the hassles, problems, or barriers that are facing us in the quality system. Our goal is to make the products and services more dependable for our customers.

Credibility

Of all the secrets that we have surveyed, credibility is the one most often in the news with the fallen leaders in organizations that have shown that they have no clue as to the actions required for one with credibility. Credibility is making certain that our actions are believable. Credibility also is related to keeping our word and delivering what we promise. It is saying what you will do and doing what you say; it is keeping your promises.

Genuine leaders never sacrifice their integrity or compromise their credibility. Leaders follow through on what they say they will do. Credible leaders do not "fake it"; they are sincere and genuine. They lead by example and exhibit behaviors, values, and qualities that others wish to emulate. Credible leaders practice what they teach. They know that they are judged by what they do and not what they say. One leader described the **Three Cs** of leadership as credibility/character, confidence, and communication.

Credible leaders are honest. Credible leaders are true to themselves since credibility has elements of personal morals and ethics. They lead by example and treat others with dignity. This ensures that the others on the team respect the leader. A leader must give respect to gain respect. A leader is capable and knows what he or she is doing, and demonstrate the willingness to put in the time and effort, to work as hard as the leader expects of the associates and lead by example. Leaders who are credible never ask another to do something that the leader would not do. They also do not compromise their credibility as it will come back to haunt them.

Credible leaders do the right thing at all times. They never compromise their values. They walk the walk and lead by example. Credible leaders are those that the followers believe in by their actions. They set the example. Although sometimes difficult, credible leaders do what they say they will do. Credible leadership is based on trust; trust, once broken, is difficult to restore. Credibility is integrity, based on straightforward honesty.

Leaders communicate the vision and then live by it. They know that if others do not see the leader "being" the vision, they will ask: Why should we? Credible leaders are the example. They are sincere, since credibility comes from the heart. One leader advised that you should be certain that when you put your head "down on the pillow" at night, that you can fall "peacefully" to sleep. That is to say, credible leaders do not have to worry about being caught or being exposed as not being someone that they pretend or masquerade to be.

Credibility is the hallmark of those who aspire to lead quality improvement efforts in any organization. These individuals must be believable as the decisions on actions to improve quality will be based in large part on their advice and recommendations. The confidence in the quality leadership efforts will be based in large part on the credibility of the leader, as perceived by others in the organization. Of all the secrets of leadership, credibility stands at the forefront of essential components of the leader's character. By its nature, credibility cannot be phony. It must be genuine if the leader is to help influence genuine improvements in quality.

Responsibility

Leaders are responsible for seeing that actions are carried out and that directions are followed. Leaders of all organizations have a primary responsibility—to nurture, build, and protect the reputations of their organizations. Responsible leaders must work diligently each day to keep those reputations intact, knowing that reputations become tarnished and grow old unless they are "polished" often.

Leaders are responsible for genuinely caring about others and treating others the way that they want to be treated. Leaders demonstrate compassion for each person in the organization and get to know them personally and genuinely care about each individual. Responsibility stems from the fact that the leader is only as good as the people around them in the organization. The leader has the responsibility to work side by side with others in the organization.

Leaders also are responsible for developing the followers in the organization. They do this by believing in the inherent goodness of others and developing their abilities. Responsible leaders remember to appreciate every associate every day for the effort that they put forth and the contribution they make.

Responsible leaders are able to accept people and their ideas when they are different than the leaders' ideas. By accepting others and their ideas, and finding ways to meld them into the organization, a responsible leader excels. The key here is that true acceptance and the responsibility that comes with it is different than tolerance.

Responsible leaders are consistent. They remove hassles and barriers to self-growth. Responsible leaders are approachable and they surround themselves with quality people who can make the organization better. Responsible leaders, given all the technical dimensions of leadership, never forget to be a human being and treat others like human beings. They build the team with trust, concern, faith in associates, and communication. Responsible leaders are consistent and fair. When they are fair and honest with everyone, loyalty and commitment of others will follow.

Leaders in all parts of the organization are responsible for improving quality. They realize that their power as a leader comes not from their titles or positions, but in the personal responsibility that they accept to make a difference in the improvement of quality. This responsibility is shared with all who can make a contribution to the quality improvement processes.

Accountability

Accountability includes your personal actions, as well as that part of the organization for which you are responsible. Accountable leaders share their success and credit with those who helped achieve the goals in the organization. They detect mistakes as soon as possible and begin fixing the process to correct mistakes in the future. Accountable leaders view mistakes as opportunities to learn, grow, and improve. They do not take mistakes personally. Accountable leaders do not repeat mistakes more than once, and they do not make rush decisions. They make fact-based decisions based on studying the issues and the impacts of the decisions and considering all aspects of an impending decision. Accountable leaders set a high level of expectations and encourage accountability in others through coaching and development. Accountable leaders do not run away from problems in the organization; they face them and solve them at the root cause.

Accountability is another of the essential qualities of those leaders who seek to improve quality in their organizations. Learning from mistakes is part of accountability as is developing and coaching others. Accountable decisions stand the test of time as they result in positive gains in quality improvements.

Self-Confidence

Self-confidence was already identified along with credibility/character and communication as one of the Three Cs of leadership. Self-confidence stems from self-knowledge. By recognizing strengths and building on them and identifying weaknesses and working to overcome them, self-confidence emerges.

Self-confidence must be blended with empathy, an understanding of the feelings of others. Self-confident leaders have faith in their abilities and rely on their inner strength. They know what they want and have the belief in themselves and their abilities to obtain it. Self-confident leaders are true to themselves and believe that the best is yet to come in the organization. They speak up and are careful not to be dominated or overwhelmed by others through their positive personal attitude.

Internal customers who are not confident are territorial and only do what is in their best interest. Those who are confident and secure work without fear and reach out to others. Without a confident team of internal customers, a leader may be able to implement the quality processes, but he or she will not be successful in achieving the levels of quality desired.

Those who lead quality improvements must exude self-confidence in their abilities. They must instill this confidence in the organization and its people to strive to be the best that they can in service of their customers.

Some Additional Thoughts on Leadership

Since leadership begins with an inner quest, before leaders challenge others, they must first challenge themselves. Self-knowledge is an important part of this quest. Once leaders know themselves, they must communicate the person discovered to those they wish to lead. Self-knowledge includes determining and accenting strengths and determining weaknesses and transforming them into strengths.

It is also important to be oneself and not try to copy someone else's leadership style. Being true to oneself is essential because when we go home at the end of the day we have to be able to live with the choices that we have made throughout the day. Leaders should be driven to being successful, yet keep both successes and failures in perspective with other areas of life (e.g., family, friends, and health). Above all, they should not be too hard or self-critical.

Leaders also should challenge their biases and stereotypes. These biases and stereotypes are what Francis Bacon called "the idols which beset men's minds." Each of us has a fragmented view of how the world works embedded in our personal paradigm. The leader's role is to put together and harmonize such views. Only by "associating" minds in this way can a leader acquire a full and objective view of the world.

Leaders must be impatiently patient. They need to transmit a sense of urgency, a feeling that life is short and that there is a great deal to accomplish. Yet, the leader cannot be unreasonable or expect results overnight; the effect on morale can be devastating. The best leaders balance a sense of urgency with tenacity and persistence.

Leaders do not blame; they learn. No one knows what the future will bring, how a market will respond or whether a new process will work. Yet, so often when a desired outcome fails to materialize, traditional managers look for scapegoats, someone to blame. That reaction freezes people's mind-sets and destroys imagination. In the sciences, researchers do not look upon a failed experiment as a mistake to be blamed on someone. Instead, they see it as an opportunity to change their view of how things work. Leaders do not fix the blame; they fix the problem. Leaders make room for all possibilities. That is what allows leaders to be realistic and imaginative at the same time.

Summary

Your personal leadership journey has already started. You are encouraged to evaluate where you are in your journey in light of the top five leadership qualities, keys, and secrets brought to focus in this chapter. Tie your personal leadership journey to your organization's leadership journey to improve quality. When the two journeys are aligned there will be no stopping you or the organization.

Your leadership journey never ends; you never reach your destination. Rather, excellent leaders know that they can continuously improve and keep trying to do so. In the words of the great leader Sir Winston Churchill; "Never, never, never, never quit."

Key Terms

Communication—One of the four foundations of leadership.

Existentialism—An analysis and understanding of individual existence in an unfathomable universe. The philosophy centers on the individual assuming ultimate responsibility for her or his actions.

Leadership Keys—Develop a vision, trust your subordinates, simplify, keep your cool, be an expert.

Leadership Qualities—Have a strong personal value or belief system; provide a compelling message or vision; recognize that the ability to adjust is a necessity; make their outcomes tangible; listen as well as, if not better than, they speak.

Leadership Secrets—Dependability, credibility, responsibility, accountability, and self-confidence.

Perseverance—One of the four foundations of leadership.

Three Cs—Credibility/character, confidence, and communication.

Trust—One of the four foundations of leadership.
Vision—One of the four foundations of leadership.

Review Questions

1. What is the concept of existential leadership and how does it relate to your personal views of leadership?
2. Who is your ideal leader and how does the leader's leadership traits interact with the followers, responsibility, results, and setting examples?

Activities in Your Organization

Listed below are some activities designed to reinforce the key chapter concepts in your organization. If you are a student and not currently working in the industry, interview an industry leader about one of these topics.

1. You analyzed the top five qualities of effective leaders using the self-assessment tool in Exhibit 12.3. After analyzing your rankings of leadership qualities, reflect on the results. Ask a trusted friend or colleague to give you some feedback about these results based on what she or he knows about your leadership qualities. Did your rankings change as a result of the insights from this trusted friend/colleague? What is your highest ranked leadership quality? How can you capitalize on this strength? What is your lowest ranked leadership quality? How can you develop this into a strength? What can you do to use these leadership qualities to improve quality in your organization?
2. You analyzed the top five keys of effective leaders using the self-assessment tool in Exhibit 12.3. After analyzing your rankings of leadership keys, reflect on the results. Ask a trusted friend or colleague to give you some feedback about these results based on what she or he knows about your leadership keys. Did your rankings change as a result of the insights from this trusted friend/colleague? What is your highest ranked leadership key? How can you capitalize on this strength? What is your lowest ranked leadership key? How can you develop this into a strength? What can you do to use these leadership keys to improve quality in your organization?
3. You analyzed the top five secrets of effective leaders using the self-assessment tool in Exhibit 12.3. After analyzing your rankings of leadership secrets, reflect on the results. Ask a trusted friend or colleague to give you some feedback about these results based on what she or he knows about your leadership secrets. Did your rankings change as a result of the insights from this trusted friend/colleague? What is your highest ranked leadership secret? How can you capitalize on this strength? What is your lowest ranked leadership secret? How can you develop this into a strength? What can you do to use these leadership secrets to improve quality in your organization?

References

Cichy, Ronald F. "Blueprint for Leadership." *Michigan Lodging.* (November–December; Vol. 13, pp. 6, 15, 1988.)

Cichy, Ronald F., and Caroline L. Cook. "Leadership Qualities: The Non-Commercial Foodservice Industry." *Restaurant Personnel Management* Volume 4, Number 8 (August 1991): 6–7.

Cichy, Ronald F., and Raymond S. Schmidgall. "Financial Executives in U.S. Clubs." *Club Management.* Volume 38, Number 5 (October 1997): 67–73.

Cichy, Ronald F., and Raymond S. Schmidgall. "Leadership Qualities of Financial Executives in the U.S. Lodging Industry." *The Cornell H.R.A. Quarterly.* Volume 37, Number 3 (April 1996): 56–62.

Cichy, Ronald F., and Michael P. Sciarini. "Do You Fit This Profile of a Hospitality Leader?" *Lodging.* Volume 15, Number 10 (June 1990): 40–42.

Cichy, Ronald F., and James B. Singerling. "Club COO Leadership: A Comparative Study of Leadership Qualities of Club Industry Chief Operating Officers." *FIU Hospitality Review.* Volume 15, Number 1 (Spring 1996): 25–36.

Cichy, Ronald F., Michael P. Sciarini, and Mark E. Patton. "Food-Service Leadership: Could Attila Run a Restaurant?" *The Cornell H.R.A. Quarterly.* Volume 33, Number 1 (February 1992): 46–55.

Cichy, Ronald F., Michael P. Sciarini, Caroline L. Cook, and Mark E. Patton. "Leadership in the Lodging and Non-Commercial Food Service Industries." *FIU Hospitality Review.* Volume 9, Number 1 (Spring 1991): 1–10.

Cichy, Ronald F., Takashige "Teddy" Aoki, Mark E. Patton, and Kerry Y. Hwang. "Shido-sei: Leadership in Japan's Commercial Food-Service Industry." *The Cornell H.R.A. Quarterly.* Volume 34, Number 1 (February 1993): 88–95.

Drucker, Peter F., *Management Challenges for the 21st Century.* New York: HarperCollins Publishers, Inc. 1999.

Hager, Dan. *The Legacy of the Leader.* East Lansing, MI: *The* School of Hospitality Business Alumni Association, 2002.

Merton, Thomas. *Contemplation in a World of Action.* Notre Dame, IN: University of Notre Dame Press, 1998.

Schmidgall, Raymond S., and Ronald F. Cichy. "Club Controllers Requirements: Skills, Knowledge, and Responsibilities." *The Bottomline.* Volume 12, Number 8 (December/January 1998): 15–18.

Schmidgall, Raymond S. and Ronald F. Cichy. "Historian versus Visionary: Leadership Traits of Lodging Financial Executives." *The Bottomline.* Volume 11, Number 5 (August/September 1996): 9–13, 28.

Zona, Guy A. *The Soul Would Have No Rainbow If the Eyes Had No Tears.* New York: Touchstone, 1994.

Relevant Web Sites

An online leadership assessment:
   http://crs.uvm.edu/gopher/nerl/personal/Assess/b.html
Effective Leadership and TQM:
   http://www.dti.gov.uk/mbp/bpgt/m9ja91001/m9ja910014.html#toc_3
Hospitality Business at MSU:
   http://www.bus.msu.edu/shb/
Leadership: An Overview:
   http://web.cba.neu.edu/~ewertheim/leader/leader.htm
Leading TQM:
   http://www.dti.gov.uk/mbp/bpgt/m9ja91001/m9ja910018.html#toc_17
Managers as Leaders:
   http://www.leadersdirect.com/mgrlead.html
RARE Hospitality International, Inc. Web Site:
   www.rarehospitality.com/
Quality Leaders Network:
   http://www.loebigink.com/qnet/default.htm

Chapter

13   *Quality Life*

Applying quality principles to personal real life situations in and of itself is a great summary of how to bring quality to life and to work in the hospitality industry.

John R. Weeman, Jr.
President
Weeman Partners in Development
Irving, TX

Learning Objectives

1. Develop a personal definition of quality.
2. Apply the principles of quality improvement to daily life by understanding the prime importance of relationships.
3. Understand the personal quality triangle.
4. Apply quality improvement principles to life.
5. Describe the steps and components of the quality life implementation process model.
6. Develop a Balanced Score Card for your quality life.

In the last chapter, we discussed the importance of leaders understanding themselves before trying to lead themselves or others. This understanding of self leads to the development of a personal vision of quality and the possibility of taking this personal definition of quality into an organization that has a matching, or closely aligned, definition. This creates a situation where a shared vision of quality exists based on shared values about quality.

Self-Understanding

The application of the principles of improving quality to our personal lives begins with **self-knowledge** that leads to **self-awareness** and **self-understanding**. Self-knowledge is a process that requires a personal commitment to exploring and getting to know oneself.

It requires honesty and candor and is based on the fact that the improvement begins by looking within. We can begin the process by asking the following questions:

- Who exactly am I at my core?
- What and who do I care about?
- How do I behave and act?

The answers to these questions provide insight into what we treasure, what is important, who is significant, and what we value in life. These answers will lead to an understanding of personal values, which are core values. These core values could include ambition, balance of family and work, caring, continuous learning, continuous quality improvement, creativity, dedication, empowerment, equality, fairness, focus, forgiveness, fun, growth, happiness, a healthy lifestyle, honesty, humor, integrity, leadership, loyalty, open communication, an open mind, passion, a positive attitude, professionalism, punctuality, reliability, respect, self-improvement, teamwork, trust, trustworthiness, unconditional love, and/or understanding.

Once personal values begin to emerge, we can utilize them to articulate a personal vision with the following questions:

- What do I want to create in my life?
- If my life were ideal, what would be happening and how would I know it?
- What are my dreams for my life in the future?

Examples of personal visions include:

- To live each day by being myself, my best.
- To be happy and successful in all personal and professional endeavors.
- To be the best leader in the hospitality business while being the best parent to my children.
- To live each day as if it were the last and to cherish the people around me.
- To be the exemplar of continuous quality improvement in both my personal and professional lives.
- To live for the moments that I will treasure forever.
- To create a lasting impression with the people I care about, give my children the best education and teach them about love and integrity, and build a strong marriage partnership based on love and honesty.

An unknown author once wrote that "Life is not measured by the number of breaths you take. It is measured by the number of moments that take your breath away." The place to begin a quality life is with the end in mind. This concept is called *back planning* and begins with the desired outcome in mind. While it combines Eastern and Western philosophies, it requires us to consider and develop answers to the following questions:

- If my life is ideally effective, how will I know it?
- What will be happening if my life is perfect?
- How will the ideal, perfect life manifest itself for me, significant others, and at work?
- What desired outcomes or results will I be achieving with self, significant others, and at work?

By envisioning the ideal future, we can plan backwards from that future. For example, if we expect the ideal future 10 years from now, what needs to be happening 5 years from today? Three years from today? One year from today? Today? This is the opposite of looking at where we are today and trying to improve from today in a linear, incremental fashion. This approach to a quality life helps create our own unique destiny. Within that destiny, each of us has a personal definition of quality.

The third necessary component for a quality life is a mission. Recall that a mission is our purpose or our reason for being. Some develop their personal mission after asking and answering the question "What distinctive source of value do I add to the world?" There is synergy between the personal and professional mission statements. The power is derived from the ways that the two are aligned and moving forward into the future together. Some examples of personal missions include:

- To be a highly effective person.
- To set a high standard for quality both in personal and professional lives. To always strive to give 100 percent of who you are and to be a role model and example for those around you.
- To be a friend to those you know, to place your life before your career, to do something you love doing, to be a positive asset to others, to never forget your role models and the people and organizations that have supported you.
- To balance quality of life between family and work, to continuously improve yourself, to develop and grow in your personal and professional lives, to build relationships with family and friends.
- To surround yourself with the people who are important to you, to have a loving and honest relationship with your spouse, to instill strong values in your children and inspire them, to continue to improve relationships with your family, to be loyal and hardworking, to be caring and effective, to contribute to the financial well-being of the family.
- To maintain balance between personal and professional, to continue to grow and develop, to follow the passion in your heart and soul, to address the challenges you will face in deliberate and honest ways.
- To be loyal to family and friends, lead a successful career that you will enjoy, stay healthy, take on challenges, live life to the fullest, believe that nothing is impossible, give your enthusiasm, devotion, and yourself to all you do.

Personal Definition of Quality

Just as with the understanding of personal vision and values, it is important to think about and articulate a personal definition of quality. Doing so will help clarify what we value when it comes to quality and what our vision is for a personal quality life. Once understood, this definition can be shared with others as part of the process of creating a shared vision.

Many of the principles we have covered about a shared vision in an organization also apply to the creation of a shared vision in our quality life. We might begin to think about our personal definition of quality by asking and answering the following questions:

- What do I personally value when it comes to quality?
- How does it relate to my personal vision for quality?
- What is my personal definition of quality?

These questions are at the core of the exploration of the principles of managing quality and continuous quality improvement in daily life. It would be most interesting to write the answers to these questions now and store them away for six months or a year. Then take them out and re-read and reconsider them, noting any changes that have occurred since they were written. One would expect an evolution in the definition throughout the quality improvement journey.

Once we have mastered the principles and practices of managing for quality, it would be terrific if these same ideas and principles would create the same level of excellence in our personal lives. Many principles do have direct application to our personal lives; we refer to this as a **Quality Life (QL).** When we originally developed this QL concept, it was at the urging of our students who told us that they saw applicability of the principles of improving quality in an organization to improving quality in one's personal life. They asked us to share examples from our lives with them so that they might benchmark our lives and learn from them. We have included a segment on QL in each of our subsequent Managing for Quality in Hospitality Business senior-level courses at Michigan State University.

Applying Quality Principles to Life

QL is the application of quality improvement principles to our personal lives. This application is largely relationship based, that is, it applies to relationships first with yourself, then with friends, and family, and also with colleagues at work. Relationships that are valued have certain characteristics; they are based on honesty and trust, for example. Valued relationships add a richness to our lives because of their character. These relationships help build individual self-esteem and self-confidence through the journey toward ongoing improvement.

Relationships have a power that results directly from the time we invest in them. In a relationship it is important for each individual to dedicate oneself to the fulfillment of the other. At the core of relationships is the notion of knowing ourselves and knowing how deeply we believe in ourselves. Relationships that are really memorable exalt the individual while recognizing and celebrating that the relationship helps the individual realize his or her full potential. Relationships are built on the foundation of individuals. Shared common vision, mission, and values make the relationship balanced, along with the sense of individual and the collective identity of the relationship.

A Personal Quality Triangle

Throughout the book, we have emphasized the need to balance the expectations of internal customers, external customers, and financial expectations using a Quality Triangle model. This model has been adapted into a personal Quality Triangle and is presented in Exhibit 13.1.

Exhibit 13.1   The Personal Quality Triangle

The self at the bottom left of the triangle is the starting point. It represents each of us as an individual. The question at this point of the triangle is "Who am I?" Self has a set of expectations that are tied to self-knowledge, self-understanding, self-esteem, and self-confidence and may have some eternal dimensions that are spiritual or religious.

The significant others at the top of the model include individuals with whom we have interpersonal relationships, including members of our families, friends, associates in organizations (e.g., clubs), and others outside of work. Questions to ask at this point include:

- Who are you?
- Who are we together?
- What are we now?
- What do we want to become?

The others in our relationships have expectations too. Some of the questions about relationships are:

- Why is this relationship important to me? To the other person?
- Are the requirements of the other person being met?
- Are my requirements being met in the relationship?
- Are both of us committed to the relationship?
- Is the other person contributing as much to the relationship as I am? What would my life be like without this relationship?
- How can the relationship be improved?

The work at the bottom right of the model represents all of the individual relationships that we have at work as they relate to our persona and roles at work. Once again, there is a different set of expectations here. Sometimes we must make choices in balancing the three sets of expectations. Sometimes they are in conflict with each other; at other times they are in harmony. For example, we cannot exclusively focus on work expectations and take unfair advantage of significant others or abuse the self in the process. There must always be some form of balance; balance in the triangle leads to balance in life.

Exhibit 13.2 illustrates how to apply the principles of managing and improving quality to our personal lives.

Our QL hinges on credibility. Credibility is making certain that our actions are believable and it is related to keeping our word. Credibility is an essential value in our families. We depend on our families for so much. In turn, they depend on us because we have built credibility through keeping our word.

When we were young, we depended on our parents and other members of our family. Early in our lives, our parents and other family members taught us the fundamentals of service by meeting our every need. In turn, our spouses, our children, and other family members have given us countless opportunities to serve them in kind and patient ways and attempt to exceed their expectations.

Quality Improvement Principle	Application to Life and Service Quality
Vision/Constancy of Purpose	Every family must have their vision or dream of what they want their family to be. And, like the organization's vision, this dream must come from the heart, mind, and soul of every family member, including the children. There would be periodic changes in the vision.
	Quality of service and customer satisfaction are strongly enhanced by everyone's commitment to the vision.
Remove Inspection	Be less critical and more supportive, especially of your spouse, where 100% support is required. Empower your children and let them make decisions early in life, because the "big decisions" come later.
	Monitored and empowered associates who have the right information and freedom are a tremendous force in this organization.
Continuous Improvement	Grow with each other as family members (both children and parents). Remember what you have learned about effective teams and think of the family as a team trying to improve on a continuous basis. Think of family challenges as you would issues at work and use the tools of intervention to improve on a continuous basis. Think of yourself continuing to improve and learn in your golden years.
Institute Leadership	There is no foundation for the adage: Who wears the pants in the family? There are two leaders working in harmony to develop the children and the family as a whole. The family culture and overall environment are established and maintained by both parents. The parents set the example, especially in the early childhood stages. Do things as a family whenever possible so the children can view first hand how to correctly react to real life situations, issues, and challenges.
	Effective leaders know they live in a "fish bowl" and take advantage by setting a good example.
Drive Out Fear	The environment in the home must be one of trust and freedom to speak. The leaders must foster ideas and accept past failures. The children must not fear their parents and must have the ability to plan their own future.
	Improvements in service quality rest in the associates' creativity and the freedom of expression.
Break Down Barriers	Do everything TOGETHER! This includes travel and vacations. It also includes family participation in each member's interests and hobbies. Most importantly, solve problems together. Do not point fingers or cast blame, but review the processes in family life to create a strong sense of team.
	Levels of customer satisfaction are increased when teams are involved in the process of CQI.
Vigorous Education Program	Promote family education at all levels and make certain that education takes precedent over all other items such as athletics and social activities, including those of the leaders. Children need to appreciate what their life is like because of their parents' influences.
	Educated associates take an early lead because they understand what quality and leadership have to do with customer satisfaction.
TEAM Approach	Conduct family meetings, at the dinner table for example, to discuss issues, find the root cause, and intervene. This is where commitments are made. This is precious time of which parents can take advantage.
	Meet with your associates on an informal basis throughout the day because these internal customers will more likely enroll in the CQI process.

Exhibit 13.2 Quality Improvement Principles Applied to a Quality Life

Process Thinking	Always focus on what and how, not who. Discourage blame at all levels. Family processes are acted out as behavior patterns in reaction to external issues.
	Blame gets us nowhere. Mentoring and process evaluation allows associates to reach their potential.
Celebrate/Recognize Success	Recognize milestones and show appreciation for accomplishments. Your spouse is your number one customer, but your children are very close behind. Always recognize and treat your children on an equal basis. Recognition leads to high self-esteem, which in turn leads to future success.
	Don't wait for the annual awards banquet to recognize positive performance. Do it every day!
Maintain Balance	Do what you have to do at work, but never let work cause problems in your home.

Exhibit 13.2   continued

Our families have had a tremendous impact on shaping our philosophy of service, and for that matter, on ways to improve quality.

Effectiveness of QL

The effectiveness of QL comes from how we interrelate with others when dealing with life's challenges and how, while even in the midst of problems, we feel the joy and fun of the journey.

Those who desire a QL are responsible for seeing that they understand their personal values and vision, as well as their personal definition of quality. These QL leaders have a primary responsibility—to nurture, build, and protect the relationships with self and others. All of us as QL leaders must work diligently each day to keep those relationships intact, knowing that relationships become tarnished and grow old unless they are "polished" often.

Self, significant others, and work all provide opportunities for meeting or exceeding expectations in a QL. Sometimes love, understanding, an overriding emotion of security and hope, laughter, and positive humor are the result. Other times, the relationships are more challenging. Ideally, each person in the relationship has a feeling of belonging and senses that, because of the relationship, they are never traveling life's path alone.

Implementation of a Quality Life

The steps for implementing a quality life are presented in Exhibit 13.3.

The implementation process begins with a commitment from ourselves as the first necessary step of understanding self. At some point in our journey through this life, each of us must decide what our driving force is. In other words, we must hear our own individual internal voice telling us who we are and what we want to do about who we are. This will help us determine our personal requirements in the form of needs, wants, and expectations.

We can transform the voices heard within into requirements. The requirements can then be sorted into the vital few, as opposed to the trivial many. This

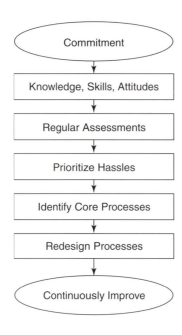

Exhibit 13.3   Quality Life Implementation Process Model

Pareto Principle application helps us focus our limited time and resources on what is really necessary for us. We develop and prioritize the requirements and then search for solutions, where necessary, and commit to those solutions. We know what we have to do and have the empowering freedom to do it; this leads to self-control and self-confidence.

Commitment also includes the pledge to treat others with dignity. By treating others positively, we avoid behaviors and feelings that would impair the relationship. This helps others and increases their commitment and loyalty to the relationship. We are each responsible for contributing to a compelling vision for all others in the relationship so the others will choose to enroll in the implementation process.

The next step is acquiring the necessary knowledge, skills, and behaviors. The goal is to share basic values based on trust and respect. Once the basic values are acquired, it is the responsibility of each to teach, guide, and mentor others. All must be included because it takes everyone in the relationship to contribute. QL requires knowledge, skills, and behaviors to elicit cooperation from others.

The third step is regular assessments. This is not to be confused with "judging" self or others; assessments of self, significant others, and work encourages making decisions based on information, not just intuition. For example, one might ask the following:

- Who is the family member?
- What is the family member's requirement?
- What does this family member need, want, or expect?

The goal during assessment is to identify and begin to analyze problems or hassles in the relationship so they can be addressed. One could ask in each relationship the following:

- Is the requirement of the other person being met?
- What could be done to improve the relationship?

This step includes a great deal of communication, specifically listening. The listening required in this step could take the form of interviews and other tools to categorize the data. Once categorized, it is relatively easy to identify recurring themes and hassles that occur over and over again.

The next step, prioritizing hassles, becomes easier when the assessment information is known. (Recall that the word "hassles" is the code name for problems, obstacles, barriers, challenges, and opportunities that you are facing.) The top priorities are those seen or experienced most frequently in all the assessments. Typically one of the most frequent hassles in relationships is related to problems in communication. One could prioritize hassles from the standpoint of self, significant others, and work, and work on improving the top one in each of the three categories simultaneously. Once the hassle is uncovered, a number of tools can be used to identify the root cause(s) and eliminate these hassles.

Next, the core processes are determined. A core process is one that is essential for meeting the needs and exceeding the expectations of self, significant others, or work, in both the short- and long-term. One of the questions to ask is: "What is it that we do that is critical?" For example, one of the critical core processes is to involve people in planning the experiences that affect them. This increases the pride and joy that they derive from that experience. It does not matter if the experience is a family vacation, a dinner at a special restaurant, or just watching a movie at home together. We want to make others feel good by contributing to the development and improvement of key processes. One of the key processes is the demonstration of loyalty to each other. In a family, for instance, this is seen as sibling loyalty rather than sibling rivalry. The relationships must be based on mutual respect and support, another core principle. If this core principle needs to be improved, the question to ask is: "What can I do to help you?"

Another core principle is to communicate openly, directly, and quickly when there is need for an improvement. Communication of essential information and feelings must take place freely and regularly in a relationship with all concerned. There should be the feeling that there is a fair contribution by all to building the relationship. In short, we must guide others in the process. This step also includes the identification of ways to measure the effectiveness of each of the core processes.

Redesigning the process is the next step. We redesign a process when we help others solve their problems. Often problems surface due to faulty planning. How can we change the process to improve the planning? The goal is to try to bring out the best in self and others. Another objective in redesigning the process is to attempt to introduce variety so boredom and fatigue do not occur in the relationships. Redesigning also includes respecting and accepting others in the relationships by accepting responsibility for self and the group. The overall objective of the redesign is the satisfaction of self and of others.

The final step is continuous improvement; a step that is never completed. This helps the relationships and the individuals have long-term staying power. If we implement this process using this model, we simply cannot have a bad family relationship, work relationship, or relationship with self. We will demonstrate that we genuinely care about others. We will link together quality and the relationships; they will become inseparable. We will view people as competent children or adults based on high levels of trust, and we will affirm that they want the same that we do—to improve continuously. We also will have the opportunity to keep learning, to always set our goals higher. We will be able to not only improve the relationships; we will also improve the planning and communication over time. We and others will be more energetically committed to a QL.

By its very nature a quality life requires us to improve each day. While the improvements may be small each day, the sum of the improvements is cumulative and helps ensure even higher levels of satisfaction. To perform at a high level mandates getting better through the elimination of one hassle at a time, each and every day. The end result is that the individual lives a higher quality life.

Use of the Tools

The tools introduced in Chapter 8 can be used in the assessment of baselines and the continuous improvement of a quality life. To determine the effectiveness of the quality life, we must regularly assess the levels of quality and improve and manage for quality when necessary.

Brainstorming is used to identify the burning issues. An example of an issue might be the balance between family and work commitments. Brainstorming also may be utilized as a tool to list all possible root causes of an issue, such as the pros and cons of moving to Corpus Christi, Texas, versus Denver, Colorado. *Nominal Group Technique* can be used to prioritize issues, such as hassles faced when leaving college after graduation and going to work full time. A *Flow Chart* presents a flow of steps in a process, such as finding that first full-time position out of college or changing positions or careers later in life. To describe these same steps in bar or line statement form, we could use a *Pareto Chart, Run Chart* or a *Histogram*. A *Pareto Chart* also may be used to help prioritize root causes, such as the causes of conflict and communication breakdowns in a family. A *Cause and Effect Diagram* helps identify and categorize all the root causes of an issue. It could be used to analyze whether a person should leave his or her current position or stay. The *PDCA Cycle* is used to develop solutions and an action plan. Unacceptable service levels could be improved by planning, doing, checking, and acting using the PDCA Cycle. The *Force Field Analysis* also helps develop solutions by seeing the entire picture in terms of driving forces and restraining forces. It could be used to assist in the analysis of whether to stay in a relationship or leave it. Once the plan is implemented, it can be monitored using a *Pareto Chart* or a *Control Chart*. For example, a personal weight loss and exercise program could be monitored with these tools. The *SQPD Guide* can clearly pinpoint quality, cost, and revenue effects of a planned intervention. It could be modified slightly to consider the quality, cost, and revenue impacts associated with moving into a career in hotel sales from a career in front office operations.

The *Balanced Score Card* is perhaps one of the most applicable tools to a total quality life. It assists in measuring the results of a personal and professional life. It can include the five basic categories, modified to fit the individual life. For example, the Customer Satisfaction, Financial/Cost, Human Resources, Marketing/Growth, and Organizational Effectiveness categories could include what is listed in Exhibit 13.4.

Begin by filling in the blanks for the year; 20__. Some prefer to use a scale of 1 (low) to 5 (high) on the Balanced Score Card. Others prefer simply to assess each item on the score card by answering "yes" or "no." Some prefer a Balanced Score Card that only has two categories: personal and professional. The personal category includes self, family, and friends. The professional or work category would consider some of the following:

- Are my personal values aligned with the organization's values?
- Is my personal vision and mission in line with the organization's vision and mission?
- Do I like my position?
- Do I want more from work than I can get from my position?
- Would I be willing to take a less stressful position at lower pay to do something I enjoy more?
- Do I like the people I work with?
- Am I satisfied with my position?
- Would another position at the same organization or a different organization be more satisfying?
- What could I do to improve my position?

FAMILY
BALANCED SCORE CARD
Year 20___

OUTCOME AREA	TARGET PERFORMANCE	CURRENT PERFORMANCE	BASELINE PERFORMANCE	MEASUREMENT TOOL	REPORTING FREQUENCY
1. Customer Satisfaction					
1.1 Improve customer (each family member) satisfaction					
1.2 View family and friends as customers					
1.3 Discover the requirements of these customers					
1.4 Develop relationships with these customers					
2. Financial/Cost					
2.1 Improve short and long term family financial position					
2.2 Financial goals to personally achieve					
2.3 Reduction in personal debt					
2.4 Save for college for children					
2.5 Save for retirement					
2.6 Keep a position with a defined salary					

Exhibit 13.4 A Sample Balanced Score Card for a Quality Life

263

FAMILY
BALANCED SCORE CARD
Year 20___

OUTCOME AREA	TARGET PERFORMANCE	CURRENT PERFORMANCE	BASELINE PERFORMANCE	MEASUREMENT TOOL	REPORTING FREQUENCY
3. Human Resources					
3.1 Improve personal relationships with family members					
3.2 Be dedicated to the needs and wants of family and friends					
3.3 Instill values and vision in children					
3.4 Be fair and honest with others					
3.5 Treat others as you would like to be treated					
4. Marketing/Growth					
4.1 Improve personal career position					
4.2 Market self to organization					
4.3 Market self to friends and family					
4.4 Continue to learn and develop					
4.5 Valued asset to all team members, personally and professionally					
4.6 Moving forward in the career					

Exhibit 13.4   continued

FAMILY
BALANCED SCORE CARD
Year 20___

OUTCOME AREA	TARGET PERFORMANCE	CURRENT PERFORMANCE	BASELINE PERFORMANCE	MEASUREMENT TOOL	REPORTING FREQUENCY
5. Organizational Effectiveness 5.1 Improve leadership skills and effectiveness with family members 5.2 New and better ways to be organized personally 5.3 Effectiveness at home 5.4 Effectiveness at work 5.5 Live life in a contented way 5.6 Be happy 5.7 Love what you do personally and professionally 5.8 Hassles reduced or eliminated 5.9 Challenges met 5.10 Results, desired outcomes achieved 5.11 Time balance between personal and professional lives 5.12 Decrease time wasted in procrastination 5.13 Threats minimized 5.14 Strengths used fully 5.15 Weaknesses compensated for or improved					

Exhibit 13.4 continued

From the Balanced Score Card we can discover what changes need to be made in our lives, both personal and professional, to realize our goals and vision. In other words, what can we change to be more proud of who we are *and* who we are becoming?

If the Balanced Score Card does not show the desired results, we need to re-align the process of our quality plan. Make the necessary changes in life to realize goals. Even though we realign our quality process, we can keep the same core values.

Summary

The understanding of self leads to development of a personal vision of quality and the possibility of taking this personal definition into an organization that has a matching definition. We create this personal vision with self-awareness, self-knowledge, and self-understanding. Once we have defined our personal vision and looked at what makes a quality life, we can begin the implementation process. This process begins with a commitment to understand ourselves and ends with the step of continuous improvement. As in our work lives, continuous improvement in our personal lives is a never-ending process.

Key Terms

Quality Life (QL)—Quality principles that have direct application to our personal lives.

Self-Awareness—Tool for creating a personal vision.

Self-Knowledge—A process that requires a personal commitment to exploring and getting to know oneself.

Self-Understanding—Tool for creating a personal vision.

Review Questions

1. What is your personal definition of quality? How do you expect it to change over the next five years?
2. What are three quality improvement principles that you have naturally applied to your life in the past? Which three do you intend to apply to your life in the future?
3. What are the three components of the personal quality triangle to maintain quality in one's life? How do you balance these?
4. What are the steps and components of the quality life implementation process? How do they apply to your life?
5. How would you build a QL culture in your family?
6. What categories will you include in your Balanced Score Card?

Activities in Your Quality Life Journey

Listed below are some activities you can do in your pursuit of a quality life.

1. The place to begin a quality life is with the end in mind. Decide what you desire for yourself, significant others, and work, and the culture you would like

to develop in your quality life. This concept, back planning, begins with the desired outcome in mind and requires you to consider and develop answers to the following questions:

- If my life is ideally effective, how will I know it?
- What will be happening if my life is perfect?
- How will the ideal, perfect life manifest itself for me, significant others, and at work?
- What desired outcomes or results will I be achieving with self, significant others, and at work?

By envisioning the ideal future, you can plan backwards from that future. For example, if we expect the ideal future 10 years from now, what needs to be happening 5 years from today? Three years from today? One year from today? Today? This approach to a quality life helps create our own unique destiny.

2. Within the destiny that you have envisioned in Activity #1, think about your personal definition of quality. Ask and answer the following question: "What do I personally value when it comes to quality, how does it relate to my personal vision for quality, and what is my personal definition of quality?" Now write the answer to the question on paper, seal it and in a self-addressed stamped envelope, and give it to a trusted friend. Ask that friend to mail the envelope to you in six months. Six months later, after you receive and open that envelope and read the earlier definition of quality, compare it to the definition of quality that you are now using. How has your personal definition of quality evolved in the past six months? What does this change mean?

3. Consider the implementation of your quality life and the steps in the process. What commitment are you willing to make as the first necessary step of understanding self? What are your vital few requirements? How would these requirements be prioritized? What knowledge, skills, and behaviors do you need to acquire? What regular assessments of self, significant others, and work will you undertake? Who do you need to communicate with during assessment? How will you collect the information, categorize the data, and identify recurring themes and hassles? How will you prioritize hassles, problems, obstacles, barriers, challenges, and opportunities that you are facing? Which tool(s) will you use to identify the root cause(s) and eliminate these hassles? How will you determine the core processes? What is it that you do that is critical? What will you do to redesign a process and help others solve their problems? How can you change the process to bring out the best in self and others? What will be included in your personal Balanced Score Card? What will you do to continuously improve (a step that is never completed)?

Relevant Web Sites

Assess Your Own Personal Quality of Life (by Diana Chaudhuri):
http://www.globalideasbank.org/BOV/BV-365.HTML
Integrating Organizational and Personal Development (by Richard Winder and Daniel Judd):
http://www.ldri.com/articles/98aqcmapcompass.html
International Society for Quality of Life Research (ISOQOL) Web Site:
http://www.isoqol.org/
National Mentoring Center:
http://www.nwrel.org/mentoring/
Quality of Life Instruments Database:
http://www.qolid.org/

Chapter

14 *Final Thoughts*

When customers perceive a match between their initial expectations and the service they consistently receive, they identify a quality outcome. To deliver quality we must fine-tune our listening skills and truly understand our customer's expectations well before service is initiated. Customer service focus is necessary to communicate progress and detect changes in customer expectations which then drive future service enhancements.

Linda Rhodes-Pauly, MS, RD
Vice President Business Development
HDS Services
Farmington Hills, MI

Learning Objectives

1. Summarize the quality improvement knowledge, skills, and attitudes you have studied in this book.
2. Describe the challenges facing our industry.

At this point we have working knowledge of the following:

- What quality is
- The importance of internal customers and their power
- What total customer focus means
- Commitment to the principles of Dr. Deming
- Using the CQI process
- The steps in the decision-making process
- How to bring quality principles to our personal lives
- How leaders use the quality principles
- Why high performance service organizations achieve excellence
- How to use empowerment and synergism
- How to use self-directed teams
- What external customer loyalty and perceived quality are
- How to use the tools of the trade
- How to build the strategic quality plan
- The importance of vision, mission, and core values
- How to implement quality—the six steps

As we have pointed out, organizations are systems with interrelated processes that directly affect the quality of the products and services created and delivered for the organization's customers. We have described an overall system for managing and improving quality that has evolved and been proven in HDS Services, a "real world" managed services organization. We have reinforced the essential elements of the system by using examples from other organizations known for managing and improving quality.

Our system approach begins with *knowing our customers* and understanding how the *requirements of customers* influence our efforts to manage and improve quality. Everything we do in the organization is in service of the organization's customers. The three broad sets of expectations in any organization—*internal customers' expectations, external customers' expectations, and financial expectations*—are of primary consideration. The expectations must be revisited and studied regularly as they relate to customer requirements, how well the organization's processes are delivering on the expectations, and the balance of all three expectations.

To manage and improve quality requires an understanding of the history of the quality movement and its basic concepts as discovered and tested by the *champions* or *gurus of quality*. These pioneers were the first to experiment with a systems approach to improve quality. The improvements, principles, and metrics they used have been improved upon and are still being used today.

Quality management views the process of change from the paradigm of customers first, beginning with internal customers (associates) and moving to external customers. The needs and expectations of these two groups are translated into processes and systems that are trumpeted in the organization's vision, mission, values, and culture. The associates must be empowered as they improve quality with their teams. Quality leaders understand that treating the organization's internal customers with respect and dignity results in these associates treating the organization's external customers in kind. *Effective teams* utilize synergy to manage and improve quality. Through collaboration, the teams serve customers in ways that are not possible when individuals are working to do so by themselves. Cross-functional action groups add a diversity of views and ways to address the improvement of quality. Self-directed teams operate by relying on team members to identify and prioritize hassles, intervene to reduce or eliminate the hassles, and improve other critical processes in the organization.

The quality perceived by *external customers* determines the levels of improvements needed in an organization. These customers must regularly be asked for honest feedback regarding quality. This feedback can be supplemented by customer complaints which can lead to the identification of quality improvement opportunities resulting in customer satisfaction.

Management helps deliver results that are better today than yesterday by facilitating the progress of the associates who serve on cross-functional action group teams, giving them the necessary resources to deliver the required improvements, providing the tools needed for associates to be effective in their efforts, and keeping internal and external customers connected. *Tools of the trade* are utilized to measure and monitor quality improvements. The goal is not these metrics, however; it is to improve the results embedded in the level of quality in the organization's products and services delivered to customers. Improving these results will enhance customer satisfaction and build customer loyalty.

William Jennings Bryan is credited with saying: "Destiny is not a matter of change; it is a matter of choice. It is not a thing to be waited for; it is a thing to be achieved." *Strategic quality planning* begins with a personal vision and results in a shared vision within the organization. These visions answer the question: "What do I want to create?" In concert with the mission and core values of the organization, the vision is the stimulus for the strategic goals and critical processes. The values, vision, and mission help build commitment from all.

Assessing quality helps us determine requirements of the customers, as well as how we are doing in the delivery of these requirements at levels that meet or exceed the customers' expectations. Assessments that are regular and ongoing lead to improvements.

The six steps of *implementing quality* include education, assessment, addressing the burning issues, determining critical processes and determining how to measure progress, redesigning the process, and continuous improvement. This implementation is a process that is never ending since implementation continuously spotlights other needed improvements.

Leading quality is the responsibility of all in the organization. If we all lead from our own position and contribute to the common good of the organization in service of that organization's customers, the customers will be satisfied. Personal leadership qualities, keys, and secrets identify strengths that can be used to the strategic advantage of the individual and the organization and weaknesses that can be improved.

A *quality life* occurs in one's personal life when the principles of managing and improving quality are implemented. And as the quality of our lives improve, the lives of those we touch will be improved as well. The organization also benefits, since quality life principles have a direct impact on the individual who ultimately contributes to the organization as a team member and internal customer.

Final Thoughts Regarding Managing for Quality

Here are some final thoughts about quality and the pathway to excellence. First, work with *a passion*, not only to succeed, but also, using your heart and using an internal customer focus as the driving force. Associates will readily recognize passion and leadership abilities, and this will make leaders and the entire team successful.

Convert good customers to **raving fans.** This is accomplished through a process of identifying customer needs and expectations, then going beyond these in ways that exceed their expectations. This works with both internal and external customers. Creating raving fans is similar to achieving a personal vision **"plus one"**—a little extra. In most cases your customers know what your objectives and strategies are for meeting their expectations. The "plus one" is the little extra, the surprise that overwhelms the customer and creates a loyal customer for life. The "plus one" separates us and our organization from the competition. In many cases, the "plus one" is a strong relationship or partnership with our customer. This revolutionary approach to customer relationship management is detailed in the book *Raving Fans* by Ken Blanchard and Sheldon Bowles.

It is you, not others who control your attitude. What is your vision for the future and how does it affect the ways you are acting today? What are your personal and professional visions? What is your goal for when you reach your next decade mark (i.e., you turn 30, or 40, or 50, or 60)?

Some spend their time complaining and identifying barriers in their lives. They are the victims to all they meet. Instead, try to do what it takes today and tomorrow and the next day and the next to reach your ideal, perfect vision of the future. Let that vision pull you into the future. And even if you stop short, you will be closer to that vision than you were yesterday or the day before. Be willing to ask for help from the others listed on your personal balanced score card. Be willing to serve others in turn. If you have the gift of serving others, focus on serving others. Extend your hospitality and kindness to strangers.

It is essential to prioritize our lives and try to achieve a balance with our family, friends, and work. It is also critical to seek and find quiet time for solitude, silence, and reflection. It is amazing how much you can hear when no one is talking. Leadership is first, foremost, and always an inner quest. We need to wake up, and learn to explore and come to know ourselves, be true to ourselves and our values, and make a contribution to life. If you have the gift of being a leader, lead diligently and responsibly with credibility. Over time, we need to focus on significance (your internal measure of the difference you are making in the lives of others) rather than success (an external metric of how you are achieving).

Early in your career, you will more than likely be performing tasks related to the lower levels of the industry's or organization's organizational structure. If you accept this status as a part of the learning experience, you will not only learn, but upper management will recognize your character and overall positive attitude. The leaders of today had to "pay their dues" as they moved through their own career paths, and so will those of you entering the corporate world. However, the future leaders who have experienced and learned the principles of the management of quality presented in this book will definitely have a head start and an advantage over others.

You will know how to make the correct decisions and how to lead your internal customers. You will recognize the associates as your pathway to future success. You will be learning all about your organization's culture, products, and services. Your peers will also have to learn the principles of managing quality and how to use the organization's assets. When you practice the principles of quality management and improvement learned from this book and from the pedagogical approach to their use as learned by the students in our course at Michigan State University, you will be miles ahead.

Be sure to mentor several associates in your organization. The higher up in the organization the person goes, the more people he or she can *mentor*. The flip side of leadership and your mentoring responsibilities is the *high visibility of the leader* and what associates expect from their leader. Most associates are seeking a learning environment, and this is the opportunity leadership must use to the organization's strategic advantage. The primary asset not seen on the organization's balance sheet is **intellectual capital.** Increasing the value of this asset is not accomplished through wealth or financial gain. This asset increases through a commitment by leadership to be a mentoring organization with mentors at all levels. Use your mentors as an example; and follow their lead. It is one thing to practice the quality principles, but to teach them adds to your knowledge and depth of their use. So take the opportunity to teach and develop your associates. They will respect you forever.

Most of us have roots in our family, our childhood and adolescent environment, and in the geographic location(s) where we were raised. This is especially true for those raised in the Quality Life (QL) environment. But, there is one additional experience you must never forget. That is your time devoted to study, perhaps at the university level, with your friends, professors, and those of us who have played a role in molding your management style. Never forget your *roots* and do not allow disputes to ruin friendships and partnerships.

Always remember the enormous *power of the team.* The teams you developed when you built your organization's strategic quality plan possessed a voice in determining your organization's future. As a team member you should express your views, but, after the team makes its decision, everyone must support the decision and their teammates.

Also, keep in mind that the organization that you join after graduation will more than likely not practice the principles of leadership and management outlined in this book. So, what will you do? Our advice would be to practice the quality improvement management philosophies in your area of responsibility. You may end up being your organization's quality champion.

Remember to *manage by walking around.* In other words, be visible and available to all associates and customers. You will learn from your associates as you intermittently leave the global area of responsibility and enter the important areas of production or point of service. You will need to take advantage of these experiences to not only confirm quality levels but more importantly to recognize associates for their contributions. Those moments of recognition will be remembered for a lifetime. Don't wait for the annual awards banquet. The recognition should be presented in an honest and sincere way. This will enhance the sense of integrity in the leadership as seen by associates.

Always remember the good things you learned from previous mentors when you were a supervisor, department head, or front line staff member. Those same attributes should be in your arsenal for teaching and setting an example. In a sense, when you share your experiences and knowledge, you can attain immortality.

Remember that *change* is a positive situation, so never become set in your ways, especially the way you manage the organization. Also, remember that most changes are driven by your actions. However, never sacrifice your values for change. Your organization should never become predictable from a strategic point of view. You do want the organization to be predictable in the level of quality it achieves. To be predictably known as the best is every leader's vision.

Always give your associates and the management team the *freedom to grow.* That means that you teach and guide, then get out of the way. Try not to compare teams in your organization with athletic teams or the military because the environment and outcomes are entirely different. While some of the quality principles apply, others definitely do not. But the primary difference lies in the outcome because failure in one's performance in the organization has much less risk than on the battlefield or in a sporting event.

However, take into account that great achievements involve higher levels of *risk.* The gurus mentioned early on in this book took great risks in promoting their philosophies of managing and improving quality. In Dr. Deming's case, these principles were totally ignored by U.S. industry following World War II, so he eventually took them to Japan and totally revolutionized the manufacturing industry in that country. In this case, American industry was the loser, but we did not lose the lesson because we recognized our mistake, recovered, and have now integrated quality and Dr. Deming's obligations into our organizations.

Remember the examples of quality presented by and in HDS Services. They are unique to the hospitality industry but can be adapted to and applied to all organizations and industries. Always remember the lessons learned from developing organizations in the classroom environment as well. You and your team members know that *quality is the pathway to excellence.*

Finally, remember to listen to the voices of quality associates as well as external customers in your organization; and family members, friends, and colleagues in your life. In your personal and professional journey, regardless of the paths, careers, and organizations you choose, patiently listen and keep listening.

Challenges Facing the Industry

The **leadership challenges** facing the hospitality industry are similar to the challenges facing other organizations in many ways. In the *The Leadership Challenge,* James M. Kouzes and Barry Z. Posner highlight the challenges facing leaders as the following:

- Heightened uncertainty
- People first
- Even more connected
- Social capital
- Global economy
- Speed
- A changing workforce
- Even more intense search for meaning

Heightened uncertainty in our world today stems from the dramatic changes that affected all of us on September 11, 2001. We now worry about terrorism and the uncertainty and possible chaos it brings. This uncertainty spilled from our personal lives into the lives of our organizations as the stock market dipped to unfamiliar lows and organizations laid off workers in record numbers. One of the positive outcomes of the system that we described for managing and improving quality is that it heightens certainty and helps us more consistently deliver what we promise.

By putting *people first* we shift the top priority from career and work to relationships with family members and friends. It has been suggested that the tragedy of September 11 brought the primary priority of relationships with family and friends into focus. In the past, in some ways we were a hospitality industry of loneliness in the center of great communities of associates who wanted to contribute their time and talents in diverse ways. In other ways, we were an industry of serious breakdowns in personal and professional relationships in the face of unparalleled growth. Some would say that we were an industry of great personal ennui (i.e., boredom) in the middle of great claims of associate empowerment. This renewed focus on relationships extends to the organization as people place more importance on trust-based relationships and interactions with each other than they do on completion of tasks. Our quality improvement system puts people first by initially defining the requirements of the two most important groups of people (i.e., internal customers and external customers) and then utilizing the talents of teams of associates to drive the improvement process in the organization.

Technology enables us to be *even more connected,* both personally and organizationally. One only has to think about the Internet, cell phones, personal digital assistants, e-mail, and other such tools that were not available in the recent past to see this is true. One of the challenges of this technology is finding ways to keep people connected face-to-face. The quality system that we described has the cross-functional action group meetings as its primary mechanism for reducing or eliminating hassles. These groups operate with people in a room having conversations about ways to improve quality. This connects people in the organization and keeps them connected through a shared vision.

Social capital is the collective value of people who know each other and understand what they are willing to do for each other. It refers to the synergy that occurs in teams that operate in mutually beneficial relationships by working toward a common goal. The relationships are built on shared values. Social capital increases when the opinions of people are valued and they are invited to give their input to help the organization improve.

The *global economy* is readily visible in the $3.5 trillion of annual revenues in the global hospitality and tourism industries. There are pressures to provide a world-class level of quality to our more highly diverse internal customer workforce, as well as for the more highly diverse and sophisticated external customer base. The principles of improving quality position an organization to compete more effectively in the global economy, since the process can define the requirements for any group of customers. The tools used help connect the organization and its people to the global economy and take advantage of global opportunities.

Speed is an important factor to consider today, as demanding customers expect quality products and services less expensively and faster. Technology has accelerated the rate at which all of us expect our needs to be met. We feel rushed and impatient because of the rising demands on our time. We are not able to focus the time or efforts that we would like on people and tasks due to the sheer number of demands on us today. Yet, the system for improving quality presented here forces us to be deliberate, to focus on relationships in our action group teams, to be purposeful in our fact-based decisions, to carefully assess the results of our efforts, and to be persistent so we can continue to get better each day.

A changing workforce has been apparent in the hospitality industry for years. Today's heterogeneous workforce brings a level of diversity to the organization unlike that at any other time in the past. This variety of talents among the internal customers permits us to serve a more diverse group of external customers. With this multiplicity of internal and external customers comes challenges and opportunities. This diversity is a strength that contributes to the system for managing and improving quality much more dramatically and with greater impact than in the days when there were unchanging, homogeneous internal and external customers. When viewed as a strength, the changing workforce helps us expand our products and services to a much broader market of external customers.

A *more intense search for meaning* relates to the fundamental need of people to know that they are making a difference in their lives, the lives of others, and in the organization. An unknown author wrote: "Real success is success with self. It is not having things, but in having mastery, having victory over oneself ." People are searching for ways to be significant, not simply successful. They see this significance in the ways that they contribute to others. One of the ways associates can make a positive contribution to others is by helping to improve their own quality of life. This will have a positive effect on the quality of life for others who are significant in their lives.

Everything we do must be *both* planned and done with counsel. If people are involved with the planning of the work, they will bring pride and joy into the workplace. The hospitality industry has no room for arrogance elevated to the level of inspiration. As leaders, we must abandon our omniscient (i.e., all-knowing) and omnipotent (i.e., all-powerful) egos to the talents of those creating and delivering the products, services, and experiences.

To cultivate a continuous quality improvement mentality, we must seek counsel, accept advice, and listen to the opinions of others on subjects dear to us. Reflection becomes integral to the process of growth and basic to our style of acting and leading. Life is a learning process. We acknowledge and affirm the value of experience and learning from failure. In these we discover the truth and help develop others.

We hope that you find that which gives your life a deep meaning for you. American writer Henry David Thoreau wrote: "If one advances in the direction of his dreams, and endeavors to live the life which he has imagined, he will meet with success unexpected in common hours." Find something worth living for, something that energizes you, something that you are passionate about, something that enables you to move forward. We cannot tell you what it might be for you. You have to find, choose, and love it. We can only encourage you to start looking right now.

Summary

The system presented in this book has, as its foundation, the understanding of quality and ways to improve it. The quality improvement process is ongoing, a never-ending journey. We have studied the dimensions of the journey in the HDS Services system and have observed the outcomes in our course. This system of managing and improving quality is part of the journey required if improvement is the goal. Regardless of whether you have a vision for improving quality in your organization or your personal life, our system can help you get started and improve. But you must be passionate about quality improvement for the system to work.

Key Terms

"Plus One"—A little extra; a surprise that overwhelms the customer and creates a loyal customer for life.

Intellectual Capital—Increases through a commitment by leadership to be a mentoring organization with mentors at all levels.

Leadership Challenges—Eight obstacles confronting leaders.

Raving Fans—Accomplished through a process of identifying customer needs and expectations, then going beyond these in ways that exceed their expectations.

Review Questions

1. What are the major topics that were presented in this book as they relate to quality?
2. What are some of the quality challenges facing the industry?
3. What is the highest priority action that you personally will take to improve quality in your organization?

Activities in Your Organization

1. Review the list at the beginning of this chapter of the broad areas we covered in this book. Are there areas listed that need elaboration and further explanation? If so, please refer back to that section of the appropriate chapter and review the material once again.
2. Several challenges facing leaders of the hospitality industry are the following:
   - Heightened uncertainty
   - People first

- Even more connected
- Social capital
- Global economy
- Speed
- A changing workforce
- Even more intense search for meaning

How do these individual challenges affect or potentially impact your organization? How can you and others in the organization use the system for managing and improving quality to address these challenges and transform them into opportunities for the organization?

3. Review the final thoughts presented in this chapter. Think about how you work with a passion. Now ask and answer these questions: What do you do to use your heart and use an internal customer focus as the driving force? What are you doing to convert your good customers to raving fans? What are you doing to lead your internal customers? How are you mentoring associates in your organization? How do you fulfill the requirement of a high visibility of the leader for the associates? What are you doing to increase the intellectual capital of the organization? How will you manage and improve quality in an organization that you join that is not practicing the principles of quality leadership and management? What do you do to view change in a positive manner, and never become set in your ways, especially the way you manage the organization? To reach great achievements, how do you encourage higher levels of risk?

References

Blanchard, Ken and Sheldon Bowles. *Raving Fans: A Revolutionary Approach to Customer Service.* New York: Morrow, William & Co., 1993.

Kouzes, James M. and Barry Z. Posner. *The Leadership Challenge.* San Francisco, CA: Jossey-Bass–A Wiley Company, 2003.

Glossary

24/72: Ideas need to be acknowledged within 24 hours, and decisions completed within 72 hours.

5Nines Program: 5Nines represents a commitment to total customer satisfaction. The 5Nines acronym refers to end-to-end availability 99.999% (5Nines) of the time or no more than five minutes of total downtime per year for customers.

85/15 Rule of Quality: 85 percent of the company's problems are process-based, not people-related (15%).

Account Retention: Number of clients signed to management contracts that are kept and maintained.

Action Group Team (AGT): A team set up to work on a specific hassle or opportunity for improvement and includes representatives from multiple departments.

Addressing the Burning Issues: These are then incorporated into action plans and formal business plans.

Affinity Diagram: Arranging responses from members of a focus group into groups of similar ideas.

Assessing Quality: The requirements of the customers as well as how the organization is doing in the delivery of requirements at levels that meet or exceed the customers' expectations.

Assessment: A baseline is critical; baseline assessments must be conducted with two major groups; external customers (clients) and internal customers (associates).

Assessment Costs: Relate to the processes of monitoring measurement and making assessments beyond the baseline.

Associate Conflicts: Can develop as a result of team arrogance and other conflicts can result from one or more team members not pulling their weight.

Associate Feedback: Includes regular performance appraisals and completion of training programs.

Associate Satisfaction: Assessment of internal customers.

Associates-First Orientation: Everything is based on satisfying the needs of internal customers. The company needs to communicate with them and listen to their concerns and ideas.

Autonomy: Associates with functional limits who are independent and do not fear failure or making mistakes.

Awareness: Each can determine what he or she is able to contribute to making the plan become a reality.

Balanced Score Card (BSC): Identifies the performance levels of the previous year and the targets for the new year and provides a means to measure actual current performance against the targets.

Baseline: The current level of quality; consisting of the results of the initial quality assessments and surveys.

Benchmarking: Helps an organization study a process at another organization and adapt, modify, and apply the process at their own organization. Process to compare others within an industry, or organizations outside of an industry, to identify, understand, and adapt best practices and processes.

Brainstorming: Technique designed to generate a large number of ideas, causes, and solutions through a process of total interaction.

Building Commitment: Inviting people to be involved and participate in things that affect them.

Casting Limits: Defines who does what in the organization.

Cause and Effect Analysis: The effect is the problem statement which was brainstormed and prioritized through nominal group technique. The goal is to select the root cause that has the largest effect and solve/address that cause.

Cause and Effect Diagram: A tool used to analyze causes of a variation; sometimes called fishbone diagram.

Celebration of Success: Upon achieving success, we celebrate and recognize associates who have participated and contributed.

Check Sheet: Used to gather data on the problem or root cause.

Collaborative Thinking Teams: Associates learning to use the information to improve products and services; they should be recognized for their efforts.

Comment Cards: When comment cards and a reply on how the problem was eliminated are posted; it is a rich testimony that action was taken. Often those who complete comment cards are either very satisfied or extremely upset.

Commitment: The process for managing and improving quality is more likely to succeed if there is a strong message that there is a commitment to make quality the core of the organization's culture.

Commodities: Products or services now fall into the same class; perceived to have similar or equal quality by customers.

Common Purpose and Vision: This must mirror the goals of the organization, but it also must be able to be adopted by all of the diverse groups in the organization.

Communication: One of the four foundations of leadership. Listening is the key skill.

Compensation: Pay for performance.

Confidence: Confidence of associates is needed for vision, values, and processes of the organization to be successful.

Consensus: A decision or position reflecting collective thinking of a team that all members participate in developing, understand fully, believe workable, can live with, and will actively support.

Continuous Improvement: Promotes creativity, enhances customer satisfaction, and challenges traditional thinking. The basic concept dictates that any form of improvement, quantitatively measured, is acceptable. Represents a step-like incremental series of better results; it is a series of planned and monitored outcomes.

Continuous Quality Improvement: Key to the managing and improving quality for both internal and external customers; the objective is to deliver results that are better today compared to those of yesterday.

Cooperation: When associates use compromise in dealing with other members of the group. Working together toward a common quality improvement goal.

Core Principles of Quality: Require that top management to be visibly committed to improving quality.

Core Values: Guide the planning process, decision making regarding which plans are the highest priorities, and the resulting action to make the plans become reality.

Corporate Perception: Defines the future of the organization.

Cost of Nonconformance: Philosophy of Armand V. Feigenbaum and his rationale regarding an organization's commitment to quality.

Critical Processes: Directly contribute to the experience that the customer has with the organization. Necessary to meet present and future needs of the organization's customers.

Critical to Quality (CTQ): CTQ is an integral part of confirming the guests' requirements. To define CTQ in Six Sigma terms, voice of the customer (VOC) data are collected and compared to the guests' CTQ requirements. Then, the gap between the requirements and the current quality level of the organization's products and services is analyzed. Once the gap is identified and quantified, the Six Sigma internal customer team can begin to focus on measuring, analyzing, improving, and controlling this gap using the define, measure, analyze, improve and control process.

Crosby Complete Management System: Crosby's 14 steps to implementing quality improvements in an organization.

Cross-Functional Teams: Composed of people in various functional departments to determine the present level of quality and work on improvements.

Current External Customers: Should never be taken for granted or forgotten.

Customer Driven: High performance service organizations cannot define their visions until their customers are understood.

Customer Feedback: May be obtained through surveys, one-on-one conversations, and focus groups.

Customer-first Orientation: Everything done should be focused on the customer.

Customer Focus: Must be continuously evaluated. This feedback may be obtained by interviewing a number (say three to five percent) of customers each quarter.

Customer Loyalty: Customers perceive greater quality, and therefore value, from the organization and are therefore loyal. Loyal customers are valuable to an organization because of their word-of-mouth advertising, as well as their long-term economic value.

Customer Retention: Preventing customers from leaving the organization; providing the opportunity to build loyal customers.

Customer Satisfaction: Follows from customer service that meets or exceeds expectations.

Customer Service: Includes both intangible aspects and tangible aspects. Tangible aspects of quality relate to technical elements; intangible parts of customer service quality are more difficult to create, deliver, and measure.

Deming Circle: Cross-functional teams encourage rapid results by having teams explore ways to enhance customer service. Repeated until improvement is achieved through identification and elimination of problems.

Deming's 14 Obligations of Top Management: These form the core of Deming's quality system and define ways for an organization to transform itself into an organization focused on quality.

Diversity: Includes race, religion, personality, personal objectives, and financial/cultural background.

DMADV: A process that Defines, Measures, Analyzes, Defines, and Verifies.

DMAIC: A process that Defines, Measures, Analyzes, Improves, and Controls existing processes.

Driving Forces: Move a situation toward change.

Economic Objectives: These drive managers to achieve success from diversity and the different talents of associates.

Education: An enrollment process.

Empowerment: Each person is given the responsibility for quality, not just simply informed of what is expected. Providing direction for what needs to be done, the tools to do it, and then getting out of the way so people can achieve the results.

Enrollment: Flourishes when concerns of members are addressed and expectations are heard. It is enhanced when individual team tasks are directly connected to a person's abilities and expertise. Enrollment is encouraged when responsibility and accountability are present. Results when people are free to choose and individual choice stems from the individual's personal vision.

Existentialism: An analysis and understanding of individual existence in an unfathomable universe. The philosophy centers on the individual assuming ultimate responsibility for her or his acts.

External Customers: The people that purchase an organization's products and services.

External Failure Costs: Involve defects in services and products as received and perceived by the external customers.

Feedback: Extremely important piece of the Continuous Quality Improvement process. We get feedback from many sources by conducting assessments of our products and services.

Financial Expectations: These vary between organizations. Businesses expect to make a profit for the stakeholders, while non-profit organizations frequently expect to generate a surplus. This profit or surplus is used to build the organization by investing for future needs and in future growth.

Flow Chart: Used to get a more complete understanding of the processes involved in providing present services; also describes how the various steps relate to one another and follow in a sequence.

Focus Groups: Focus groups with internal customers may help discover that associates are starved for information about customer feedback. Focus groups also are suited to external customers.

Follow Up: The manager's need for immediacy of information from an associate.

Force Field Analysis: It simply presents the driving forces that move a situation toward change, and restraining forces that block that movement and prevent change.

Formal Feedback: Formal methods for obtaining customer feedback include traffic studies, questionnaires sent to randomly selected customers, surveys, personal interviews, and technology-based data mining.

Former Customers: A great deal to be learned from them because they had the opportunity to compare our products and services with those of other organizations.

Functional Limits: Principles that allow associates to concentrate on important and clearly defined areas of responsibility.

Goals: Provide the what, when, where, and how of doing business.

Group Input: Another way to obtain associate input is in a group setting, specifically during a meeting of a Work (i.e., departmental) Group Team.

High Performance Service Organizations: View quality as a strategic objective that is part of the organization's overall strategic business plan.

High Performance Teams Process Model: Team Formation, Team Framework, Team Management, Team Participation, Team Monitoring and Evaluation, inputs and outputs.

Idea Teams (IT): The teams meet with area managers as a Quality Improvement Team (QIT) to ensure ideas are being implemented and improvements are being made.

Identification of Critical Processes: To include customer (both internal and external) satisfaction, associate turnover, client retention, and other important areas.

Implementation Costs: Expenses related to getting started.

Implementing Quality: Six steps include educating, assessing, addressing the burning issues, determining critical processes and how to measure progress, redesigning the process, and continuous improvement.

Indicators: Used to measure the quality of products and services.

Informal Feedback: The goal is to capture, retain, sort, and act on this information. For example, to have associates complete a brief form at the end of the shift that details product comments, service comments, and suggestions/ideas for improvement.

Intangible Aspects: More difficult to create, deliver, and measure. Examples are a smile by the person working behind the counter, a friendly greeting and genuine "thank you" by the person changing a customer's oil; makes the service experience memorable.

Intellectual Capital: Increases through a commitment by leadership to be a mentoring organization with mentors at all levels.

Internal Customers/Associates: Staff members who are selected, oriented, and trained to create and deliver the products and services of the organization.

Internal Failure Costs: Related to rejects inside the organization's operations. They also involve costs associated with product design and redesign resulting from intervention.

Interventions: The action taken after the root causes of the problem are identified and prioritized, and solutions are developed.

ISO 9000: International Organization for Standardization. This organization develops quality standards. These standards are objective measurements against which an organization can be measured and certified.

Juran's Ten Steps to Quality Improvement: A way to organize an interconnected quality network to maximize an organization's delivery of quality products and services.

Key Functions: Have the greatest impact on the quality of products, services, and experiences ultimately created for and delivered to the customers.

Leadership: The process of taking people somewhere with an idea, creating a compelling vision to help them see into the future and then leading them to that future.

Leadership Challenges: Eight barriers confronting leaders.

Leadership Keys: Develop a vision, trust your subordinates, simplify, keep your cool, and be an expert.

Leadership Qualities: Have a strong personal value or belief system; provide a compelling message or vision; recognize that the ability to adjust is a necessity; make their outcomes tangible; and listen as well as, if not better than, they speak.

Leadership Secrets: Dependability, credibility, responsibility, accountability, and self-confidence.

Leadership Skills: In addition to the service excellence overview, it is essential to develop these in the organization.

Leading Quality: Responsibility of everyone in the organization since leadership is intimately related to managing and improving quality.

Learning Organization: Process of managing for quality exists and flourishes within the organization.

Machiavellian Managers: The needs and expectations of their companies, and the managers, drive all actions.

Malcolm Baldrige National Quality Award: Established by the United States Congress in 1987, it was named after a former U.S. Secretary of Commerce and recognizes U.S. companies who have achieved excellence through implementation of quality-improvement programs. It was created to enhance the competitiveness of U.S. businesses by promoting quality through awareness and recognition of quality achievements of U.S. businesses.

Management by Fact: Decisions are based on facts, not feelings or emotions.

Management Contact: Should take place regularly because the personal interaction can harvest a great deal of information.

Managing by Walking Around (MBWA): Managers should never go directly to their office upon arrival at work; they should tour the organization or part of the organization and interact with as many associates as possible.

Metrics: These measurements are for tracking the key indicators of effectiveness for each department in the organization. Think of these metrics as instruments on the dashboard of a vehicle. Like these dashboard instruments, we only look at a few (e.g., the speedometer and the fuel gauge indicator) regularly.

Mission: Seeks to clarify how the organization adds value by contributing to the world in a unique way. Defines the purpose of the organization and what the organization does.

Mission Statement: A mission statement answers the questions: Why do we exist? What is our purpose? In what interest do we function/operate?

National Institute of Standards and Technology: An agency of the U.S. Department of Commerce's Technology Administration.

New Business: The lifeblood of an organization that intends to grow.

Niche: Defines and delineates the identity of the business.

Nominal Group Technique (NGT): Used to give everyone the opportunity to equally voice their opinions and prioritize.

One Half Plus One Method: Used in the case where there are many items to prioritize.

Organizational Memory: The culture that takes place at the individual, team, and organization levels.

Organizational Systems: Define how things are done based on experience, organization standards, and customer expectations. Organizational systems also explain who is involved and why.

Orientation: Where people understand how to make the vision and mission real if they are to make contributions in positive ways. They must understand their role and how it contributes to the success of the organization as it exceeds the expectations of customers; also includes discussions of the philosophies and standards of the organization.

Paradigm: A way of seeing the world; places the customers first, beginning with internal customers and then shifting to external customers.

Pareto Chart: Used to determine which problems to resolve in what order, separate vital few from trivial many.

Participative Management: Getting input and creative ideas from all team members. The level of stress in the organization is reduced because individuals can receive more information.

Partnering: Creates opportunities for synergism and growth; partnerships and alliances also provide a perfect environment for expanding the knowledge and understanding of managing for quality in the organization.

PDCA Cycle: Plan, Do, Check, and Act.

Perseverance: One of the four foundations of leadership. Tenacity.

Personal Vision: Provides the view of the future for which a person exists. Answers the question: What do I want to create in my life?

Piggyback Input: Build on the ideas of others during brainstorming.

"Plus One": A little extra; a surprise that overwhelms the customer and creates a loyal customer for life.

Preferred Partner: A vision for providing management and consulting services.

Preventing Hassles: Achieved by doing things right the first time and avoiding problems, barriers, failures, obstacles, and red beads.

Process Analysis Team: The primary processes identified by the Steering Team are reviewed, modified, and eventually improved by this team.

Process Improvement for Service Excellence: To identify the top concerns facing each category of customers.

Product Development Process: Used to identify the customers.

Prospective Customers: Excellent source of information regarding how the organization stacks up against the competition and how the organization's products and services can be modified to better meet the needs of future clients.

Quality: Doing the right things right

Quality Improvement Team (QIT): Composed of managers/workgroup leaders, this team's primary responsibility is to make decisions and monitor quality activities.

Quality in Fact: The customer wants us to meet the specifications and the technical aspects of the product and service.

Quality in Perception: Wanting customers to *love* the services.

Quality Indicators: Used to measure the degree and/or frequency of conformance to the valid requirements.

Quality Life (QL): Quality principles that have direct application to our personal lives. Results from the effective application of quality principles to one's personal life; also have a direct impact on the individual who ultimately must make a contribution to the organization as a team member and internal customer of the organization.

Quality Perceived: Products and services of one organization compared to similar products and services available from other organizations; and as the value added when a product or service is created and delivered.

Quality Quotient (QQ): The measurement of the management's and associates' knowledge and use of the quality improvement principles.

Questionnaires and Surveys: Results are posted for all internal customers to review and the results are sent to action group teams and work group teams for identification and prioritization of the process problems and resolutions.

Raving Fans: Accomplished through a process of identifying customer needs and expectations, then going beyond these in ways that exceed their expectations.

Realigning the Processes: Redesigning to continuously improve a process.

Recognition: Based on the performance of the teams and the individuals and consists of rewards for service excellence performance.

Recognition of Associate Success: Recognition does not have to wait for awards banquets and the annual evaluation. It can be done almost on a daily basis, and it is particularly effective when it takes place in front of the associate's peers.

Red Beads: Hassles, barriers, problems, obstacles, or failures.

Respect: Respect should be earned; some level of respect is required for success and synergetic gain.

Restraining Forces: Block movement and prevent change.

Restricting Forces: Point out that many of the techniques that worked in the past will not work in the future.

Rollout Plan: Process of gathering statistical information must be established, and, undoubtedly, some quality-related equipment will have to be purchased; administrative functions such as program start-up, performance report establishment, and audit must be completed as well.

Run Chart: Used to monitor a process to determine how the results are changing over a long period of time.

Run/Control Chart: Used to measure the long-term effects of the root causes and present them graphically over a period of time that is meaningful to the possible resolution. It identifies shifts or changes in the average result.

Sampling of Products: Sometimes works well in obtaining feedback in a foodservice organization. This practice can lead to discussions about which items to add to the menu.

Sanitation Scores: This assessment is essential for any hospitality organization or service business, since customers expect cleanliness and safety. Also is done system-wide and two awards are given annually: the Outstanding Sanitation Award for most improved sanitation is given to the unit that has the greatest numerical improvement and the highest corporate sanitation score is given to the unit with the highest score for the year.

Secret Shoppers: Attempt to obtain insights into their products and services from the customers' perspectives. Individuals are retained by the company to anonymously evaluate the service experiences.

Selection: The goal is to screen applicants and identify people who share the organization's vision, mission, and values.

Self-Awareness: Tool for creating a personal vision.

Self-Directed Teams: Teams that work with little oversight or direction from management. Utilized to drive change and improve performance.

Self-Knowledge: A process that requires a personal commitment to exploring and getting to know oneself.

Self-Understanding: Tool for creating a personal vision.

Senior Quality Improvement Team (SQIT): The organization's executive team. It is the overseer of quality improvement initiatives. Defines policies and procedures for the management of quality in daily operations; directs, coordinates, refines, and approves recommendations in the process of continuous quality improvement.

Service Excellence: Something that you must want to do and enjoy to truly be successful. It is essential to strive to improve a little bit every day.

Service Excellence Overview: It's important to ask and answer the following question: What barriers are standing in your way to providing world-class service? Everyone in the organization must have an opportunity to participate in the answer to this question.

Service Guarantees: Promises made to customers.

Shared Vision: A vision that all embrace in the organization.

Sharing Information: To have all associates enroll in the vision, mission, and core values of the organization, management must teach and share as much information as possible.

Shopping the Competition: Allows an organization to see how competitors take essentially the same commodities (i.e., products) and add value with their own unique services.

Six Sigma: A concept derived from statistics, that uses the Greek letter Sigma to measure how far from perfection a product deviates.

Steering Team: This team is formed to get everyone involved and acclimated to managing quality improvements, removing barriers to quality, and identifying all the company's primary processes. This team includes senior management.

Strategic Goals: The action plans; each should be identified with a prime mover (associate, manager, supervisor, and team) that will drive the goal.

Strategic Plan: Part of the process to raise awareness among associates and managers, so each can determine what he or she is able to contribute to making the plan become a reality.

Strategic Planning Process: Provides a comprehensive approach that helps position the organization for the long-term and addresses key strategic issues in the near term.

Strategic Quality Plan: Result of Strategic Quality Planning Process Model.

Strategic Quality Plan Development (SQPD) Guide: The SQPD Guide permits the listing our objective, the plans for action, and the impact of these actions on quality, cost and revenue, as well as the organization's proforma financial statements.

Strategic Quality Planning: Begins with a personal vision, which transforms into a shared vision within the organization. This vision is the driver behind strategic goals and critical processes.

Strategic Quality Planning Process Model: Ties together vision, mission, core values, strategic goals, critical processes, and results.

Strategic Results: Outcomes produced in an organization.

Stretch Goals: Frequently the way that improvements get started.

Structure: Gives the organization more direction and continuity.

Statements of Core Value: (same as core values)

S.W.O.T. Analysis: Organization's internal and/or external strengths, weaknesses, opportunities, and threats.

Surveys: Tools used to asses external customers and internal customers.

Symbiosis: Helping each other and increased effectiveness, which is a result of working together.

Synergism: Decisions that produce services and products that no individual alone would have been able to achieve.

Systems Perspective: Includes the core values and concepts of a system; leadership, strategic planning, customer and market focus measurement, analysis, and knowledge management, human resource focus, process management and business results.

Taguchi Loss Function: Formula developed to calculate the costs associated with lack of quality.

Tangible Aspects: Technical elements, such as pressing a shirt at a laundry or the act of changing the oil and filling all the fluids in an automobile.

Targets: Action Group Teams (AGT) develop strategies to reach or surpass these; must be measurable.

Team: A team is two or more individuals who work together as a cohesive unit to achieve a specific and shared goal that requires interdependent action and collaboration.

Team Champions: Individuals that are responsible for ensuring that all are trained properly.

Team Deployment: Initiating continuous quality improvement.

Teamwork: Using the strengths of individuals and the synergy of teams to serve customers.

The Better Way: A manager sees change happening and wants to help make it happen.

Thinking Outside the Box: Demands time and commitment from key internal customers within the learning organization and the organization's culture and core values.

Three Cs: Credibility/character, Confidence, and Communication.

Threshold: Specifically related to an indicator and may be thought of as a "yard stick" of what is an acceptable level of performance.

Tools of the Trade: Combined into systems and used along with solid management principles to improve quality; set of measurements or metrics linked to ongoing procedures for testing whether the organization is meeting, exceeding, or falling below the standards. Help measure and monitor quality improvements.

Top Box Teams: A team that has a goal of converting low customer satisfaction scores to high customer satisfaction scores.

Total Customer Satisfaction Teams: Encourages associates to shape their work environment through problem solving and goal accomplishment.

Total Quality Control (TQC): A system for integrating quality development, maintenance, and improvement into the groups of an organization.

Total Quality Management (TQM): Bottom line performance will take care of itself in an organization that is committed to and practices managing for quality.

Traditional Organizations: The organization operated with a culture of fear and hostility. Associates were afraid that when problems occurred they would be blamed, so they waited for precise directions by top management before acting.

Traffic Studies: Require visits to the competition two or three times during the same part of the day.

Training: Includes specific knowledge, skills, and attitudes so that the new associate may understand and successfully contribute to the mission and needs of the functional area and the organization.

Trifecta: Changing management cultures.

Trust: One of the four foundations of leadership. An environment of trust within the team brings about openness, effective communication, and creativity.

Valid Quality Requirements: Based on the needs and expectations of customers.

Validation of Training: Training is validated by associates and managers in each functional area. Additional validation is provided by customers, both internal and external.

Value Added Selling: Value added results in new salesproposals leading to a key result, new business.

Value Limits: These are contained in operational guidelines such as the organization's core principles of management; establish limits or a framework within which to manage and operate.

Values: Describe how people in the organization tend to behave and act.

Value System: In an organization, helps empowered associates make the right decisions.

VANO Manager: Visual, Appearance/Accounting, Numbers Only manager

Vision: A picture of the ideal future; answers the question "what do we want to create?" One of the four foundations of leadership. Forward looking.

Vision Statements: (same as vision)

Voice of Customer (VOC): VOC is the process of gathering, analyzing, and integrating customer input back into the organization's decision making.

Work Flow Process: Feigenbaum's concept of how improvement in one component of a process helps improve other areas of the organization.

Work Group Team (WGT): A group of associates based in the functional area in which they work. The goal is to have members of this team become more self-directed by self-managing. Work groups are given an issue or issues to resolve and, when resolution is achieved, the group is dissolved. The tenure of the work group is measured by the complexity of the issue and the time required for successful resolution.

Index

Your Tools of the Trade

These Tools of the Trade are designed to be used by you. Simply tear out the appropriate tool and use it for practice application in the "Activities in Your Organization" section of the chapter. Tear out the forms and copy them when more are needed. Additional forms may be used in class projects, as well as in your organization. These are *your* Tools of the Trade.

BALANCED SCORE CARD

OUTCOME AREA	TARGET PERFORMANCE	CURRENT PERFORMANCE	BASELINE PERFORMANCE	MEASUREMENT TOOL	REPORTING FREQUENCY
1. Financial/Cost					
2. Marketing/Growth					

BALANCED SCORE CARD

OUTCOME AREA	TARGET PERFORMANCE	CURRENT PERFORMANCE	BASELINE PERFORMANCE	MEASUREMENT TOOL	REPORTING FREQUENCY
3. Customer Satisfaction					
4. Organizational Effectiveness					

BALANCED SCORE CARD

OUTCOME AREA	TARGET PERFORMANCE	CURRENT PERFORMANCE	BASELINE PERFORMANCE	MEASUREMENT TOOL	REPORTING FREQUENCY
5. Human Resources					

BALANCED SCORE CARD

OUTCOME AREA	TARGET PERFORMANCE	CURRENT PERFORMANCE	BASELINE PERFORMANCE	MEASUREMENT TOOL	REPORTING FREQUENCY
1. Financial/Cost					
2. Marketing/Growth					

BALANCED SCORE CARD

OUTCOME AREA	TARGET PERFORMANCE	CURRENT PERFORMANCE	BASELINE PERFORMANCE	MEASUREMENT TOOL	REPORTING FREQUENCY
3. Customer Satisfaction					
4. Organizational Effectiveness					

BALANCED SCORE CARD

OUTCOME AREA	TARGET PERFORMANCE	CURRENT PERFORMANCE	BASELINE PERFORMANCE	MEASUREMENT TOOL	REPORTING FREQUENCY
5. Human Resources					

BALANCED SCORE CARD

OUTCOME AREA	TARGET PERFORMANCE	CURRENT PERFORMANCE	BASELINE PERFORMANCE	MEASUREMENT TOOL	REPORTING FREQUENCY
1. Financial/Cost					
2. Marketing/Growth					

BALANCED SCORE CARD

OUTCOME AREA	TARGET PERFORMANCE	CURRENT PERFORMANCE	BASELINE PERFORMANCE	MEASUREMENT TOOL	REPORTING FREQUENCY
3. Customer Satisfaction					
4. Organizational Effectiveness					

BALANCED SCORE CARD

OUTCOME AREA	TARGET PERFORMANCE	CURRENT PERFORMANCE	BASELINE PERFORMANCE	MEASUREMENT TOOL	REPORTING FREQUENCY
5. Human Resources					

CAUSE AND EFFECT DIAGRAM

EFFECT

CAUSES

PROBLEM

PEOPLE

PROCEDURES

EQUIPMENT

PRODUCTS

ENVIRONMENT

CAUSE AND EFFECT DIAGRAM

EFFECT

CAUSES

PROBLEM

PEOPLE

PROCEDURES

EQUIPMENT

PRODUCTS

ENVIRONMENT

CAUSE AND EFFECT DIAGRAM

EFFECT

CAUSES

PROBLEM

PEOPLE

PROCEDURES

EQUIPMENT

PRODUCTS

ENVIRONMENT

CAUSE AND EFFECT DIAGRAM

EFFECT

CAUSES

PROBLEM

MANPOWER

METHODS

MACHINERY

MATERIALS

ENVIRONMENT

CAUSE AND EFFECT DIAGRAM

EFFECT

CAUSES

PROBLEM

MANPOWER

MACHINERY

METHODS

MATERIALS

ENVIRONMENT

CAUSE AND EFFECT DIAGRAM

EFFECT

CAUSES

PROBLEM

MANPOWER

MACHINERY

METHODS

MATERIALS

ENVIRONMENT

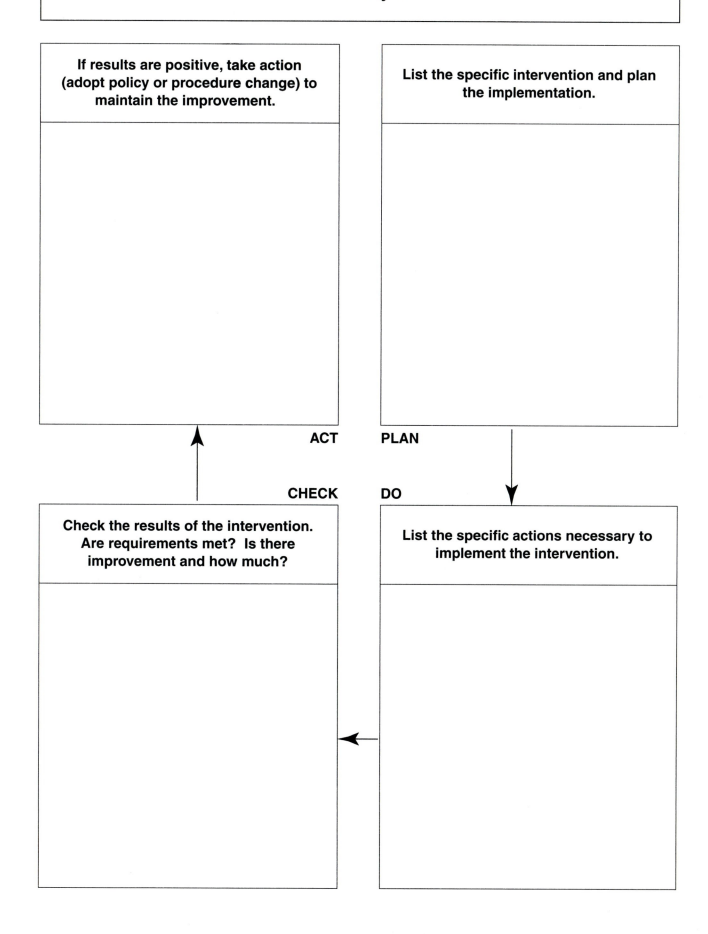

PDCA Cycle

If results are positive, take action (adopt policy or procedure change) to maintain the improvement.

List the specific intervention and plan the implementation.

ACT **PLAN**

CHECK **DO**

Check the results of the intervention. Are requirements met? Is there improvement and how much?

List the specific actions necessary to implement the intervention.

PDCA Cycle

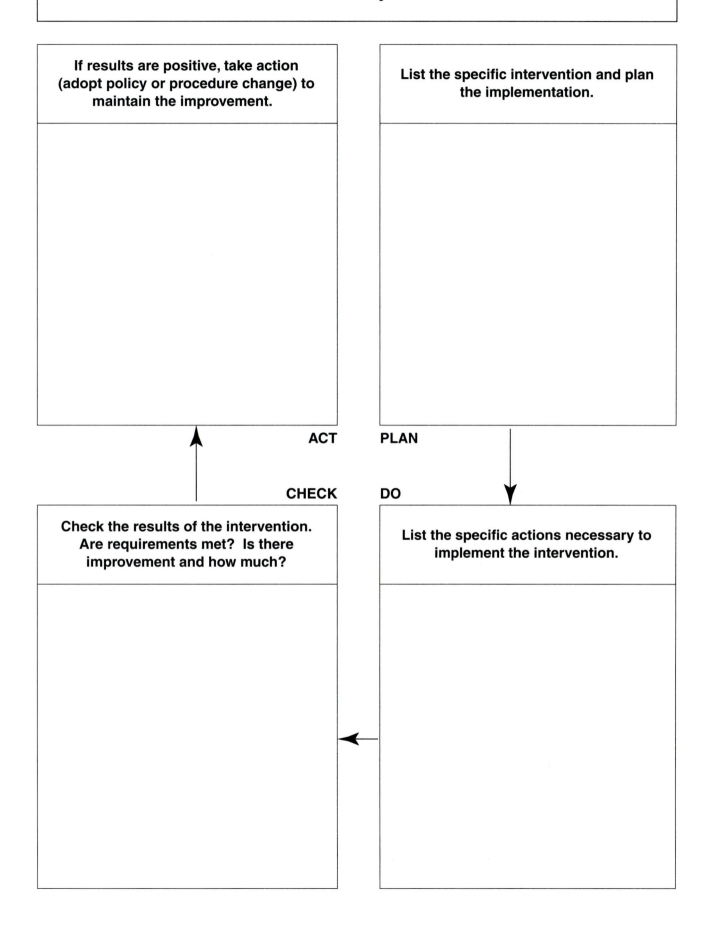

If results are positive, take action (adopt policy or procedure change) to maintain the improvement.

List the specific intervention and plan the implementation.

ACT

PLAN

CHECK

DO

Check the results of the intervention. Are requirements met? Is there improvement and how much?

List the specific actions necessary to implement the intervention.

PDCA Cycle

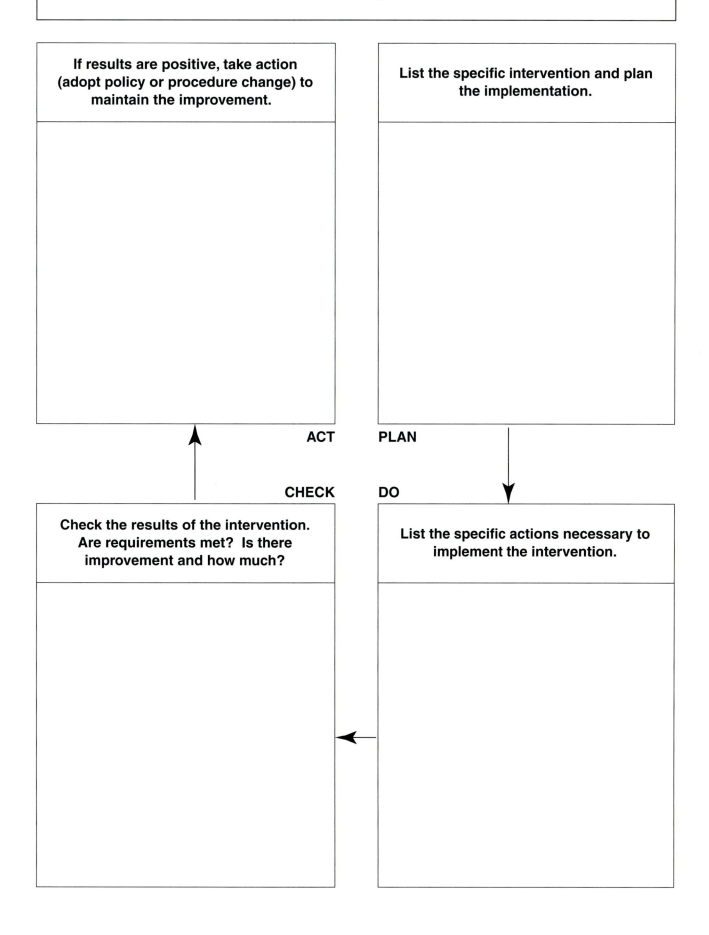

If results are positive, take action (adopt policy or procedure change) to maintain the improvement.

List the specific intervention and plan the implementation.

ACT

PLAN

CHECK

DO

Check the results of the intervention. Are requirements met? Is there improvement and how much?

List the specific actions necessary to implement the intervention.

STRATEGIC QUALITY PLAN DEVELOPMENT GUIDE

DEPARTMENT: _____

TEAM MEMBERS: _____
_____

OBJECTIVE	ACTION PLAN	COST/REVENUE/QUALITY IMPACT
		C = R = Q =
		C = R = Q =
		C = R = Q =
		C = R = Q =
		C = R = Q =